SQL Server Advanced Data Types

JSON, XML, and Beyond

Peter A. Carter

Apress®

SQL Server Advanced Data Types: JSON, XML, and Beyond

Peter A. Carter
London, UK

ISBN-13 (pbk): 978-1-4842-3900-1   ISBN-13 (electronic): 978-1-4842-3901-8
https://doi.org/10.1007/978-1-4842-3901-8

Library of Congress Control Number: 2018955129

Managing Director, Apress Media LLC: Welmoed Spahr
Acquisitions Editor: Jonathan Gennick
Development Editor: Laura Berendson
Coordinating Editor: Jill Balzano

Cover designed by eStudioCalamar

Cover image designed by Freepik (www.freepik.com)

Distributed to the book trade worldwide by Springer Science+Business Media New York, 233 Spring Street, 6th Floor, New York, NY 10013. Phone 1-800-SPRINGER, fax (201) 348-4505, e-mail orders-ny@springer-sbm.com, or visit www.springeronline.com. Apress Media, LLC is a California LLC and the sole member (owner) is Springer Science+Business Media Finance Inc (SSBM Finance Inc). SSBM Finance Inc is a **Delaware** corporation.

For information on translations, please e-mail rights@apress.com, or visit www.apress.com/rights-permissions.

Apress titles may be purchased in bulk for academic, corporate, or promotional use. eBook versions and licenses are also available for most titles. For more information, reference our Print and eBook Bulk Sales web page at www.apress.com/bulk-sales.

Any source code or other supplementary material referenced by the author in this book is available to readers on GitHub via the book's product page, located at www.apress.com/9781484239001. For more detailed information, please visit www.apress.com/source-code.

Printed on acid-free paper

Given the cover art, this book could only be dedicated to my son, Reuben.

Table of Contents

About the Author

Peter A. Carter is a SQL Server expert with more than 15 years' experience in database development, administration, and platform engineering. He is currently a consultant, based in London. Peter has written a number of books across a variety of SQL Server topics, including security, high availability, and automation.

About the Technical Reviewer

**Ian Stirk** is a freelance SQL Server consultant based in London. In addition to his day job, he is an author, creator of software utilities, and technical reviewer who regularly writes book reviews for www.i-programmer.info.

He covers every aspect of SQL Server and has a specialist interest in performance and scalability. If you require help with your SQL Server systems, feel free to contact him at ian_stirk@yahoo.com or www.linkedin.com/in/ian-stirk-bb9a31.

Ian would like to thank Peter Carter, Jonathan Gennick, and Jill Balzano for making this book experience easier for him.

None of us stands alone, and with this in mind, Ian would like to thank these special people: Pat Richards, Bhargava Ganti, Jon McCabe, Nick Fairway, Aida Samuel, Paul Fuller, Vikki Singini, Rob Lee, Gerald Hemming, and Jordy Mumba.

Ian's fee for his work on this book has been donated to the Deworm the World Initiative (www.givingwhatwecan.org/report/deworm/).

Introduction

SQL Server Advanced Data Types attempts to demystify the complex data types that are available to developers in modern versions of SQL Server. Over the last couple of years, I have noticed that many SQL developers have heard of each of the complex data types available in SQL Server but often avoid using them, as they are not sure how these are best utilized. This has led to suboptimal solutions being developed, such as an incident that I recently experienced in which a very good and seasoned SQL developer implemented complex hierarchical logic using self joins, because he did not feel confident implementing the HierarchyID data type.

That inspired me to write this book—to help SQL and other developers responsible for writing T-SQL, as part of their applications, to better understand the complex data types available in SQL Server and give them the confidence to use these complex structures appropriately.

The book starts by exploring the simple, conventional data types that are available in SQL Server and reminds readers why making the right choices about data types can be so important. The book then moves on to offer in-depth discussions about the complex data types in SQL Server, namely, XML, JSON, HierarchyID, GEOGRAPHY, and GEOMETRY. Many of the code examples in the book are based on real-world problems and solutions that I have encountered in my time as an SQL Server consultant in London.

Many of the code examples in this book use the WideWorldImporters sample database. The GitHub repo for this database can be found at github.com/Microsoft/sql-server-samples/tree/master/samples/databases/wide-world-importers and the .bak file can be downloaded from github.com/Microsoft/sql-server-samples/releases/download/wide-world-importers-v1.0/WideWorldImporters-Standard.bak.

CHAPTER 1

SQL Server Data Types

SQL Server 2017 provides a wide range of basic data types that can store data, such as character strings, numeric data, binary data, and dates. In this chapter, I will review each of the basic data types available in SQL Server, looking at the differences between similar data types. I will also discuss the importance of using the correct data type for each use case.

Tip The following sections discuss the acceptable ranges for each data type. It is worth noting, however, that all data types can also be set to NULL, indicating that the value is unknown.

Numeric Data Types

Some numeric data types in SQL Server are exact, while others are approximate. If a data type is exact, it stores a number to a fixed precision. If a data type is approximate, in many cases, it will store a very close approximation of a number, instead of the number itself.

The numeric data types supported by SQL Server are listed in Table 1-1.

© Peter A. Carter 2018
P. A. Carter, *SQL Server Advanced Data Types*,
https://doi.org/10.1007/978-1-4842-3901-8_1

Table 1-1. Numeric Data Types

Data Type	Description	Storage Size	Range	Exact/ Approximate
BIT	A flag that can be set to 0 or 1, the string values True and False can also be inserted into a column of data type BIT and are converted to 1 or 0, respectively.	1 byte for every 8 bit columns in a table	0 to 1	Exact
TINYINT	Stores a whole number, with no decimal points	1 byte	0 to 255	Exact
SMALLINT	Stores a whole number, with no decimal points	2 bytes	to 2^15 to 2^15 to 1	Exact
INT	Stores a whole number, with no decimal points	4 bytes	to 2^31 to 2^31 to 1	Exact
BIGINT	Stores a whole number, with no decimal points	8 bytes	to 2^63 to 2^63 to 1	Exact

| DECIMAL | Stores a number with fixed decimal precision. When using DECIMAL, you must specify precision and scale. The precision is the maximum number of digits that can be stored, while the scale is the maximum number of digits that follow the decimal point. For example, 123.456 could be stored with a precision of 6 and a scale of 3. DECIMAL is functionally equivalent to NUMERIC. | The storage space required depends on the precision, as below:

• 1-9 – 5 bytes
• 10-19 – 9 bytes
• 20-28 – 13 bytes
• 29-38 – 17 bytes | to 10^38+
1 to 10^38 to 1 | Exact |

(continued)

Table 1-1. (*continued*)

Data Type	Description	Storage Size	Range	Exact/ Approximate
NUMERIC	Stores a number with fixed decimal precision. When using NUMERIC, you must specify precision and scale. The precision is the maximum number of digits that can be stored, while the scale is the maximum number of digits that follow the decimal point. For example, 123.456 could be stored with a precision of 6 and a scale of 3. NUMERIC is functionally equivalent to DECIMAL.	The storage space required depends on the precision, as below: • 1-9 – 5 bytes • 10-19 – 9 bytes • 20-28 - 13 bytes • 29-38 – 17 bytes	to 10^38+1 to 10^38 to 1	Exact

FLOAT	Stores a number with approximate precision. FLOAT accepts a single precision value between 1 and 53. If a value between 1 and 24 is entered, it is translated to 24, which is also known as single precision. If a number between 25 and 54 is passed, it is treated as 54, also known as double precision. If FLOAT is used without specifying a precision, single precision is used. A FLOAT with single precision is a synonym for REAL.	The amount of storage space required, depends on the precision, as below: • Single precision (7 digits) – 4 bytes • sDouble precision (15 digits) – 8 bytes	Single precision: to 1.79E+308 to 2.23E to 308 Double precision: 2.23E to 308 to 1.79E+308	Approximate
REAL	Stores a number with approximate precision. REAL uses single precision and is a synonym for FLOAT(24)	4 bytes	1.79E+308 to 2.23E to 308	Approximate

(continued)

Table 1-1. (*continued*)

Data Type	Description	Storage Size	Range	Exact/ Approximate
SMALLMONEY	Stores small monetary values with a precision of four decimal places. Currency symbols, such as £ or $, can be passed into the data type as a prefix but are not stored by SQL Server.	4 bytes	to 214,748.3648 to 214,748.3647	Exact
MONEY	Stores large monetary values with a precision of four decimal places. Currency symbols, such as £ or $, can be passed into the data type as a prefix but are not stored by SQL Server.	8 bytes	to922,337,203,685, 477.5808 to 922,337,203,685, 477.5807	Exact

---

Tip   The caret (^) operator means to the power. For example, 2^15-1 means 2 to the power of 15 minus 1, which equates to 32,767.

To see how a number behaves, using each of the numeric formats, we will use the number 2.5888712345678923456789 and convert it to each of the numeric data types, to examine its behavior. In SQL Server, there are two functions that we can use to change the data type of a value: CAST and CONVERT.

The CAST function uses the syntax in Listing 1-1.

Listing 1-1. CAST Syntax

```
CAST( expression AS datatype[(length)] )
```

The expression can be either a value that you wish to convert, a column in a table, or any other valid expression. The datatype should be the target data type for the expression. length is optional and based on the target data type. For example, if you were using CAST to change the data type of an INT to a DECIMAL, length would consist of the required precision and scale. If you were casting a value to a string, the length would be the maximum length of the string.

The CONVERT function uses the syntax in Listing 1-2.

Listing 1-2. CONVERT Syntax

```
CONVERT( datatype[(length)], expression [, style] )
```

The style option of the CONVERT function allows the developer to supply additional information about how to translate the expression. The style options that are available for numeric data types can be found in Table 1-2.

Table 1-2. *Numeric Data Type Style Options*

Style Code	Data Types	Output
0	FLOAT & REAL	The default value for FLOAT and REAL. A maximum of six digits. Uses scientific notation, if required
1	FLOAT & REAL	Eight digits. Always uses scientific notation
2	FLOAT & REAL	Sixteen digits. Always uses scientific notation
3	FLOAT & REAL	Seventeen digits, with lossless conversion
0	SMALLMONEY & MONEY	The default value for SMALLMONEY and MONEY. No comma separation, and two digits to the right of the decimal point
1	SMALLMONEY & MONEY	Comma separation every three digits on the left of the decimal point. Two digits to the right of the decimal point
2	SMALLMONEY & MONEY	No comma separation. Four digits to the right of the decimal point
126	SMALLMONEY & MONEY	Used when converting to character data types. No comma separation. Four digits to the right of the decimal point

The script in Listing 1-3 shows how to use the CAST function to translate the number 2.5888712345678923456789 to each numeric data type.

Note   BIT is excluded, as the conversion does not make sense. If it were included, however, it would CAST to 1.

Listing 1-3. Casting a Number to Each Data Type

```
SELECT
          CAST(2.588871234567892345678 AS TINYINT) AS 'TINYINT'
        , CAST(2.588871234567892345678 AS SMALLINT) AS
          'SMALLINT'
        , CAST(2.588871234567892345678 AS INT) AS 'INT'
        , CAST(2.588871234567892345678 AS BIGINT) AS 'BIGINT'
        , CAST(2.588871234567892345678 AS DECIMAL(23,22)) AS
          'DECIMAL'
        , CAST(2.588871234567892345678 AS DECIMAL(18,17)) AS
          'DECIMAL ROUNDED'
        , CAST(2.588871234567892345678 AS NUMERIC(23,22)) AS
          'NUMERIC'
        , CAST(2.588871234567892345678 AS FLOAT(24)) AS
          'SINGLE FLOAT'
        , CAST(2.588871234567892345678 AS FLOAT(53)) AS
          'DOUBLE FLOAT'
        , CAST(2.588871234567892345678 AS REAL) AS 'REAL'
        , CAST(2.588871234567892345678 AS SMALLMONEY) AS
          'SMALLMONEY'
        , CAST(2.588871234567892345678 AS MONEY) AS 'MONEY'
```

9

The results of the query in Listing 1-3 can be found in Figure 1-1.

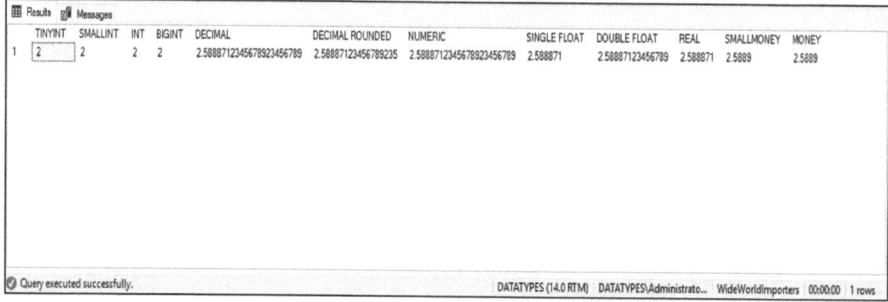

Figure 1-1. *Results of casting to numeric data types*

Character Strings

SQL Server can store both Unicode and non-Unicode strings. Strings can also be stored either as a fixed length or a variable length. The character data types supported by SQL Server are listed in Table 1-3.

Table 1-3. *Character Data Types*

Data Type	Description	Storage Size	Maximum Length	Variable/Fixed
CHAR	Stores a string of non-Unicode characters, with a fixed length. When using CHAR, you must pass in a value, to indicate the maximum length of the string. If the string is shorter than the maximum length, the string will be padded with whitespace.	Maximum string length × 1 byte	8000 characters	Fixed
VARCHAR	Stores a string of non-Unicode characters with a variable size, depending on the string that is stored. When using VARCHAR, you must either specify a maximum length for the string or specify MAX. When MAX is specified, the data type can store up to 2GB.	The length of the string stored × 1 byte	2GB	Variable
NCHAR	Stores a string of Unicode characters with a fixed length. When using CHAR, you must pass in a value, to indicate the maximum length of the string. If the string is shorter than the maximum length, the string will be padded with whitespace.	Maximum string length × 2 bytes	4000 characters	Fixed

(continued)

11

Table 1-3. (*continued*)

Data Type	Description	Storage Size	Maximum Length	Variable/Fixed
NVARCHAR	Stores a string of Unicode characters with a variable size, depending on the string that is stored. When using VARCHAR, you must either specify a maximum length for the string or specify MAX. When MAX is specified, the data type can store up to 2GB.	The length of the string stored × 2 bytes	2GB	Variable
TEXT	A deprecated data type that should not be used. Stores non-Unicode strings with a variable length	The length of the string stored × 1 byte	2GB	Variable
NTEXT	A deprecated data type that should not be used. Stores Unicode strings with a variable length	The length of the string stored × 2 bytes	2GB	Variable

The script in Listing 1-4 uses the DATALENGTH system function to demonstrate the difference in storage size for a 15-character string, cast as each character data type.

Listing 1-4. Examining the Storage Size of Strings

```
SELECT
      DATALENGTH(CAST('My String Value' AS NCHAR(20))) AS
      'NCHAR'
    , DATALENGTH(CAST('My String Value' AS NVARCHAR(20))) AS
      'NVARCHAR'
    , DATALENGTH(CAST('My String Value' AS CHAR(20))) AS 'CHAR'
    , DATALENGTH(CAST('My String Value' AS VARCHAR(20))) AS
      'VARCHAR'
```

The results of Listing 1-4 can be found in Figure 1-2.

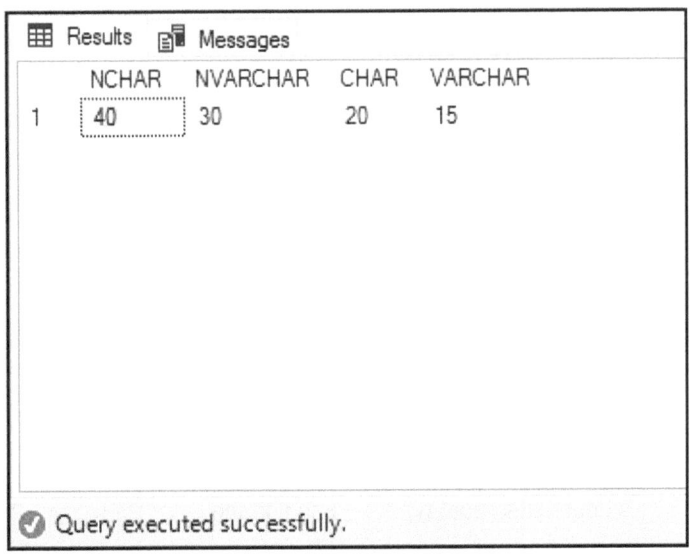

Figure 1-2. *Results of comparing string storage sizes*

Binary Data Types

SQL Server can store binary data, such as a word document or a photo, using native binary data types. Binary data types are also used to store data that has been encrypted using a key or certificate. The binary data types available in SQL Server are detailed in Table 1-4.

Table 1-4. *Binary Data Types*

Data Type	Description	Storage Size	Maximum Length	Variable/ Fixed
BINARY	Stores binary data with a fixed length. When using BINARY, you must specify the data length in bytes. If the data stored is shorter than the specified length, it will be padded.	Equal to maximum number of allowed bytes	8000 bytes	Fixed
VARBINARY	Stores binary data with a variable length. When using VARBINARY, you must specify either the maximum length of the data in bytes or specify MAX. When MAX is specified, data up to a maximum of 2GB can be stored.	Equal to the actual number of bytes stored, plus 2 bytes	2GB	Variable
IMAGE	A deprecated data type that should not be used. Stores binary data with a variable length	Equal to the actual number of bytes stored, plus 2 bytes	2GB	Variable

Tip   For detailed information about encrypting data, please refer to *Securing SQL Server* (Apress, 2016), which can be found at www.apress.com/gp/book/9781484222645.

The style options available for BINARY data when using the CONVERT function are detailed in Table 1-5.

Table 1-5. *Style Options for BINARY Data*

Style Code	Output
0	The default value for binary data. Converts ASCII characters to binary bytes, or vice versa
1	Converts a character string into binary data. Validates that there are an even number of hexadecimal bytes and that the first character is 0x
2	Converts binary data into a character string. Each byte will be converted into two hexadecimal characters. Data that overflows the data type will be truncated. If the data is shorter than a fixed length data type, it will be padded.

The script in Listing 1-5 demonstrates how to read a password that has been encrypted and stored in a VARBINARY column and convert it back to a character string. The script first creates the required objects and encrypts the password.

Listing 1-5. Decrypting an Encrypted Password and Converting It Back to a Character String

```
--Create a certificate that will encrypt the symmetric key

CREATE CERTIFICATE PasswordCert
        ENCRYPTION BY PASSWORD = 'MySecurePa$$word'
```

```
        WITH SUBJECT = 'Cert for securing passwords table' ;
```

--Create a symmetric key that will encrypt the password

```
CREATE SYMMETRIC KEY PasswordKey
        WITH ALGORITHM = AES_128
        ENCRYPTION BY CERTIFICATE PasswordCert ;
```

--Create a table to store the password

```
CREATE TABLE dbo.Passwords
(
        Password    VARBINARY(256)
) ;
```

--Open the symmetric key, so that it can be used

```
OPEN SYMMETRIC KEY PasswordKey
        DECRYPTION BY CERTIFICATE PasswordCert
        WITH PASSWORD = 'MySecurePa$$word' ;
```

--Encrypt a password and insert it into the table

```
INSERT INTO dbo.Passwords
SELECT ENCRYPTBYKEY(KEY_GUID('PasswordKey'), 'Pa$$w0rd') ;
```

--Decrypt and read the password
--The first column in the result set shows the password as the
decrypted value but still binary format
--The second column in the result set shows the password
decrypted and converted back to a character string

```
SELECT
        DECRYPTBYKEY(Password) AS 'Decrypted Password In
        Binary'
      , CAST(DECRYPTBYKEY(Password) AS CHAR(8)) AS 'Decrypted
        Password As Character String'
```

```
FROM dbo.Passwords

--Close the symmetric key

CLOSE SYMMETRIC KEY PasswordKey ;
```

The results of the select statement against the table created in Listing 1-5 can be found in Figure 1-3.

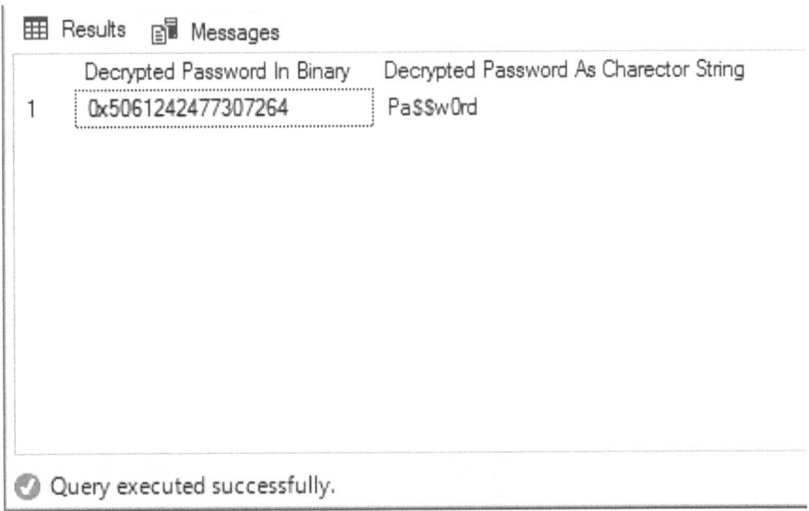

Figure 1-3. *Results of converting binary data to a character string*

Dates and Times

SQL Server can store accurate date and time information, including UTC offsets. The details of each supported date and time data type can be found in Table 1-6.

Table 1-6. Date and Time Data Types

Data Type	Description	Storage Size	Accuracy
DATE	Stores a date	3 bytes	Date
TIME	Stores a time of day. When using TIME, you can specify a fractional second precision, to a maximum of 7. slf omitted, the default is 7.	Depending on the fractional second precision, as follows: • 0-2 – 3 bytes • 3-4 – 4 bytes • 5-7 – 5 bytes	100 nanoseconds
DATETIME	Stores a date and a time with fractional seconds	8 bytes	Rounded to .000, .003, or .007 seconds
SMALLDATETIME	Stores a date and a time to the grain of 1 minute	4 bytes	One minute

DATETIME2	Stores a date and time with fractional seconds. DATETIME2 is more accurate than DATETIME and stores a larger range of dates. When using DATETIME2, you can specify a fractional second precision, to a maximum of 7. If omitted, the default is 7	Depending on the fractional second precision, as follows: • 0-2 – 6 bytes • 3-4 – 7 bytes • 5-7 – 8 bytes	100 nanoseconds
DATETIMEOFFSET	Stores a date and time, with time zone awareness. When using DATETIMEOFFSET, you can specify a fractional second precision, to a maximum of 7. If omitted, the default is 7. When storing a date and time, you can pass a UTC offset of -14 to +14	10 bytes	100 nanoseconds

Table 1-7 details allowable style options for date and time data types when using the CONVERT function.

Table 1-7. *Date and Time Styles*

Style Code	Standard	Input/Output
0 or 100	Default for datetime and smalldatetime	mon dd yyyy hh:miAM (or PM)
1	US	mm/dd/yy
2	ANSI	yy.mm.dd
3	British & French	dd/mm/yy
4	German	dd.mm.yy
5	Italian	dd-mm-yy
6		dd mon yy
7		Mon dd, yy
8 or 108		hh:mi:ss
9 or 109	Default style (100) + time (ms)	mon dd yyyy hh:mi:ss:mmmAM (or PM)
10	USA	mm-dd-yy
11	Japan	yy/mm/dd
12	ISO	yymmdd
13 or 113		dd mon yyyy hh:mi:ss:mmm(24h)
20 or 120	ODBC canonical	yyyy-mm-dd hh:mi:ss(24h)
21 or 121	ODBC canonical with time (ms) Default for time, date, datetime2, and datetimeoffset	yyyy-mm-dd hh:mi:ss.mmm(24h)

(continued)

Table 1-7. (*continued*)

Style Code	Standard	Input/Output
101	US	mm/dd/yyyy
102	ANSI	yyyy.mm.dd
1-3	British & French	dd/mm/yyyy
104	German	dd.mm.yyyy
105	Italian	dd-mm-yyyy
106	European default	dd mon yyyy
107		Mon dd, yyyy
110	USA	mm-dd-yyyy
111	Japan	yyyy/mm/dd
112	ISO	yyyymmdd
13 or 113	European default (106) + time (ms)	dd mon yyyy hh:mi:ss:mmm(24h)
114		hh:mi:ss:mmm(24h)
126	ISO8601	yyyy-mm-ddThh:mi:ss.mmm mmmm not displayed if 0
127	ISO8601 with time zone	yyyy-mm-ddThh:mi:ss.mmmZ mmmm not displayed if 0
130	Hijri	dd mon yyyy hh:mi:ss:mmmAM mon is the Hijri Unicode representation of the month name
131	Hijri	dd/mm/yyyy hh:mi:ss:mmmAM mon is the Hijri Unicode representation of the month name

The script in Listing 1-6 shows how a date and time value will be displayed when cast to each of the date and time data types. The script uses the SYSUTCDATETIME function to retrieve the current system date and time.

Listing 1-6. Casingt a Value to Each of the Date and Time Data Types

```
SELECT
    CAST(SYSUTCDATETIME() AS time(7)) AS 'TIME'
    ,CAST(SYSUTCDATETIME() AS date) AS 'DATE'
    ,CAST(SYSUTCDATETIME() AS smalldatetime) AS 'SMALLDATETIME'
    ,CAST(SYSUTCDATETIME() AS datetime) AS 'DATETIME'
    ,CAST(SYSUTCDATETIME() AS datetime2(7)) AS 'DATETIME2'
    ,CAST(SYSUTCDATETIME() AS datetimeoffset(7)) AS
    'DATETIMEOFFSET' ;
```

The results of running the query in Listing 1-6 can be found in Figure 1-4.

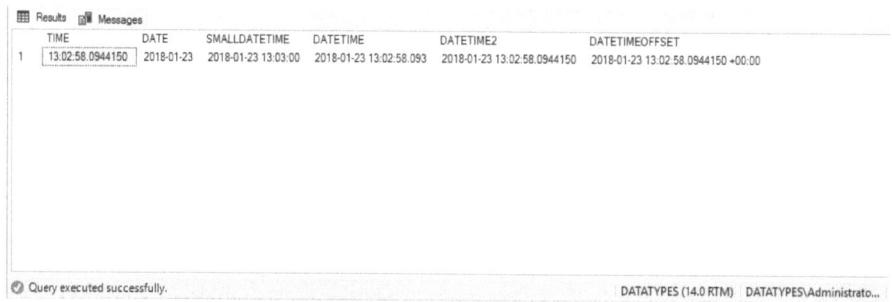

Figure 1-4. *Results of casting a value to each date and time data type*

Miscellaneous Standard Data Types

SQL Server offers many other standard data types that can be used for specialized purposes. A description of these data types can be found in Table 1-8.

Table 1-8. *Miscellaneous Data Types*

Data Type	Description	Size	Allowable Usage
CURSOR	Stores a cursor with a variable or stored procedure output	Variable	Variable or stored procedure OUTPUT parameter
TIMESTAMP	Exposes a system-generated, unique binary value. Used for versioning a row within a table	8 bytes	Table, variable, stored procedure parameter
UNIQUEIDENTIFIER	Stored a GUID (Globally Unique Identifier)	16 bytes	Table, variable, stored procedure parameter
SQL VARIANT	Can store data of multiple data types. Can be used when you do not know the data type of the data that will be input, but this is a very bad practice	Variable	Table, variable, stored procedure parameter
TABLE	Stores a result set within a variable, to be used at a later time	Variable	Variable

The script in Listing 1-7 creates a value of the data type UNIQUEIDENTIFIER, which has been created using the NEWID system function.

Listing 1-7. Creating a UNIQUEIDENTIFIER

```
SELECT NEWID() ;
```

The results of running the query in Listing 1-7 can be found in Figure 1-5.

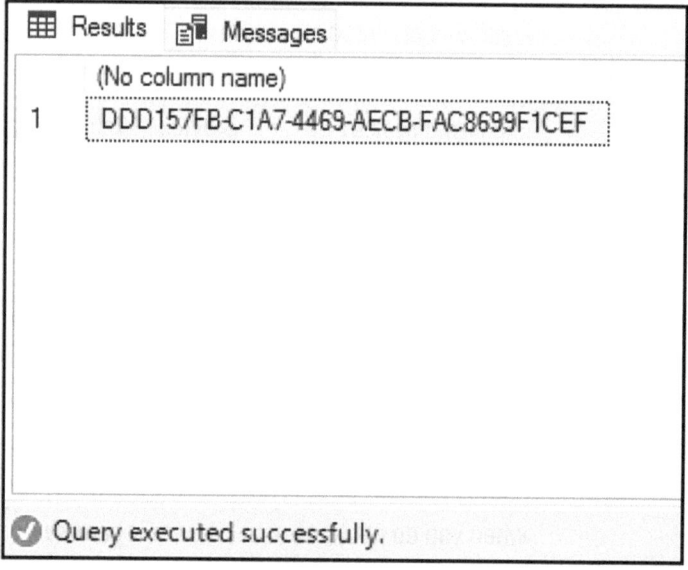

Figure 1-5. *Viewing a* UNIQUEIDENTIFIER *created with* NEWID

Summary of Advanced Data Types

SQL Server provides several advanced data types. These data types will be discussed throughout this book, but a summary can be found in Table 1-9.

Table 1-9. *Advanced Data Types*

Data Type	Description
HIERARCHYID	HierarchyID can be used to store hierarchical data, such as a BoM (bill of materials) of department structure, in a hexadecimal form. The data type exposes numerous methods that allow developers to easily navigate the hierarchy.
XML	Used to store data in native XML format. FLWOR (discussed in Chapter 4) statements can then be used against the data.
JSON	Stores data in a native JSON format. SQL Server provides functions to convert data to and from JSON, extract values from JSON, and modify JSON data.
GEOGRAPHY	Stores location data, using the round earth model. The data type exposes a number of methods that can be used to interact with the geospatial data.
GEOMETRY	Stores location data, using the flat earth model. The data type exposes a number of methods that can be used to interact with the geospatial data.

The available style options when using the CONVERT function with XML data are detailed in Table 1-10.

Table 1-10. *Style Options for XML Data*

Style Code	Output
0	The default value. Discards unneeded whitespace and does not allow an internal DTD to be created
1	Preserves all whitespace
2	Discards unneeded whitespace but allows limited DTD processing
3	Preserves whitespace and allows limited DTD processing

Why Is Using the Correct Data Type Important?

The most commonly used, and most commonly misused, data type in SQL Server is INT. When developers must store whole numbers, INT is always the default choice. Often, however, developers must only store small values. An INT uses 4 bytes of data, whereas if a SMALLINT would suffice, only 2 bytes of storage would be used. In cases in which you have small lookup tables, with less than 255 rows, a TINYINT could be used as the primary key, only using 1 byte of storage per row.

You're probably thinking to yourself at this point that storage is relatively cheap these days. Do 2 or 3 bytes of data here and there really matter? To answer that question, you should not only think in terms of storage but in terms of memory usage and application performance.

Imagine that you have a fact table containing 1 billion rows that you must join to five dimension tables, each containing 30,000 rows. If you have used the INT data type for the primary key in each of these dimensions, that column would be 117KB in each of the dimension tables, but the corresponding foreign key column in the fact table would be 3.72GB! Now let's multiply that by 5, so that each dimension table is covered. We are now at 18.6GB. This is how much data SQL Server will have to read from disk into memory before probably spooling out again, to TempDB, in order to join the tables in your query. If we had used the SMALLINT data type for our dimension tables instead, SQL Server would only have to consume 9.3GB of data.

Another consideration when choosing data types is ensuring that the same data type is used when the same data is stored in multiple columns. For example, imagine that you have an ETL process that pulls data from an OLTP database into a data warehouse. You may populate the data warehouse by running queries that join or filter tables on columns such as dates. If the data types are not consistent between columns—for example, a date is stored as the DATE data type in one table and stored as a DATETIME2 in another column—then implicit casting operations will occur. These have negative impacts on performance and even stop optimal indexes from being used.

Tip   If data type casting is required, I generally recommend doing this manually, with the CAST or CONVERT functions, instead of allowing implicit conversions. This can make code easier to understand when debugging

---

Summary

SQL Server provides a large amount of data types out of the box that will accommodate the needs of most development scenarios. Numeric values can be stored as whole numbers, or with either exact or approximate decimal precision. Character data can be stored with Unicode or non-Unicode character sets. SQL Server can also store dates, times, or both. You also have the option of recording time zone information.

Values can be converted between different data types using either the CAST or CONVERT functions. When using the CONVERT function, additional translation information can be provided, via styles.

When developing using SQL Server, it is very important to use the correct data type. When choosing a data type, a developer should use the most limiting data type that will store all required values. If a data type with a more expansive range is erroneously used, then, as a database scales, a severe impact of memory utilization and performance may be witnessed.

CHAPTER 2

Understanding XML

XML (Extensible Markup Language) is a markup language, similar to HTML, that was designed for the purpose of storing and transporting data. Like HTML, XML consists of tags. Unlike HTML, however, these tags are not predefined. Instead, they are defined by the document author. An XML document has a tree structure, beginning with a root node and containing child nodes (also known as child elements). Each element can contain data but also `1..n` attributes.

This chapter will assist you in your understanding of XML, by explaining the structure of an XML document, before diving into the difference between XML fragments and well-formed XML, XML schemas, and how XML data is often used in SQL Server.

Understanding XML

Each attribute can contain data that describes the element. For example, imagine that you require details of sales orders to be stored in XML format. It would be sensible to assume that each sales order be stored in a separate element within the document. But what about that sales order properties, such as order date, customer ID, product IDs, quantities, and prices? These pieces of information could either be stored as child elements of the sales order element, or they could be stored as attributes of the sales order element. There are no set rules for when you should use child elements

© Peter A. Carter 2018
P. A. Carter, *SQL Server Advanced Data Types*,
https://doi.org/10.1007/978-1-4842-3901-8_2

or attributes to describe properties of an element. This choice is at the discretion of the document author.

The XML document in Listing 2-1 provides a sample XML document that holds the details of sales orders for a fictional organization. In this example, the document author has chosen to use an element to store each sales order and a nested element to store each line item of the order. The details of each sales order and line item are stored in attributes of the elements.

Listing 2-1. Sales Orders Stored Using Attribute-Centric Approach

```
<SalesOrders>
  <SalesOrder OrderDate="2013-03-07" CustomerID="57" OrderID="3168">
    <LineItem StockItemID="176" Quantity="5" UnitPrice="240.00" />
    <LineItem StockItemID="143" Quantity="108"
    UnitPrice="18.00" />
    <LineItem StockItemID="136" Quantity="3" UnitPrice="32.00" />
    <LineItem StockItemID="92" Quantity="48" UnitPrice="18.00" />
  </SalesOrder>
  <SalesOrder OrderDate="2013-03-22" CustomerID="57" OrderID="4107">
    <LineItem StockItemID="153" Quantity="40" UnitPrice="4.50" />
    <LineItem StockItemID="36" Quantity="9" UnitPrice="13.00" />
    <LineItem StockItemID="208" Quantity="108" UnitPrice="2.70" />
  </SalesOrder>
  <SalesOrder OrderDate="2013-04-09" CustomerID="57" OrderID="4980">
    <LineItem StockItemID="102" Quantity="10" UnitPrice="35.00" />
    <LineItem StockItemID="144" Quantity="24" UnitPrice="18.00" />
    <LineItem StockItemID="79" Quantity="36" UnitPrice="18.00" />
    <LineItem StockItemID="217" Quantity="10" UnitPrice="25.00" />
  </SalesOrder>
  <SalesOrder OrderDate="2016-01-09" CustomerID="57" OrderID="64608">
    <LineItem StockItemID="156" Quantity="40" UnitPrice="15.00" />
    <LineItem StockItemID="56" Quantity="7" UnitPrice="13.00" />
  </SalesOrder>
```

```
  <SalesOrder OrderDate="2016-05-25" CustomerID="57"
  OrderID="73148">
    <LineItem StockItemID="31" Quantity="7" UnitPrice="13.00" />
    <LineItem StockItemID="103" Quantity="2" UnitPrice="35.00" />
  </SalesOrder>
</SalesOrders>
```

The XML in Listing 2-1 can be generated by running the query in Listing 2-2 against the WideWorldImporters database.

Listing 2-2. Generating Attribute-Centric XML

```
SELECT
          SalesOrder.OrderDate
        , SalesOrder.CustomerID
        , SalesOrder.OrderID
        , LineItem.StockItemID
        , LineItem.Quantity
        , LineItem.UnitPrice
FROM Sales.Orders SalesOrder
INNER JOIN Sales.OrderLines LineItem
        ON LineItem.OrderID = SalesOrder.OrderID
WHERE SalesOrder.OrderID IN
(
3168,
4107,
4980,
64608,
73148
)
FOR XML AUTO, ROOT('SalesOrders') ;
```

> **Note**   The FOR XML clause is used to convert the results of a query into XML format. FOR XML is discussed in Chapter 3.

The XML document in Listing 2-2 stores the same information as the document in Listing 2-3. This time, however, the document author has used an element-centric approach, instead of an attribute-centric approach. Therefore, the data is stored in child elements, as opposed to attributes.

Listing 2-3. Sales Orders Stored Using Element-Centric Approach

```
<SalesOrders>
  <SalesOrder>
    <OrderDate>2013-03-07</OrderDate>
    <CustomerID>57</CustomerID>
    <OrderID>3168</OrderID>
    <LineItem>
      <StockItemID>176</StockItemID>
      <Quantity>5</Quantity>
      <UnitPrice>240.00</UnitPrice>
    </LineItem>
    <LineItem>
      <StockItemID>143</StockItemID>
      <Quantity>108</Quantity>
      <UnitPrice>18.00</UnitPrice>
    </LineItem>
    <LineItem>
      <StockItemID>136</StockItemID>
      <Quantity>3</Quantity>
      <UnitPrice>32.00</UnitPrice>
    </LineItem>
```

```
  <LineItem>
    <StockItemID>92</StockItemID>
    <Quantity>48</Quantity>
    <UnitPrice>18.00</UnitPrice>
  </LineItem>
</SalesOrder>
<SalesOrder>
  <OrderDate>2013-03-22</OrderDate>
  <CustomerID>57</CustomerID>
  <OrderID>4107</OrderID>
  <LineItem>
    <StockItemID>153</StockItemID>
    <Quantity>40</Quantity>
    <UnitPrice>4.50</UnitPrice>
  </LineItem>
  <LineItem>
    <StockItemID>36</StockItemID>
    <Quantity>9</Quantity>
    <UnitPrice>13.00</UnitPrice>
  </LineItem>
  <LineItem>
    <StockItemID>208</StockItemID>
    <Quantity>108</Quantity>
    <UnitPrice>2.70</UnitPrice>
  </LineItem>
</SalesOrder>
<SalesOrder>
  <OrderDate>2013-04-09</OrderDate>
  <CustomerID>57</CustomerID>
  <OrderID>4980</OrderID>
```

```
  <LineItem>
    <StockItemID>102</StockItemID>
    <Quantity>10</Quantity>
    <UnitPrice>35.00</UnitPrice>
  </LineItem>
  <LineItem>
    <StockItemID>144</StockItemID>
    <Quantity>24</Quantity>
    <UnitPrice>18.00</UnitPrice>
  </LineItem>
  <LineItem>
    <StockItemID>79</StockItemID>
    <Quantity>36</Quantity>
    <UnitPrice>18.00</UnitPrice>
  </LineItem>
  <LineItem>
    <StockItemID>217</StockItemID>
    <Quantity>10</Quantity>
    <UnitPrice>25.00</UnitPrice>
  </LineItem>
</SalesOrder>
<SalesOrder>
  <OrderDate>2016-01-09</OrderDate>
  <CustomerID>57</CustomerID>
  <OrderID>64608</OrderID>
  <LineItem>
    <StockItemID>156</StockItemID>
    <Quantity>40</Quantity>
    <UnitPrice>15.00</UnitPrice>
```

```
    </LineItem>
    <LineItem>
      <StockItemID>56</StockItemID>
      <Quantity>7</Quantity>
      <UnitPrice>13.00</UnitPrice>
    </LineItem>
  </SalesOrder>
  <SalesOrder>
    <OrderDate>2016-05-25</OrderDate>
    <CustomerID>57</CustomerID>
    <OrderID>73148</OrderID>
    <LineItem>
      <StockItemID>31</StockItemID>
      <Quantity>7</Quantity>
      <UnitPrice>13.00</UnitPrice>
    </LineItem>
    <LineItem>
      <StockItemID>103</StockItemID>
      <Quantity>2</Quantity>
      <UnitPrice>35.00</UnitPrice>
    </LineItem>
  </SalesOrder>
</SalesOrders>
```

The XML document in Listing 2-3 can be generated by running the query in Listing 2-4.

Listing 2-4. Generating Element-Centric XML

```
SELECT
        SalesOrder.OrderDate
      , SalesOrder.CustomerID
      , SalesOrder.OrderID
```

```
        , LineItem.StockItemID
        , LineItem.Quantity
        , LineItem.UnitPrice
FROM Sales.Orders SalesOrder
INNER JOIN Sales.OrderLines LineItem
        ON LineItem.OrderID = SalesOrder.OrderID
WHERE SalesOrder.OrderID IN
(
3168,
4107,
4980,
64608,
73148
)
FOR XML AUTO, ELEMENTS, ROOT('SalesOrders') ;
```

Note   The FOR XML clause is discussed in Chapter 3.

The picture in Figure 2-1 calls out each noteworthy aspect of the attribute-centric document from Listing 2-1.

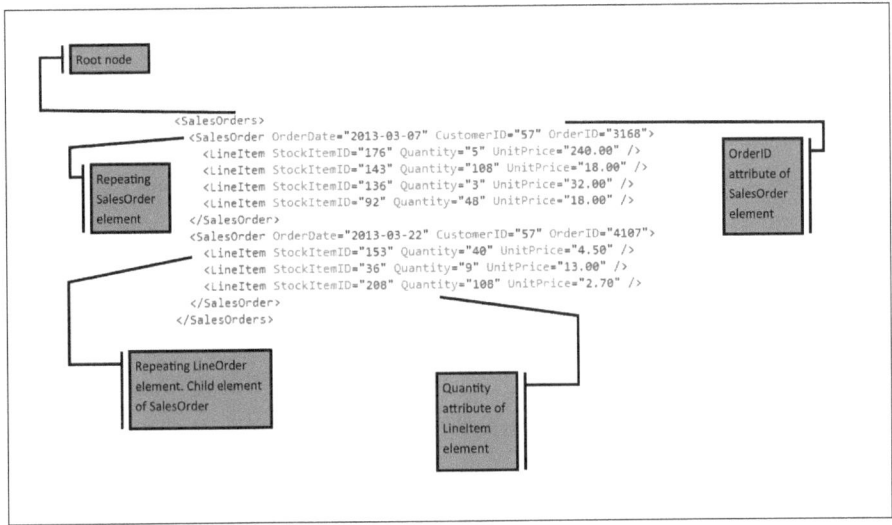

Figure 2-1. *Aspects of an XML document*

There are several things to note when looking at this XML document. First, elements begin with the element name, encapsulated within angle brackets. They end with the element name, preceded by a backslash and enclosed in angle brackets. Any elements that fall between these two tags are child elements of the tag.

Attributes are enclosed in double quotation marks and reside within the beginning tag of an element. For example, OrderID is an attribute of the <SalesOrder> element.

It is acceptable to have repeating elements. You can see that <SalesOrder> is a repeating element, as two separate sales orders are stored in this XML document. The <SalesOrders> element is the document's root element and is the only element that is not allowed to be complex. This means that it cannot have attributes and cannot be repeating. Attributes can never repeat within an element. Therefore, if you require a node to repeat, you should use a nested element as opposed to an attribute.

Well-Formed XML

SQL Server supports both XML fragments and well-formed XML. Using well-formed XML is favorable, as there is a degree of validation. Therefore, you should always try to use well-formed XML, where possible. For an XML document to be well-formed, certain requirements must be met, and these requirements are listed following:

- XML documents must have a single, non-repeating root element.

- XML elements must have a closing tag.

- XML elements must be properly nested, with closing tags in the reverse order of opening tags.

- XML attribute values must be quoted with double-quotation marks.

- Each attribute name must be unique within an element.

Tip   XML tags are case-sensitive.

Although SQL Server supports XML fragments (XML documents that are not well-formed), the syntax must still be syntactically correct. For example, consider the script in Listing 2-5. The XML document is syntactically incorrect, because the root node is missing a closing angle bracket.

Listing 2-5. ·Syntactically Incorrect XML

```
DECLARE @Example XML ;

SET @Example =
'<SalesOrder OrderDate="2013-03-07" CustomerID="57"
OrderID="3168">
    <LineItem StockItemID="176" Quantity="5" UnitPrice="240.00" />
    <LineItem StockItemID="143" Quantity="108"
    UnitPrice="18.00" />
    <LineItem StockItemID="136" Quantity="3" UnitPrice="32.00" />
    <LineItem StockItemID="92" Quantity="48" UnitPrice="18.00" />
  </SalesOrder>
  <SalesOrder OrderDate="2013-03-22" CustomerID="57"
  OrderID="4107">
    <LineItem StockItemID="153" Quantity="40" UnitPrice="4.50" />
    <LineItem StockItemID="36" Quantity="9" UnitPrice="13.00" />
    <LineItem StockItemID="208" Quantity="108" UnitPrice="2.70" />
  </SalesOrder' ;

  SELECT @Example ;
```

Running the script in Listing 2-5 will produce the error shown in Figure 2-2.

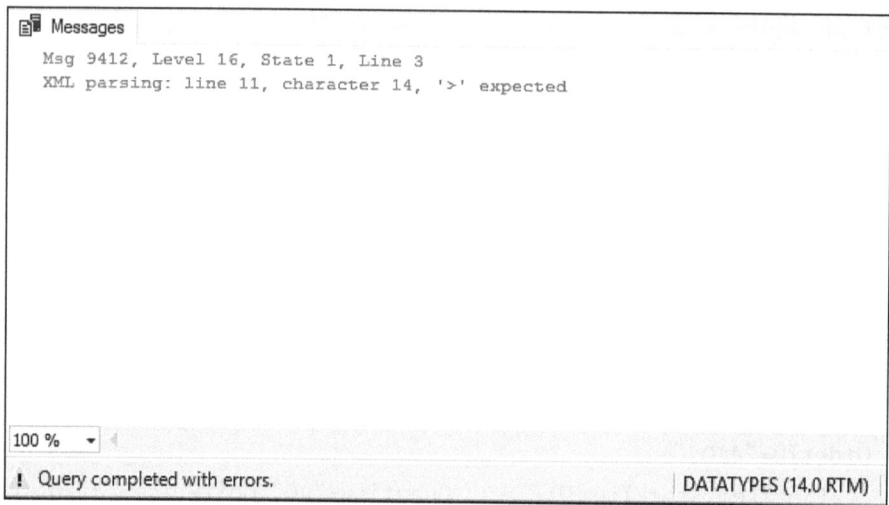

Figure 2-2. XML syntax error

If we were to correct the syntax error and rerun the script (Listing 2-6), the script would run and return an XML document as the result set, even though the document is not well-formed. It is not well-formed, because there is not a root node.

Listing 2-6. XML Fragment

```
DECLARE @Example XML ;

SET @Example =
 '<SalesOrder OrderDate="2013-03-07" CustomerID="57"
 OrderID="3168">
    <LineItem StockItemID="176" Quantity="5" UnitPrice="240.00" />
    <LineItem StockItemID="143" Quantity="108" UnitPrice="18.00" />
    <LineItem StockItemID="136" Quantity="3" UnitPrice="32.00" />
```

```
   <LineItem StockItemID="92" Quantity="48" UnitPrice="18.00" />
</SalesOrder>
<SalesOrder OrderDate="2013-03-22" CustomerID="57"
OrderID="4107">
   <LineItem StockItemID="153" Quantity="40" UnitPrice="4.50" />
   <LineItem StockItemID="36" Quantity="9" UnitPrice="13.00" />
   <LineItem StockItemID="208" Quantity="108" UnitPrice="2.70" />
</SalesOrder>' ;

SELECT @Example ;
```

The results of running the script in Listing 2-6 are shown in Figure 2-3.

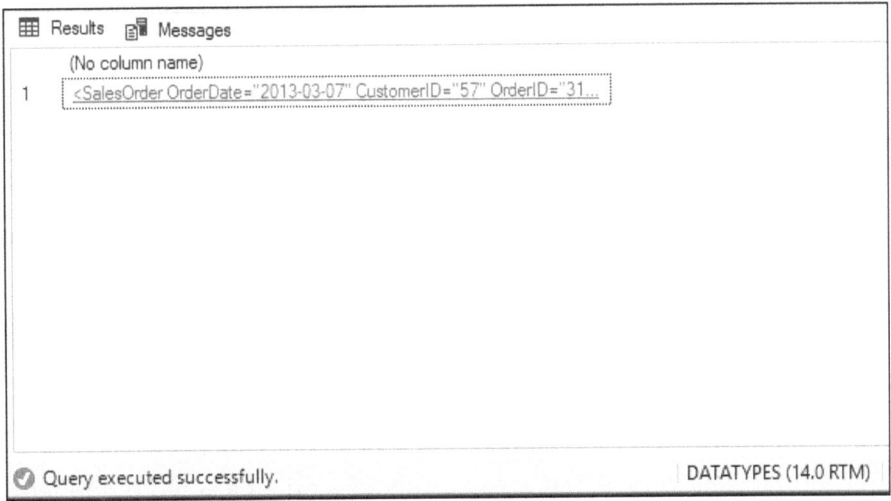

Figure 2-3. *XML fragment*

To make the XML document returned, well-formed XML, we would have to add the root node, as demonstrated in Listing 2-7.

41

Listing 2-7. Well-Formed XML

```
DECLARE @Example XML ;

SET @Example =
'<SalesOrders>
  <SalesOrder OrderDate="2013-03-07" CustomerID="57"
  OrderID="3168">
    <LineItem StockItemID="176" Quantity="5" UnitPrice="240.00" />
    <LineItem StockItemID="143" Quantity="108" UnitPrice="18.00" />
    <LineItem StockItemID="136" Quantity="3" UnitPrice="32.00" />
    <LineItem StockItemID="92" Quantity="48" UnitPrice="18.00" />
  </SalesOrder>
  <SalesOrder OrderDate="2013-03-22" CustomerID="57"
  OrderID="4107">
    <LineItem StockItemID="153" Quantity="40" UnitPrice="4.50" />
    <LineItem StockItemID="36" Quantity="9" UnitPrice="13.00" />
    <LineItem StockItemID="208" Quantity="108" UnitPrice="2.70" />
  </SalesOrder>
</SalesOrders>' ;

SELECT @Example ;
```

Newcomers to XML are often confused by the difference between a well-formed XML document and a valid XML document. Even if an XML document is well-formed, it is not considered valid, unless its components conform to the details provided in an associated schema. The original form of the XML schema was known as a DTD (document type definition), but now it is known as an XSD (XML schema definition). DTD schemas are not supported by SQL Server, so the focus of this chapter will be on understanding XSD schemas.

Understanding XSD Schemas

The format of an XML document can be defined by an XSD schema. An XSD schema will define the document's structure, including data types, if complex types (complex elements) are allowed, and how many times an element must occur (or is limited to occurring) within a document. It also defines the sequence of elements and if an element is mandatory. The main components of an XSD schema are as follows:

- Element declarations, defining the properties of an elements:

  - Element name

  - Element default value

  - Element type

  - Elements integrity constraints

- Attribute declarations, defining the properties of an attribute

  - Attribute name

  - Attribute default value

  - Attribute type

  - Attribute constraints

- Simple and complex types

- Model group and attribute group definitions

- Element particle and attribute use

If an element is bound to a primitive data type and does not include child elements or attributes, it is a simple type. If an element has child elements, attributes, or other special properties, such as being bound to an ordered sequence, it must be defined as a complex type.

Model groups and attribute groups are named groups of nodes that can be reused in multiple type definitions. Element particles and attribute uses define the complex properties of a node. For attributes, this might include the optionality of the node. For an element, this may also be minimum and maximum occurrences of the node.

Listing 2-8 shows a schema declaration for the well-formed XML document in Listing 2-7.

Listing 2-8. XSD Schema

```
<xs:schema attributeFormDefault="unqualified"
elementFormDefault="qualified" xmlns:xs="http://www.
w3.org/2001/XMLSchema">
  <xs:element name="SalesOrders">
    <xs:complexType>
      <xs:sequence>
        <xs:element name="SalesOrder" maxOccurs="unbounded"
        minOccurs="0">
          <xs:complexType>
            <xs:sequence>
              <xs:element name="LineItem" maxOccurs="unbounded"
              minOccurs="0">
                <xs:complexType>
                  <xs:simpleContent>
                    <xs:extension base="xs:string">
                      <xs:attribute type="xs:short"
                      name="StockItemID" use="optional"/>
                      <xs:attribute type="xs:byte"
                      name="Quantity" use="optional"/>
                      <xs:attribute type="xs:float"
                      name="UnitPrice" use="optional"/>
                    </xs:extension>
```

```
        </xs:simpleContent>
      </xs:complexType>
    </xs:element>
  </xs:sequence>
  <xs:attribute type="xs:date" name="OrderDate"
  use="optional"/>
  <xs:attribute type="xs:byte" name="CustomerID"
  use="optional"/>
  <xs:attribute type="xs:short" name="OrderID"
  use="optional"/>
      </xs:complexType>
    </xs:element>
  </xs:sequence>
  </xs:complexType>
  </xs:element>
</xs:schema>
```

Tip   There are free online tools that will create an XSD schema, based on an XML document. For example, `FreeFormatter.com` offers an XSD generation tool, which can be found at `www.freeformatter.com/xsd-generator.html`. Alternatively, Visual Studio can also automatically generate schemas.

An XML document must be well-formed for it to be bound to a schema. If an XML document is bound to a schema, it is called valid, or typed, XML. SQL Server supports the use of XSD schemas through XML schema collections, which are discussed in Chapter 4.

45

XML Usage Scenarios in SQL Server

The ability to work with XML in SQL Server can be very useful, in many different cases. For example, imagine that you have a middleware application that pulls sales orders from a web site and pushes them into an SQL Server database. SQL Server's ability to work with XML data allows a developer to use native SQL Server tooling to shred that XML sales order into a relational table structure. XML documents can be shredded into relational values by using the XQuery Nodes method or the OPENXML() function. Both will be discussed in Chapter 4. Conversely, imagine that you must pass sales orders to a middleware system that requires an XML document. This could also be achieved using SQL Server. You simply run a query to retrieve the relational data and append the FOR XML clause, which will convert the data to XML. FOR XML will be discussed in Chapter 3.

SQL Server's support for schema validation also means that an application can validate its data against a schema supplied by an SQL Server developer before sending it across the network. SQL Server can also validate a document against an XML schema before passing it to an application. Essentially, you can create a data contract between the different layers of an application, saving time and allowing for better error-handling.

In another use case, for storing data as XML in SQL Server, imagine that you have an XML document that contains detailed product definitions and descriptions. You could, of course, simply maintain this file as an XML file in the file system, but storing the document in SQL Server allows you to query this XML document and join the results to relational information that is stored in an SQL Server database. XML documents can be queried in SQL Server, using XQuery, which is discussed in Chapter 4.

Many SQL Server data structures are stored in XML format. For example, the following SQL Server features all rely on XML data structures:

- Extended events

- Event information within DDL triggers

- Event notifications

- Data collectors

Native SQL Server support for XML allows developers and administrators to interact with this data.

If you are reading this book and come from an application development background, then, at this point, you might be thinking "surely, everybody just uses JSON these days. Why bother with XML?" JSON is a much more lightweight document format, which is discussed in Chapters 6–9 of this book. XML still has functionality that is not supported by JSON, however. For example, if you wish to use the following functionality, you will require XML, rather than JSON:

- Schema validation

- XPath

- Namespaces

- XLST

Summary

XML is a markup language like HTML. Instead of having predefined tags, however, the tags are defined by the document author. An XML document consists of elements and attributes and can store data in a semi-structured tree format.

SQL Server supports XML fragments, well-formed XML documents, and valid (schema-bound) XML documents. To be well-formed, an XML document must contain a single root node, and an XML document cannot be schema-bound, unless it is well-formed. The phrases *XML document* and *XML instance* are often used interchangeably (including in this chapter). Strictly speaking, however, XML document refers to XML that is well-formed, whereas an XML instance could refer to either a well-formed XML document or an XML fragment.

XML documents can be bound to a DTD (document type definition) or an XSD (XML schema definition) schema. SQL Server only supports storing XSD schemas, however. XSD schemas are implemented in SQL Server, through an XML schema collection.

CHAPTER 3

Constructing XML with T-SQL

T-SQL allows you to convert relational results sets into XML, by using the FOR XML clause in your SELECT statement. There are four modes that can be used with the FOR XML clause; FOR XML RAW, FOR XML AUTO, FOR XML PATH, and FOR XML EXPLICIT. This chapter will demonstrate how the FOR XML clause works in RAW mode, AUTO mode, PATH mode, and EXPLICIT mode. As the chapter progresses, we will move from simple to more complex examples.

Using FOR XML RAW

The simplest and easiest to understand of the FOR XML modes is FOR XML RAW. This mode will transform each row in a relational result set into an element within a flat XML document. Consider the query in Listing 3-1, which extracts details of sales orders from the WideWorldImporters database.

Listing 3-1. WideWorldImporters Sales Order Query

```
SELECT
        SalesOrder.OrderDate
      , Customers.CustomerName
      , SalesOrder.OrderID
      , LineItem.StockItemID
```

© Peter A. Carter 2018
P. A. Carter, *SQL Server Advanced Data Types*,
https://doi.org/10.1007/978-1-4842-3901-8_3

```
            , LineItem.Quantity
            , LineItem.UnitPrice
FROM Sales.Orders SalesOrder
INNER JOIN Sales.OrderLines LineItem
        ON LineItem.OrderID = SalesOrder.OrderID
INNER JOIN Warehouse.StockItems Product
        ON Product.StockItemID = LineItem.StockItemID
INNER JOIN Sales.Customers Customers
        ON Customers.CustomerID = SalesOrder.CustomerID
WHERE customers.CustomerName = 'Agrita Abele' ;
```

This query extracts the details of orders placed by a customer called Agrita Abele. A partial output of the query can be found in Figure 3-1.

	OrderDate	CustomerName	OrderID	StockItemName	Quantity	UnitPrice
1	2016-05-19	Agrita Abele	72787	Developer joke mug - when your hammer is C++ (Black)	2	13.00
2	2016-05-19	Agrita Abele	72787	Developer joke mug - when your hammer is C++ (White)	9	13.00
3	2016-05-27	Agrita Abele	73350	DBA joke mug - you might be a DBA if (Black)	4	13.00
4	2016-05-27	Agrita Abele	73350	Developer joke mug - that's a hardware problem (Black)	3	13.00
5	2016-05-19	Agrita Abele	72770	"The Gu" red shirt XML tag t-shirt (Black) 5XL	120	18.00
6	2016-05-18	Agrita Abele	72637	"The Gu" red shirt XML tag t-shirt (Black) XXL	24	18.00
7	2016-05-27	Agrita Abele	73350	Halloween zombie mask (Light Brown) S	24	18.00
8	2016-05-18	Agrita Abele	72669	Halloween skull mask (Gray) M	60	18.00
9	2016-05-19	Agrita Abele	72787	Furry gorilla with big eyes slippers (Black) XL	9	32.00
10	2016-05-27	Agrita Abele	73350	Tape dispenser (Blue)	90	32.00
11	2016-05-18	Agrita Abele	72713	Tape dispenser (Red)	20	32.00
12	2016-05-19	Agrita Abele	72770	Superhero action jacket (Blue) S	8	25.00
13	2016-05-27	Agrita Abele	73350	RC toy sedan car with remote control (Red) 1/50 scale	2	25.00
14	2016-05-18	Agrita Abele	72637	Superhero action jacket (Blue) 3XS	1	25.00
15	2016-05-19	Agrita Abele	72770	Black and orange handle with care despatch tape 48mmx100m	96	4.10
16	2016-05-18	Agrita Abele	72671	Alien officer hoodie (Black) 4XL	6	35.00
17	2016-05-18	Agrita Abele	72637	Furry animal socks (Pink) S	96	5.00
18	2016-05-18	Agrita Abele	72669	Permanent marker black 5mm nib (Black) 5mm	84	2.70
19	2016-05-27	Agrita Abele	73340	Superhero action jacket (Blue) 5XL	2	34.00
20	2016-05-27	Agrita Abele	73356	Chocolate sharks 250g	192	8.55
21	2016-05-19	Agrita Abele	72787	Novelty chilli chocolates 250g	240	8.55
22	2016-05-18	Agrita Abele	72671	Packing knife with metal insert blade (Yellow) 9mm	35	1.89
23	2016-05-18	Agrita Abele	72671	Shipping carton (Brown) 480x270x320mm	150	2.74
24	2016-05-19	Agrita Abele	72770	Shipping carton (Brown) 356x229x229mm	175	1.14
25	2016-05-19	Agrita Abele	72787	Ride on big wheel monster truck (Black) 1/12 scale	4	345.00
26	2016-05-18	Agrita Abele	72669	10 mm Anti static bubble wrap (Blue) 10m	70	26.00
27	2016-05-27	Agrita Abele	73340	32 mm Double sided bubble wrap 50m	20	112.00

Query executed successfully.   DATATYPES (14.0 RTM) | DATATYPES\Admin

Figure 3-1. *WideWorldImporters sales order output*

If we were to add a FOR XML clause using RAW mode, the results would be returned in the form of an XML fragment. The amended query in Listing 3-2 will return the XML document, instead of a relational result set.

Listing 3-2. WideWorldImporters Sales Orders Using FOR XML RAW

```
SELECT
          SalesOrder.OrderDate
        , Customers.CustomerName
        , SalesOrder.OrderID
        , Product.StockItemName
        , LineItem.Quantity
        , LineItem.UnitPrice
FROM Sales.Orders SalesOrder
INNER JOIN Sales.OrderLines LineItem
        ON LineItem.OrderID = SalesOrder.OrderID
INNER JOIN Warehouse.StockItems Product
        ON Product.StockItemID = LineItem.StockItemID
INNER JOIN Sales.Customers Customers
        ON Customers.CustomerID = SalesOrder.CustomerID
WHERE customers.CustomerName = 'Agrita Abele'
FOR XML RAW ;
```

Listing 3-3 illustrates the XML fragment that is returned.

Listing 3-3. WideWorldImporters Sales Orders Using FOR XML RAW

```
<row OrderDate="2016-05-19" CustomerName="Agrita Abele"
OrderID="72787" StockItemName="Developer joke mug - when your
hammer is C++ (Black)" Quantity="2" UnitPrice="13.00" />
<row OrderDate="2016-05-19" CustomerName="Agrita Abele"
OrderID="72787" StockItemName="Developer joke mug - when your
hammer is C++ (White)" Quantity="9" UnitPrice="13.00" />
```

```xml
<row OrderDate="2016-05-27" CustomerName="Agrita Abele"
OrderID="73350" StockItemName="DBA joke mug - you might be a
DBA if (Black)" Quantity="4" UnitPrice="13.00" />
<row OrderDate="2016-05-27" CustomerName="Agrita Abele"
OrderID="73350" StockItemName="Developer joke mug - that's a
hardware problem (Black)" Quantity="3" UnitPrice="13.00" />
<row OrderDate="2016-05-19" CustomerName="Agrita Abele"
OrderID="72770" StockItemName="&quot;The Gu&quot; red shirt XML
tag t-shirt (Black) 5XL" Quantity="120" UnitPrice="18.00" />
<row OrderDate="2016-05-18" CustomerName="Agrita Abele"
OrderID="72637" StockItemName="&quot;The Gu&quot; red shirt XML
tag t-shirt (Black) XXL" Quantity="24" UnitPrice="18.00" />
<row OrderDate="2016-05-27" CustomerName="Agrita Abele"
OrderID="73350" StockItemName="Halloween zombie mask (Light
Brown) S" Quantity="24" UnitPrice="18.00" />
<row OrderDate="2016-05-18" CustomerName="Agrita Abele"
OrderID="72669" StockItemName="Halloween skull mask (Gray) M"
Quantity="60" UnitPrice="18.00" />
<row OrderDate="2016-05-19" CustomerName="Agrita Abele"
OrderID="72787" StockItemName="Furry gorilla with big eyes
slippers (Black) XL" Quantity="9" UnitPrice="32.00" />
<row OrderDate="2016-05-27" CustomerName="Agrita Abele"
OrderID="73350" StockItemName="Tape dispenser (Blue)"
Quantity="90" UnitPrice="32.00" />
<row OrderDate="2016-05-18" CustomerName="Agrita Abele"
OrderID="72713" StockItemName="Tape dispenser (Red)"
Quantity="20" UnitPrice="32.00" />
<row OrderDate="2016-05-19" CustomerName="Agrita Abele"
OrderID="72770" StockItemName="Superhero action jacket (Blue)
S" Quantity="8" UnitPrice="25.00" />
```

```
<row OrderDate="2016-05-27" CustomerName="Agrita Abele"
OrderID="73350" StockItemName="RC toy sedan car with remote
control (Red) 1/50 scale" Quantity="2" UnitPrice="25.00" />
<row OrderDate="2016-05-18" CustomerName="Agrita Abele"
OrderID="72637" StockItemName="Superhero action jacket (Blue)
3XS" Quantity="1" UnitPrice="25.00" />
<row OrderDate="2016-05-19" CustomerName="Agrita Abele"
OrderID="72770" StockItemName="Black and orange handle with care
despatch tape  48mmx100m" Quantity="96" UnitPrice="4.10" />
<row OrderDate="2016-05-18" CustomerName="Agrita Abele"
OrderID="72671" StockItemName="Alien officer hoodie (Black)
4XL" Quantity="6" UnitPrice="35.00" />
<row OrderDate="2016-05-18" CustomerName="Agrita Abele"
OrderID="72637" StockItemName="Furry animal socks (Pink) S"
Quantity="96" UnitPrice="5.00" />
<row OrderDate="2016-05-18" CustomerName="Agrita Abele"
OrderID="72669" StockItemName="Permanent marker black 5mm nib
(Black) 5mm" Quantity="84" UnitPrice="2.70" />
<row OrderDate="2016-05-27" CustomerName="Agrita Abele"
OrderID="73340" StockItemName="Superhero action jacket (Blue)
5XL" Quantity="2" UnitPrice="34.00" />
<row OrderDate="2016-05-27" CustomerName="Agrita Abele"
OrderID="73356" StockItemName="Chocolate sharks 250g"
Quantity="192" UnitPrice="8.55" />
<row OrderDate="2016-05-19" CustomerName="Agrita Abele"
OrderID="72787" StockItemName="Novelty chilli chocolates 250g"
Quantity="240" UnitPrice="8.55" />
<row OrderDate="2016-05-18" CustomerName="Agrita Abele"
OrderID="72671" StockItemName="Packing knife with metal insert
blade (Yellow) 9mm" Quantity="35" UnitPrice="1.89" />
```

```
<row OrderDate="2016-05-18" CustomerName="Agrita Abele"
OrderID="72671" StockItemName="Shipping carton (Brown)
480x270x320mm" Quantity="150" UnitPrice="2.74" />
<row OrderDate="2016-05-19" CustomerName="Agrita Abele"
OrderID="72770" StockItemName="Shipping carton (Brown)
356x229x229mm" Quantity="175" UnitPrice="1.14" />
<row OrderDate="2016-05-19" CustomerName="Agrita Abele"
OrderID="72787" StockItemName="Ride on big wheel monster truck
(Black) 1/12 scale" Quantity="4" UnitPrice="345.00" />
<row OrderDate="2016-05-18" CustomerName="Agrita Abele"
OrderID="72669" StockItemName="10 mm Anti static bubble wrap
(Blue) 10m" Quantity="70" UnitPrice="26.00" />
<row OrderDate="2016-05-27" CustomerName="Agrita Abele"
OrderID="73340" StockItemName="32 mm Double sided bubble wrap
50m" Quantity="20" UnitPrice="112.00" />
<row OrderDate="2016-05-18" CustomerName="Agrita Abele"
OrderID="72669" StockItemName="Office cube periscope (Black)"
Quantity="20" UnitPrice="18.50" />
<row OrderDate="2016-05-27" CustomerName="Agrita Abele"
OrderID="73356" StockItemName="Ride on vintage American toy
coupe (Black) 1/12 scale" Quantity="10" UnitPrice="285.00" />
```

The first thing that we should note about this XML instance is that it is an XML fragment, as opposed to a well-formed XML document, because there is no root node. The <row> element cannot be the root node, because it repeats. This means that we cannot validate the XML against a schema. Therefore, when using the FOR XML clause, you should consider using the ROOT keyword. This will force a root element, with a name of your choosing, to be created within the document. This is demonstrated in Listing 3-4.

Listing 3-4. Adding a Root Node

```
SELECT
          SalesOrder.OrderDate
        , Customers.CustomerName
        , SalesOrder.OrderID
        , Product.StockItemName
        , LineItem.Quantity
        , LineItem.UnitPrice
FROM Sales.Orders SalesOrder
INNER JOIN Sales.OrderLines LineItem
        ON LineItem.OrderID = SalesOrder.OrderID
INNER JOIN Warehouse.StockItems Product
        ON Product.StockItemID = LineItem.StockItemID
INNER JOIN Sales.Customers Customers
        ON Customers.CustomerID = SalesOrder.CustomerID
WHERE customers.CustomerName = 'Agrita Abele'
FOR XML RAW, ROOT('SalesOrders') ;
```

Partial output of the resulting well-formed XML document can be found in Listing 3-5.

Listing 3-5. Output of XML Document with Root Node

```
<SalesOrders>
  <row OrderDate="2016-05-19" CustomerName="Agrita Abele"
  OrderID="72787" StockItemName="Developer joke mug - when your
  hammer is C++ (Black)" Quantity="2" UnitPrice="13.00" />
  <row OrderDate="2016-05-19" CustomerName="Agrita Abele"
  OrderID="72787" StockItemName="Developer joke mug - when your
  hammer is C++ (White)" Quantity="9" UnitPrice="13.00" />
```

```
<row OrderDate="2016-05-27" CustomerName="Agrita Abele"
OrderID="73350" StockItemName="DBA joke mug - you might be a
DBA if (Black)" Quantity="4" UnitPrice="13.00" />
<row OrderDate="2016-05-27" CustomerName="Agrita Abele"
OrderID="73350" StockItemName="Developer joke mug - that's a
hardware problem (Black)" Quantity="3" UnitPrice="13.00" />
<row OrderDate="2016-05-19" CustomerName="Agrita Abele"
OrderID="72770" StockItemName="&quot;The Gu&quot; red shirt XML
tag t-shirt (Black) 5XL" Quantity="120" UnitPrice="18.00" />
<row OrderDate="2016-05-18" CustomerName="Agrita Abele"
OrderID="72637" StockItemName="&quot;The Gu&quot; red shirt XML
tag t-shirt (Black) XXL" Quantity="24" UnitPrice="18.00" />
<row OrderDate="2016-05-27" CustomerName="Agrita Abele"
OrderID="73350" StockItemName="Halloween zombie mask (Light
Brown) S" Quantity="24" UnitPrice="18.00" />
<row OrderDate="2016-05-18" CustomerName="Agrita Abele"
OrderID="72669" StockItemName="Halloween skull mask (Gray) M"
Quantity="60" UnitPrice="18.00" />
<row OrderDate="2016-05-19" CustomerName="Agrita Abele"
OrderID="72787" StockItemName="Furry gorilla with big eyes
slippers (Black) XL" Quantity="9" UnitPrice="32.00" />
<row OrderDate="2016-05-27" CustomerName="Agrita Abele"
OrderID="73350" StockItemName="Tape dispenser (Blue)"
Quantity="90" UnitPrice="32.00" />
<row OrderDate="2016-05-18" CustomerName="Agrita Abele"
OrderID="72713" StockItemName="Tape dispenser (Red)"
Quantity="20" UnitPrice="32.00" />
<row OrderDate="2016-05-19" CustomerName="Agrita Abele"
OrderID="72770" StockItemName="Superhero action jacket (Blue)
S" Quantity="8" UnitPrice="25.00" />
```

```
<row OrderDate="2016-05-27" CustomerName="Agrita Abele"
OrderID="73350" StockItemName="RC toy sedan car with remote
control (Red) 1/50 scale" Quantity="2" UnitPrice="25.00" />
<row OrderDate="2016-05-18" CustomerName="Agrita Abele"
OrderID="72637" StockItemName="Superhero action jacket (Blue)
3XS" Quantity="1" UnitPrice="25.00" />
<row OrderDate="2016-05-19" CustomerName="Agrita Abele"
OrderID="72770" StockItemName="Black and orange handle with care
despatch tape  48mmx100m" Quantity="96" UnitPrice="4.10" />
<row OrderDate="2016-05-18" CustomerName="Agrita Abele"
OrderID="72671" StockItemName="Alien officer hoodie (Black)
4XL" Quantity="6" UnitPrice="35.00" />
<row OrderDate="2016-05-18" CustomerName="Agrita Abele"
OrderID="72637" StockItemName="Furry animal socks (Pink) S"
Quantity="96" UnitPrice="5.00" />
<row OrderDate="2016-05-18" CustomerName="Agrita Abele"
OrderID="72669" StockItemName="Permanent marker black 5mm nib
(Black) 5mm" Quantity="84" UnitPrice="2.70" />
<row OrderDate="2016-05-27" CustomerName="Agrita Abele"
OrderID="73340" StockItemName="Superhero action jacket (Blue)
5XL" Quantity="2" UnitPrice="34.00" />
<row OrderDate="2016-05-27" CustomerName="Agrita Abele"
OrderID="73356" StockItemName="Chocolate sharks 250g"
Quantity="192" UnitPrice="8.55" />
<row OrderDate="2016-05-19" CustomerName="Agrita Abele"
OrderID="72787" StockItemName="Novelty chilli chocolates
250g" Quantity="240" UnitPrice="8.55" />
<row OrderDate="2016-05-18" CustomerName="Agrita Abele"
OrderID="72671" StockItemName="Packing knife with metal
insert blade (Yellow) 9mm" Quantity="35" UnitPrice="1.89" />
```

```
<row OrderDate="2016-05-18" CustomerName="Agrita Abele"
OrderID="72671" StockItemName="Shipping carton (Brown)
480x270x320mm" Quantity="150" UnitPrice="2.74" />
<row OrderDate="2016-05-19" CustomerName="Agrita Abele"
OrderID="72770" StockItemName="Shipping carton (Brown)
356x229x229mm" Quantity="175" UnitPrice="1.14" />
<row OrderDate="2016-05-19" CustomerName="Agrita Abele"
OrderID="72787" StockItemName="Ride on big wheel monster
truck (Black) 1/12 scale" Quantity="4" UnitPrice="345.00" />
<row OrderDate="2016-05-18" CustomerName="Agrita Abele"
OrderID="72669" StockItemName="10 mm Anti static bubble wrap
(Blue) 10m" Quantity="70" UnitPrice="26.00" />
<row OrderDate="2016-05-27" CustomerName="Agrita Abele"
OrderID="73340" StockItemName="32 mm Double sided bubble wrap
50m" Quantity="20" UnitPrice="112.00" />
<row OrderDate="2016-05-18" CustomerName="Agrita Abele"
OrderID="72669" StockItemName="Office cube periscope (Black)"
Quantity="20" UnitPrice="18.50" />
<row OrderDate="2016-05-27" CustomerName="Agrita Abele"
OrderID="73356" StockItemName="Ride on vintage American toy
coupe (Black) 1/12 scale" Quantity="10" UnitPrice="285.00" />
</SalesOrders>
```

The other important thing to note about the document is that it is completely flat. There is no nesting. This means that the document's granularity is at the level of line item, which does not make a lot of sense.

It is also worthy of note that all data is contained in attributes, as opposed to elements. We can alter this behavior by using the ELEMENTS keyword in the FOR XML clause. The ELEMENTS keyword will cause all data to be contained within child elements, as opposed to attributes. This is demonstrated in the modified query that can be found in Listing 3-6.

Listing 3-6. Using the ELEMENTS Keyword

```
SELECT
         SalesOrder.OrderDate
       , Customers.CustomerName
       , SalesOrder.OrderID
       , Product.StockItemName
       , LineItem.Quantity
       , LineItem.UnitPrice
FROM Sales.Orders SalesOrder
INNER JOIN Sales.OrderLines LineItem
       ON LineItem.OrderID = SalesOrder.OrderID
INNER JOIN Warehouse.StockItems Product
       ON Product.StockItemID = LineItem.StockItemID
INNER JOIN Sales.Customers Customers
       ON Customers.CustomerID = SalesOrder.CustomerID
WHERE customers.CustomerName = 'Agrita Abele'
FOR XML RAW, ELEMENTS, ROOT('SalesOrders') ;
```

The well-formed XML document that is returned can be seen in Listing 3-7.

Listing 3-7. Using the ELEMENTS Keyword

```
<SalesOrders>
  <row>
    <OrderDate>2016-05-19</OrderDate>
    <CustomerName>Agrita Abele</CustomerName>
    <OrderID>72787</OrderID>
    <StockItemName>Developer joke mug - when your hammer is C++
    (Black)</StockItemName>
    <Quantity>2</Quantity>
    <UnitPrice>13.00</UnitPrice>
  </row>
```

```
<row>
  <OrderDate>2016-05-19</OrderDate>
  <CustomerName>Agrita Abele</CustomerName>
  <OrderID>72787</OrderID>
  <StockItemName>Developer joke mug - when your hammer is C++
  (White)</StockItemName>
  <Quantity>9</Quantity>
  <UnitPrice>13.00</UnitPrice>
</row>
<row>
  <OrderDate>2016-05-27</OrderDate>
  <CustomerName>Agrita Abele</CustomerName>
  <OrderID>73350</OrderID>
  <StockItemName>DBA joke mug - you might be a DBA if
  (Black)</StockItemName>
  <Quantity>4</Quantity>
  <UnitPrice>13.00</UnitPrice>
</row>
<row>
  <OrderDate>2016-05-27</OrderDate>
  <CustomerName>Agrita Abele</CustomerName>
  <OrderID>73350</OrderID>
  <StockItemName>Developer joke mug - that's a hardware
  problem (Black)</StockItemName>
  <Quantity>3</Quantity>
  <UnitPrice>13.00</UnitPrice>
</row>
<row>
  <OrderDate>2016-05-19</OrderDate>
  <CustomerName>Agrita Abele</CustomerName>
  <OrderID>72770</OrderID>
```

```
  <StockItemName>"The Gu" red shirt XML tag t-shirt (Black)
  5XL</StockItemName>
  <Quantity>120</Quantity>
  <UnitPrice>18.00</UnitPrice>
</row>
<row>
  <OrderDate>2016-05-18</OrderDate>
  <CustomerName>Agrita Abele</CustomerName>
  <OrderID>72637</OrderID>
  <StockItemName>"The Gu" red shirt XML tag t-shirt (Black)
  XXL</StockItemName>
  <Quantity>24</Quantity>
  <UnitPrice>18.00</UnitPrice>
</row>
<row>
  <OrderDate>2016-05-27</OrderDate>
  <CustomerName>Agrita Abele</CustomerName>
  <OrderID>73350</OrderID>
  <StockItemName>Halloween zombie mask (Light Brown) S</
  StockItemName>
  <Quantity>24</Quantity>
  <UnitPrice>18.00</UnitPrice>
</row>
<row>
  <OrderDate>2016-05-18</OrderDate>
  <CustomerName>Agrita Abele</CustomerName>
  <OrderID>72669</OrderID>
```

```
  <StockItemName>Halloween skull mask (Gray)
  M</StockItemName>
  <Quantity>60</Quantity>
  <UnitPrice>18.00</UnitPrice>
</row>
<row>
  <OrderDate>2016-05-19</OrderDate>
  <CustomerName>Agrita Abele</CustomerName>
  <OrderID>72787</OrderID>
  <StockItemName>Furry gorilla with big eyes slippers (Black)
  XL</StockItemName>
  <Quantity>9</Quantity>
  <UnitPrice>32.00</UnitPrice>
</row>
<row>
  <OrderDate>2016-05-27</OrderDate>
  <CustomerName>Agrita Abele</CustomerName>
  <OrderID>73350</OrderID>
  <StockItemName>Tape dispenser (Blue)</StockItemName>
  <Quantity>90</Quantity>
  <UnitPrice>32.00</UnitPrice>
</row>
<row>
  <OrderDate>2016-05-18</OrderDate>
  <CustomerName>Agrita Abele</CustomerName>
  <OrderID>72713</OrderID>
  <StockItemName>Tape dispenser (Red)</StockItemName>
  <Quantity>20</Quantity>
  <UnitPrice>32.00</UnitPrice>
</row>
```

```
<row>
  <OrderDate>2016-05-19</OrderDate>
  <CustomerName>Agrita Abele</CustomerName>
  <OrderID>72770</OrderID>
  <StockItemName>Superhero action jacket (Blue)
  S</StockItemName>
  <Quantity>8</Quantity>
  <UnitPrice>25.00</UnitPrice>
</row>
<row>
  <OrderDate>2016-05-27</OrderDate>
  <CustomerName>Agrita Abele</CustomerName>
  <OrderID>73350</OrderID>
  <StockItemName>RC toy sedan car with remote control (Red)
  1/50 scale</StockItemName>
  <Quantity>2</Quantity>
  <UnitPrice>25.00</UnitPrice>
</row>
<row>
  <OrderDate>2016-05-18</OrderDate>
  <CustomerName>Agrita Abele</CustomerName>
  <OrderID>72637</OrderID>
  <StockItemName>Superhero action jacket (Blue)
  3XS</StockItemName>
  <Quantity>1</Quantity>
  <UnitPrice>25.00</UnitPrice>
</row>
<row>
  <OrderDate>2016-05-19</OrderDate>
  <CustomerName>Agrita Abele</CustomerName>
  <OrderID>72770</OrderID>
```

```
  <StockItemName>Black and orange handle with care despatch
  tape  48mmx100m</StockItemName>
  <Quantity>96</Quantity>
  <UnitPrice>4.10</UnitPrice>
</row>
<row>
  <OrderDate>2016-05-18</OrderDate>
  <CustomerName>Agrita Abele</CustomerName>
  <OrderID>72671</OrderID>
  <StockItemName>Alien officer hoodie (Black)
  4XL</StockItemName>
  <Quantity>6</Quantity>
  <UnitPrice>35.00</UnitPrice>
</row>
<row>
  <OrderDate>2016-05-18</OrderDate>
  <CustomerName>Agrita Abele</CustomerName>
  <OrderID>72637</OrderID>
  <StockItemName>Furry animal socks (Pink) S</StockItemName>
  <Quantity>96</Quantity>
  <UnitPrice>5.00</UnitPrice>
</row>
<row>
  <OrderDate>2016-05-18</OrderDate>
  <CustomerName>Agrita Abele</CustomerName>
  <OrderID>72669</OrderID>
  <StockItemName>Permanent marker black 5mm nib (Black)
  5mm</StockItemName>
  <Quantity>84</Quantity>
  <UnitPrice>2.70</UnitPrice>
</row>
```

```
<row>
  <OrderDate>2016-05-27</OrderDate>
  <CustomerName>Agrita Abele</CustomerName>
  <OrderID>73340</OrderID>
  <StockItemName>Superhero action jacket (Blue)
  5XL</StockItemName>
  <Quantity>2</Quantity>
  <UnitPrice>34.00</UnitPrice>
</row>
<row>
  <OrderDate>2016-05-27</OrderDate>
  <CustomerName>Agrita Abele</CustomerName>
  <OrderID>73356</OrderID>
  <StockItemName>Chocolate sharks 250g</StockItemName>
  <Quantity>192</Quantity>
  <UnitPrice>8.55</UnitPrice>
</row>
<row>
  <OrderDate>2016-05-19</OrderDate>
  <CustomerName>Agrita Abele</CustomerName>
  <OrderID>72787</OrderID>
  <StockItemName>Novelty chilli chocolates
  250g</StockItemName>
  <Quantity>240</Quantity>
  <UnitPrice>8.55</UnitPrice>
</row>
<row>
  <OrderDate>2016-05-18</OrderDate>
  <CustomerName>Agrita Abele</CustomerName>
  <OrderID>72671</OrderID>
```

```
    <StockItemName>Packing knife with metal insert blade
    (Yellow) 9mm</StockItemName>
    <Quantity>35</Quantity>
    <UnitPrice>1.89</UnitPrice>
  </row>
  <row>
    <OrderDate>2016-05-18</OrderDate>
    <CustomerName>Agrita Abele</CustomerName>
    <OrderID>72671</OrderID>
    <StockItemName>Shipping carton (Brown) 480x270x320mm
    </StockItemName>
    <Quantity>150</Quantity>
    <UnitPrice>2.74</UnitPrice>
  </row>
  <row>
    <OrderDate>2016-05-19</OrderDate>
    <CustomerName>Agrita Abele</CustomerName>
    <OrderID>72770</OrderID>
    <StockItemName>Shipping carton (Brown) 356x229x229mm
    </StockItemName>
    <Quantity>175</Quantity>
    <UnitPrice>1.14</UnitPrice>
  </row>
  <row>
    <OrderDate>2016-05-19</OrderDate>
    <CustomerName>Agrita Abele</CustomerName>
    <OrderID>72787</OrderID>
    <StockItemName>Ride on big wheel monster truck (Black)
    1/12 scale</StockItemName>
```

```
  <Quantity>4</Quantity>
  <UnitPrice>345.00</UnitPrice>
</row>
<row>
  <OrderDate>2016-05-18</OrderDate>
  <CustomerName>Agrita Abele</CustomerName>
  <OrderID>72669</OrderID>
  <StockItemName>10 mm Anti static bubble wrap (Blue) 10m
  </StockItemName>
  <Quantity>70</Quantity>
  <UnitPrice>26.00</UnitPrice>
</row>
<row>
  <OrderDate>2016-05-27</OrderDate>
  <CustomerName>Agrita Abele</CustomerName>
  <OrderID>73340</OrderID>
  <StockItemName>32 mm Double sided bubble wrap 50m
  </StockItemName>
  <Quantity>20</Quantity>
  <UnitPrice>112.00</UnitPrice>
</row>
<row>
  <OrderDate>2016-05-18</OrderDate>
  <CustomerName>Agrita Abele</CustomerName>
  <OrderID>72669</OrderID>
  <StockItemName>Office cube periscope (Black)</StockItemName>
  <Quantity>20</Quantity>
  <UnitPrice>18.50</UnitPrice>
</row>
```

```
<row>
  <OrderDate>2016-05-27</OrderDate>
  <CustomerName>Agrita Abele</CustomerName>
  <OrderID>73356</OrderID>
  <StockItemName>Ride on vintage American toy coupe (Black)
  1/12 scale</StockItemName>
  <Quantity>10</Quantity>
  <UnitPrice>285.00</UnitPrice>
</row>
</SalesOrders>
```

You can see that the element-centric document still returns one element, called <row>, per row in the relational result set. Instead of the data being contained in attributes, however, it is stored in the form of child elements. Each child element has been given the name of the column, from which the data has been returned. The data is still flat, however. There is no hierarchy based on logic or physical table structure.

It is possible to give the <row> element a more meaningful name. In our example, the most meaningful name would be <LineItem>. Listing 3-8 demonstrates how we can use an optional argument in our FOR XML clause, to generate this name for the element.

Listing 3-8. Generating a Name for the <row> Element

```
SELECT
            SalesOrder.OrderDate
        , Customers.CustomerName
        , SalesOrder.OrderID
        , Product.StockItemName
        , LineItem.Quantity
        , LineItem.UnitPrice
```

```
FROM Sales.Orders SalesOrder
INNER JOIN Sales.OrderLines LineItem
        ON LineItem.OrderID = SalesOrder.OrderID
INNER JOIN Warehouse.StockItems Product
        ON Product.StockItemID = LineItem.StockItemID
INNER JOIN Sales.Customers Customers
        ON Customers.CustomerID = SalesOrder.CustomerID
WHERE customers.CustomerName = 'Agrita Abele'
FOR XML RAW ('LineItem'), ELEMENTS, ROOT('SalesOrders') ;
```

The resulting XML document can be found in Listing 3-9.

Listing 3-9. Generating a Name for the `<row>` Element Results

```
<SalesOrders>
  <LineItem>
    <OrderDate>2016-05-19</OrderDate>
    <CustomerName>Agrita Abele</CustomerName>
    <OrderID>72787</OrderID>
    <StockItemName>Developer joke mug - when your hammer is
    C++ (Black)</StockItemName>
    <Quantity>2</Quantity>
    <UnitPrice>13.00</UnitPrice>
  </LineItem>
  <LineItem>
    <OrderDate>2016-05-19</OrderDate>
    <CustomerName>Agrita Abele</CustomerName>
    <OrderID>72787</OrderID>
    <StockItemName>Developer joke mug - when your hammer is
    C++ (White)</StockItemName>
    <Quantity>9</Quantity>
    <UnitPrice>13.00</UnitPrice>
  </LineItem>
```

```xml
<LineItem>
  <OrderDate>2016-05-27</OrderDate>
  <CustomerName>Agrita Abele</CustomerName>
  <OrderID>73350</OrderID>
  <StockItemName>DBA joke mug - you might be a DBA if
  (Black)</StockItemName>
  <Quantity>4</Quantity>
  <UnitPrice>13.00</UnitPrice>
</LineItem>
<LineItem>
  <OrderDate>2016-05-27</OrderDate>
  <CustomerName>Agrita Abele</CustomerName>
  <OrderID>73350</OrderID>
  <StockItemName>Developer joke mug - that's a hardware
  problem (Black)</StockItemName>
  <Quantity>3</Quantity>
  <UnitPrice>13.00</UnitPrice>
</LineItem>
<LineItem>
  <OrderDate>2016-05-19</OrderDate>
  <CustomerName>Agrita Abele</CustomerName>
  <OrderID>72770</OrderID>
  <StockItemName>"The Gu" red shirt XML tag t-shirt (Black) 5XL
  </StockItemName>
  <Quantity>120</Quantity>
  <UnitPrice>18.00</UnitPrice>
</LineItem>
<LineItem>
  <OrderDate>2016-05-18</OrderDate>
  <CustomerName>Agrita Abele</CustomerName>
  <OrderID>72637</OrderID>
```

```
  <StockItemName>"The Gu" red shirt XML tag t-shirt (Black)
  XXL</StockItemName>
  <Quantity>24</Quantity>
  <UnitPrice>18.00</UnitPrice>
</LineItem>
<LineItem>
  <OrderDate>2016-05-27</OrderDate>
  <CustomerName>Agrita Abele</CustomerName>
  <OrderID>73350</OrderID>
  <StockItemName>Halloween zombie mask (Light Brown) S
  </StockItemName>
  <Quantity>24</Quantity>
  <UnitPrice>18.00</UnitPrice>
</LineItem>
<LineItem>
  <OrderDate>2016-05-18</OrderDate>
  <CustomerName>Agrita Abele</CustomerName>
  <OrderID>72669</OrderID>
  <StockItemName>Halloween skull mask (Gray) M</StockItemName>
  <Quantity>60</Quantity>
  <UnitPrice>18.00</UnitPrice>
</LineItem>
<LineItem>
  <OrderDate>2016-05-19</OrderDate>
  <CustomerName>Agrita Abele</CustomerName>
  <OrderID>72787</OrderID>
  <StockItemName>Furry gorilla with big eyes slippers (Black)
  XL</StockItemName>
  <Quantity>9</Quantity>
  <UnitPrice>32.00</UnitPrice>
</LineItem>
```

```xml
<LineItem>
  <OrderDate>2016-05-27</OrderDate>
  <CustomerName>Agrita Abele</CustomerName>
  <OrderID>73350</OrderID>
  <StockItemName>Tape dispenser (Blue)</StockItemName>
  <Quantity>90</Quantity>
  <UnitPrice>32.00</UnitPrice>
</LineItem>
<LineItem>
  <OrderDate>2016-05-18</OrderDate>
  <CustomerName>Agrita Abele</CustomerName>
  <OrderID>72713</OrderID>
  <StockItemName>Tape dispenser (Red)</StockItemName>
  <Quantity>20</Quantity>
  <UnitPrice>32.00</UnitPrice>
</LineItem>
<LineItem>
  <OrderDate>2016-05-19</OrderDate>
  <CustomerName>Agrita Abele</CustomerName>
  <OrderID>72770</OrderID>
  <StockItemName>Superhero action jacket (Blue)
  S</StockItemName>
  <Quantity>8</Quantity>
  <UnitPrice>25.00</UnitPrice>
</LineItem>
<LineItem>
  <OrderDate>2016-05-27</OrderDate>
  <CustomerName>Agrita Abele</CustomerName>
  <OrderID>73350</OrderID>
  <StockItemName>RC toy sedan car with remote control (Red)
  1/50 scale</StockItemName>
```

```
  <Quantity>2</Quantity>
  <UnitPrice>25.00</UnitPrice>
</LineItem>
<LineItem>
  <OrderDate>2016-05-18</OrderDate>
  <CustomerName>Agrita Abele</CustomerName>
  <OrderID>72637</OrderID>
  <StockItemName>Superhero action jacket (Blue)
  3XS</StockItemName>
  <Quantity>1</Quantity>
  <UnitPrice>25.00</UnitPrice>
</LineItem>
<LineItem>
  <OrderDate>2016-05-19</OrderDate>
  <CustomerName>Agrita Abele</CustomerName>
  <OrderID>72770</OrderID>
  <StockItemName>Black and orange handle with care despatch
  tape  48mmx100m</StockItemName>
  <Quantity>96</Quantity>
  <UnitPrice>4.10</UnitPrice>
</LineItem>
<LineItem>
  <OrderDate>2016-05-18</OrderDate>
  <CustomerName>Agrita Abele</CustomerName>
  <OrderID>72671</OrderID>
  <StockItemName>Alien officer hoodie (Black)
  4XL</StockItemName>
  <Quantity>6</Quantity>
  <UnitPrice>35.00</UnitPrice>
</LineItem>
```

```
<LineItem>
  <OrderDate>2016-05-18</OrderDate>
  <CustomerName>Agrita Abele</CustomerName>
  <OrderID>72637</OrderID>
  <StockItemName>Furry animal socks (Pink) S</StockItemName>
  <Quantity>96</Quantity>
  <UnitPrice>5.00</UnitPrice>
</LineItem>
<LineItem>
  <OrderDate>2016-05-18</OrderDate>
  <CustomerName>Agrita Abele</CustomerName>
  <OrderID>72669</OrderID>
  <StockItemName>Permanent marker black 5mm nib (Black)
  5mm</StockItemName>
  <Quantity>84</Quantity>
  <UnitPrice>2.70</UnitPrice>
</LineItem>
<LineItem>
  <OrderDate>2016-05-27</OrderDate>
  <CustomerName>Agrita Abele</CustomerName>
  <OrderID>73340</OrderID>
  <StockItemName>Superhero action jacket (Blue)
  5XL</StockItemName>
  <Quantity>2</Quantity>
  <UnitPrice>34.00</UnitPrice>
</LineItem>
<LineItem>
  <OrderDate>2016-05-27</OrderDate>
  <CustomerName>Agrita Abele</CustomerName>
  <OrderID>73356</OrderID>
  <StockItemName>Chocolate sharks 250g</StockItemName>
```

```
  <Quantity>192</Quantity>
  <UnitPrice>8.55</UnitPrice>
</LineItem>
<LineItem>
  <OrderDate>2016-05-19</OrderDate>
  <CustomerName>Agrita Abele</CustomerName>
  <OrderID>72787</OrderID>
  <StockItemName>Novelty chilli chocolates 250g
  </StockItemName>
  <Quantity>240</Quantity>
  <UnitPrice>8.55</UnitPrice>
</LineItem>
<LineItem>
  <OrderDate>2016-05-18</OrderDate>
  <CustomerName>Agrita Abele</CustomerName>
  <OrderID>72671</OrderID>
  <StockItemName>Packing knife with metal insert blade
  (Yellow) 9mm</StockItemName>
  <Quantity>35</Quantity>
  <UnitPrice>1.89</UnitPrice>
</LineItem>
<LineItem>
  <OrderDate>2016-05-18</OrderDate>
  <CustomerName>Agrita Abele</CustomerName>
  <OrderID>72671</OrderID>
  <StockItemName>Shipping carton (Brown) 480x270x320mm
  </StockItemName>
  <Quantity>150</Quantity>
  <UnitPrice>2.74</UnitPrice>
</LineItem>
```

```
<LineItem>
  <OrderDate>2016-05-19</OrderDate>
  <CustomerName>Agrita Abele</CustomerName>
  <OrderID>72770</OrderID>
  <StockItemName>Shipping carton (Brown) 356x229x229mm
  </StockItemName>
  <Quantity>175</Quantity>
  <UnitPrice>1.14</UnitPrice>
</LineItem>
<LineItem>
  <OrderDate>2016-05-19</OrderDate>
  <CustomerName>Agrita Abele</CustomerName>
  <OrderID>72787</OrderID>
  <StockItemName>Ride on big wheel monster truck (Black)
  1/12 scale</StockItemName>
  <Quantity>4</Quantity>
  <UnitPrice>345.00</UnitPrice>
</LineItem>
<LineItem>
  <OrderDate>2016-05-18</OrderDate>
  <CustomerName>Agrita Abele</CustomerName>
  <OrderID>72669</OrderID>
  <StockItemName>10 mm Anti static bubble wrap (Blue) 10m
  </StockItemName>
  <Quantity>70</Quantity>
  <UnitPrice>26.00</UnitPrice>
</LineItem>
<LineItem>
  <OrderDate>2016-05-27</OrderDate>
  <CustomerName>Agrita Abele</CustomerName>
  <OrderID>73340</OrderID>
```

```
      <StockItemName>32 mm Double sided bubble wrap 50m
      </StockItemName>
      <Quantity>20</Quantity>
      <UnitPrice>112.00</UnitPrice>
    </LineItem>
    <LineItem>
      <OrderDate>2016-05-18</OrderDate>
      <CustomerName>Agrita Abele</CustomerName>
      <OrderID>72669</OrderID>
      <StockItemName>Office cube periscope (Black)</
      StockItemName>
      <Quantity>20</Quantity>
      <UnitPrice>18.50</UnitPrice>
    </LineItem>
    <LineItem>
      <OrderDate>2016-05-27</OrderDate>
      <CustomerName>Agrita Abele</CustomerName>
      <OrderID>73356</OrderID>
      <StockItemName>Ride on vintage American toy coupe (Black)
      1/12 scale</StockItemName>
      <Quantity>10</Quantity>
      <UnitPrice>285.00</UnitPrice>
    </LineItem>
</SalesOrders>
```

Using FOR XML AUTO

Unlike FOR XML RAW, for XML AUTO can return nested results. It is also refreshingly simple to use, because it will automatically nest the data, based on the joins within your query. The modified query in Listing 3-10 uses AUTO mode to return a hierarchical XML document.

Listing 3-10. Using FOR XML AUTO

```
SELECT
            SalesOrder.OrderDate
        , Customers.CustomerName
        , SalesOrder.OrderID
        , Product.StockItemName
        , LineItem.Quantity
        , LineItem.UnitPrice
FROM Sales.Orders SalesOrder
INNER JOIN Sales.OrderLines LineItem
        ON LineItem.OrderID = SalesOrder.OrderID
INNER JOIN Warehouse.StockItems Product
        ON Product.StockItemID = LineItem.StockItemID
INNER JOIN Sales.Customers Customers
        ON Customers.CustomerID = SalesOrder.CustomerID
WHERE customers.CustomerName = 'Agrita Abele'
FOR XML AUTO ;
```

The XML fragment that is returned by this query can be partially seen in Listing 3-11.

Listing 3-11. Using FOR XML AUTO Results

```
<SalesOrder OrderDate="2016-05-19" OrderID="72787">
  <Customers CustomerName="Agrita Abele">
    <Product StockItemName="Developer joke mug - when your
    hammer is C++ (Black)">
      <LineItem Quantity="2" UnitPrice="13.00" />
    </Product>
```

```
      <Product StockItemName="Developer joke mug - when your
      hammer is C++ (White)">
        <LineItem Quantity="9" UnitPrice="13.00" />
      </Product>
    </Customers>
  </SalesOrder>
  <SalesOrder OrderDate="2016-05-27" OrderID="73350">
    <Customers CustomerName="Agrita Abele">
      <Product StockItemName="DBA joke mug - you might be a DBA
      if (Black)">
        <LineItem Quantity="4" UnitPrice="13.00" />
      </Product>
      <Product StockItemName="Developer joke mug - that's a
      hardware problem (Black)">
        <LineItem Quantity="3" UnitPrice="13.00" />
      </Product>
    </Customers>
  </SalesOrder>
  <SalesOrder OrderDate="2016-05-19" OrderID="72770">
    <Customers CustomerName="Agrita Abele">
      <Product StockItemName="&quot;The Gu&quot; red shirt XML
      tag t-shirt (Black) 5XL">
        <LineItem Quantity="120" UnitPrice="18.00" />
      </Product>
    </Customers>
  </SalesOrder>
  <SalesOrder OrderDate="2016-05-18" OrderID="72637">
    <Customers CustomerName="Agrita Abele">
```

```
      <Product StockItemName="&quot;The Gu&quot; red shirt XML
      tag t-shirt (Black) XXL">
        <LineItem Quantity="24" UnitPrice="18.00" />
      </Product>
    </Customers>
  </SalesOrder>
  <SalesOrder OrderDate="2016-05-27" OrderID="73350">
    <Customers CustomerName="Agrita Abele">
      <Product StockItemName="Halloween zombie mask (Light Brown) S">
        <LineItem Quantity="24" UnitPrice="18.00" />
      </Product>
    </Customers>
  </SalesOrder>
  <SalesOrder OrderDate="2016-05-18" OrderID="72669">
    <Customers CustomerName="Agrita Abele">
      <Product StockItemName="Halloween skull mask (Gray) M">
        <LineItem Quantity="60" UnitPrice="18.00" />
      </Product>
    </Customers>
  </SalesOrder>
  <SalesOrder OrderDate="2016-05-19" OrderID="72787">
    <Customers CustomerName="Agrita Abele">
      <Product StockItemName="Furry gorilla with big eyes
      slippers (Black) XL">
        <LineItem Quantity="9" UnitPrice="32.00" />
      </Product>
    </Customers>
  </SalesOrder>
  <SalesOrder OrderDate="2016-05-27" OrderID="73350">
    <Customers CustomerName="Agrita Abele">
      <Product StockItemName="Tape dispenser (Blue)">
        <LineItem Quantity="90" UnitPrice="32.00" />
```

```
    </Product>
  </Customers>
</SalesOrder>
<SalesOrder OrderDate="2016-05-18" OrderID="72713">
  <Customers CustomerName="Agrita Abele">
    <Product StockItemName="Tape dispenser (Red)">
      <LineItem Quantity="20" UnitPrice="32.00" />
    </Product>
  </Customers>
</SalesOrder>
<SalesOrder OrderDate="2016-05-19" OrderID="72770">
  <Customers CustomerName="Agrita Abele">
    <Product StockItemName="Superhero action jacket (Blue) S">
      <LineItem Quantity="8" UnitPrice="25.00" />
    </Product>
  </Customers>
</SalesOrder>
<SalesOrder OrderDate="2016-05-27" OrderID="73350">
  <Customers CustomerName="Agrita Abele">
    <Product StockItemName="RC toy sedan car with remote
    control (Red) 1/50 scale">
      <LineItem Quantity="2" UnitPrice="25.00" />
    </Product>
  </Customers>
</SalesOrder>
<SalesOrder OrderDate="2016-05-18" OrderID="72637">
  <Customers CustomerName="Agrita Abele">
    <Product StockItemName="Superhero action jacket (Blue) 3XS">
      <LineItem Quantity="1" UnitPrice="25.00" />
    </Product>
  </Customers>
</SalesOrder>
```

```xml
<SalesOrder OrderDate="2016-05-19" OrderID="72770">
  <Customers CustomerName="Agrita Abele">
    <Product StockItemName="Black and orange handle with care
    despatch tape  48mmx100m">
      <LineItem Quantity="96" UnitPrice="4.10" />
    </Product>
  </Customers>
</SalesOrder>
<SalesOrder OrderDate="2016-05-18" OrderID="72671">
  <Customers CustomerName="Agrita Abele">
    <Product StockItemName="Alien officer hoodie (Black) 4XL">
      <LineItem Quantity="6" UnitPrice="35.00" />
    </Product>
  </Customers>
</SalesOrder>
<SalesOrder OrderDate="2016-05-18" OrderID="72637">
  <Customers CustomerName="Agrita Abele">
    <Product StockItemName="Furry animal socks (Pink) S">
      <LineItem Quantity="96" UnitPrice="5.00" />
    </Product>
  </Customers>
</SalesOrder>
<SalesOrder OrderDate="2016-05-18" OrderID="72669">
  <Customers CustomerName="Agrita Abele">
    <Product StockItemName="Permanent marker black 5mm nib
    (Black) 5mm">
      <LineItem Quantity="84" UnitPrice="2.70" />
    </Product>
  </Customers>
</SalesOrder>
```

```xml
<SalesOrder OrderDate="2016-05-27" OrderID="73340">
  <Customers CustomerName="Agrita Abele">
    <Product StockItemName="Superhero action jacket (Blue) 5XL">
      <LineItem Quantity="2" UnitPrice="34.00" />
    </Product>
  </Customers>
</SalesOrder>
<SalesOrder OrderDate="2016-05-27" OrderID="73356">
  <Customers CustomerName="Agrita Abele">
    <Product StockItemName="Chocolate sharks 250g">
      <LineItem Quantity="192" UnitPrice="8.55" />
    </Product>
  </Customers>
</SalesOrder>
<SalesOrder OrderDate="2016-05-19" OrderID="72787">
  <Customers CustomerName="Agrita Abele">
    <Product StockItemName="Novelty chilli chocolates 250g">
      <LineItem Quantity="240" UnitPrice="8.55" />
    </Product>
  </Customers>
</SalesOrder>
<SalesOrder OrderDate="2016-05-18" OrderID="72671">
  <Customers CustomerName="Agrita Abele">
    <Product StockItemName="Packing knife with metal insert
    blade (Yellow) 9mm">
      <LineItem Quantity="35" UnitPrice="1.89" />
    </Product>
    <Product StockItemName="Shipping carton (Brown)
    480x270x320mm">
      <LineItem Quantity="150" UnitPrice="2.74" />
    </Product>
  </Customers>
```

```xml
</SalesOrder>
<SalesOrder OrderDate="2016-05-19" OrderID="72770">
  <Customers CustomerName="Agrita Abele">
    <Product StockItemName="Shipping carton (Brown) 356x229x229mm">
      <LineItem Quantity="175" UnitPrice="1.14" />
    </Product>
  </Customers>
</SalesOrder>
<SalesOrder OrderDate="2016-05-19" OrderID="72787">
  <Customers CustomerName="Agrita Abele">
    <Product StockItemName="Ride on big wheel monster truck
    (Black) 1/12 scale">
      <LineItem Quantity="4" UnitPrice="345.00" />
    </Product>
  </Customers>
</SalesOrder>
<SalesOrder OrderDate="2016-05-18" OrderID="72669">
  <Customers CustomerName="Agrita Abele">
    <Product StockItemName="10 mm Anti static bubble wrap
    (Blue) 10m">
      <LineItem Quantity="70" UnitPrice="26.00" />
    </Product>
  </Customers>
</SalesOrder>
<SalesOrder OrderDate="2016-05-27" OrderID="73340">
  <Customers CustomerName="Agrita Abele">
    <Product StockItemName="32 mm Double sided bubble wrap 50m">
      <LineItem Quantity="20" UnitPrice="112.00" />
    </Product>
  </Customers>
</SalesOrder>
```

```
<SalesOrder OrderDate="2016-05-18" OrderID="72669">
  <Customers CustomerName="Agrita Abele">
    <Product StockItemName="Office cube periscope (Black)">
      <LineItem Quantity="20" UnitPrice="18.50" />
    </Product>
  </Customers>
</SalesOrder>
<SalesOrder OrderDate="2016-05-27" OrderID="73356">
  <Customers CustomerName="Agrita Abele">
    <Product StockItemName="Ride on vintage American toy coupe
    (Black) 1/12 scale">
      <LineItem Quantity="10" UnitPrice="285.00" />
    </Product>
  </Customers>
</SalesOrder>
```

You can see that when AUTO mode is used, the FOR XML clause has automatically nested the data based on the JOIN clauses within the query. Each element has been assigned a name, based on the table alias of the table from which it was retrieved. Just as with RAW mode, we can use the ROOT keyword to add a root node and make the document well-formed. We can also make the document element-centric with the ELEMENTS keyword.

If you look closely at the document in Listing 3-11, you will notice that the resulting hierarchy is not ideal. <Customers> is nested under <SalesOrders>, and <LineItem> is nested under <Product>. In this document, however, you would naturally expect the hierarchy to be <Customers> <SalesOrders> <LineItem> <Product>. To achieve this, we would have to rewrite the query, as per Listing 3-12.

Listing 3-12. Rewriting the Query to Nest Data Correctly

```
SELECT
            Customers.CustomerName
        , SalesOrder.OrderDate
        , SalesOrder.OrderID
        , LineItem.Quantity
        , LineItem.UnitPrice
        , Product.StockItemName
FROM Sales.Orders SalesOrder
INNER JOIN Sales.OrderLines LineItem
        ON LineItem.OrderID = SalesOrder.OrderID
INNER JOIN Warehouse.StockItems Product
        ON Product.StockItemID = LineItem.StockItemID
INNER JOIN Sales.Customers Customers
        ON Customers.CustomerID = SalesOrder.CustomerID
WHERE customers.CustomerName = 'Agrita Abele'
FOR XML AUTO ;
```

Note that the order of columns has changed, so that the Customers table is referenced before the SalesOrders table, which, in turn, is referenced before the OrderLines table. The StockItems table is the last to be referenced. You will also notice that we did not have to change the order of the joins, to produce the document shown in Listing 3-13.

Listing 3-13. Results of Rewritten Query

```
<Customers CustomerName="Agrita Abele">
  <SalesOrder OrderDate="2016-05-19" OrderID="72787">
    <LineItem Quantity="2" UnitPrice="13.00">
      <Product StockItemName="Developer joke mug - when your
      hammer is C++ (Black)" />
    </LineItem>
```

```
  <LineItem Quantity="9" UnitPrice="13.00">
    <Product StockItemName="Developer joke mug - when your
    hammer is C++ (White)" />
  </LineItem>
</SalesOrder>
<SalesOrder OrderDate="2016-05-27" OrderID="73350">
  <LineItem Quantity="4" UnitPrice="13.00">
    <Product StockItemName="DBA joke mug - you might be a DBA
    if (Black)" />
  </LineItem>
  <LineItem Quantity="3" UnitPrice="13.00">
    <Product StockItemName="Developer joke mug - that's a
    hardware problem (Black)" />
  </LineItem>
</SalesOrder>
<SalesOrder OrderDate="2016-05-19" OrderID="72770">
  <LineItem Quantity="120" UnitPrice="18.00">
    <Product StockItemName="&quot;The Gu&quot; red shirt XML
    tag t-shirt (Black) 5XL" />
  </LineItem>
</SalesOrder>
<SalesOrder OrderDate="2016-05-18" OrderID="72637">
  <LineItem Quantity="24" UnitPrice="18.00">
    <Product StockItemName="&quot;The Gu&quot; red shirt XML
    tag t-shirt (Black) XXL" />
  </LineItem>
</SalesOrder>
<SalesOrder OrderDate="2016-05-27" OrderID="73350">
  <LineItem Quantity="24" UnitPrice="18.00">
    <Product StockItemName="Halloween zombie mask
    (Light Brown) S" />
  </LineItem>
```

```
    </SalesOrder>
    <SalesOrder OrderDate="2016-05-18" OrderID="72669">
      <LineItem Quantity="60" UnitPrice="18.00">
        <Product StockItemName="Halloween skull mask (Gray) M" />
      </LineItem>
    </SalesOrder>
    <SalesOrder OrderDate="2016-05-19" OrderID="72787">
      <LineItem Quantity="9" UnitPrice="32.00">
        <Product StockItemName="Furry gorilla with big eyes
        slippers (Black) XL" />
      </LineItem>
    </SalesOrder>
    <SalesOrder OrderDate="2016-05-27" OrderID="73350">
      <LineItem Quantity="90" UnitPrice="32.00">
        <Product StockItemName="Tape dispenser (Blue)" />
      </LineItem>
    </SalesOrder>
    <SalesOrder OrderDate="2016-05-18" OrderID="72713">
      <LineItem Quantity="20" UnitPrice="32.00">
        <Product StockItemName="Tape dispenser (Red)" />
      </LineItem>
    </SalesOrder>
    <SalesOrder OrderDate="2016-05-19" OrderID="72770">
      <LineItem Quantity="8" UnitPrice="25.00">
        <Product StockItemName="Superhero action jacket (Blue) S" />
      </LineItem>
    </SalesOrder>
    <SalesOrder OrderDate="2016-05-27" OrderID="73350">
      <LineItem Quantity="2" UnitPrice="25.00">
        <Product StockItemName="RC toy sedan car with remote
        control (Red) 1/50 scale" />
```

```
    </LineItem>
  </SalesOrder>
  <SalesOrder OrderDate="2016-05-18" OrderID="72637">
    <LineItem Quantity="1" UnitPrice="25.00">
      <Product StockItemName="Superhero action jacket (Blue) 3XS" />
    </LineItem>
  </SalesOrder>
  <SalesOrder OrderDate="2016-05-19" OrderID="72770">
    <LineItem Quantity="96" UnitPrice="4.10">
      <Product StockItemName="Black and orange handle with care
      despatch tape  48mmx100m" />
    </LineItem>
  </SalesOrder>
  <SalesOrder OrderDate="2016-05-18" OrderID="72671">
    <LineItem Quantity="6" UnitPrice="35.00">
      <Product StockItemName="Alien officer hoodie (Black) 4XL" />
    </LineItem>
  </SalesOrder>
  <SalesOrder OrderDate="2016-05-18" OrderID="72637">
    <LineItem Quantity="96" UnitPrice="5.00">
      <Product StockItemName="Furry animal socks (Pink) S" />
    </LineItem>
  </SalesOrder>
  <SalesOrder OrderDate="2016-05-18" OrderID="72669">
    <LineItem Quantity="84" UnitPrice="2.70">
      <Product StockItemName="Permanent marker black 5mm nib
      (Black) 5mm" />
    </LineItem>
  </SalesOrder>
```

```xml
<SalesOrder OrderDate="2016-05-27" OrderID="73340">
  <LineItem Quantity="2" UnitPrice="34.00">
    <Product StockItemName="Superhero action jacket (Blue) 5XL" />
  </LineItem>
</SalesOrder>
<SalesOrder OrderDate="2016-05-27" OrderID="73356">
  <LineItem Quantity="192" UnitPrice="8.55">
    <Product StockItemName="Chocolate sharks 250g" />
  </LineItem>
</SalesOrder>
<SalesOrder OrderDate="2016-05-19" OrderID="72787">
  <LineItem Quantity="240" UnitPrice="8.55">
    <Product StockItemName="Novelty chilli chocolates 250g" />
  </LineItem>
</SalesOrder>
<SalesOrder OrderDate="2016-05-18" OrderID="72671">
  <LineItem Quantity="35" UnitPrice="1.89">
    <Product StockItemName="Packing knife with metal insert
    blade (Yellow) 9mm" />
  </LineItem>
  <LineItem Quantity="150" UnitPrice="2.74">
    <Product StockItemName="Shipping carton (Brown)
    480x270x320mm" />
  </LineItem>
</SalesOrder>
<SalesOrder OrderDate="2016-05-19" OrderID="72770">
  <LineItem Quantity="175" UnitPrice="1.14">
    <Product StockItemName="Shipping carton (Brown)
    356x229x229mm" />
  </LineItem>
</SalesOrder>
```

```
<SalesOrder OrderDate="2016-05-19" OrderID="72787">
  <LineItem Quantity="4" UnitPrice="345.00">
    <Product StockItemName="Ride on big wheel monster truck
    (Black) 1/12 scale" />
  </LineItem>
</SalesOrder>
<SalesOrder OrderDate="2016-05-18" OrderID="72669">
  <LineItem Quantity="70" UnitPrice="26.00">
    <Product StockItemName="10 mm Anti static bubble wrap
    (Blue) 10m" />
  </LineItem>
</SalesOrder>
<SalesOrder OrderDate="2016-05-27" OrderID="73340">
  <LineItem Quantity="20" UnitPrice="112.00">
    <Product StockItemName="32 mm Double sided bubble wrap 50m" />
  </LineItem>
</SalesOrder>
<SalesOrder OrderDate="2016-05-18" OrderID="72669">
  <LineItem Quantity="20" UnitPrice="18.50">
    <Product StockItemName="Office cube periscope (Black)" />
  </LineItem>
</SalesOrder>
<SalesOrder OrderDate="2016-05-27" OrderID="73356">
  <LineItem Quantity="10" UnitPrice="285.00">
    <Product StockItemName="Ride on vintage American toy
    coupe (Black) 1/12 scale" />
  </LineItem>
</SalesOrder>
</Customers>
```

Nesting based on table joins is not always sufficient. In this example, it would be possible for some `<LineItem>` elements to contain multiple `<Product>` elements, which is obviously not correct. There cannot be more than one product per line on a sales order. This is because the primary key of the Sales.OrderLines table has not been included in the query, meaning that not every set of tuples returned from the Sales.OrderLines table must be unique. The values for `UnitPrice` and `OrderQty` happened to be repeated. If this occurred, `FOR XML AUTO` would group them. If the primary key had been included, the issue could not occur.

Using FOR XML PATH

Sometimes, you need more control over the shape of the resultant XML document than can be provided by either RAW mode or AUTO mode. When you have a requirement to define custom output, PATH mode can be used. PATH mode offers great flexibility, as it allows you to define the location of each node within the resultant XML. This is achieved by specifying how each column in the query maps to the XML, with the use of column names or aliases.

If a column alias begins with the @ symbol, an attribute will be created. If no @ symbol is used, the column will map to an element. Columns that will become attributes must be specified before columns that will be sibling nodes but defined as elements.

If you wish to define a node's location in the hierarchy, you can use the / symbol. For example, if you required the order date to appear nested under an element called `<OrderHeader>`, you could specify its column alias as `'/OrderHeader/OrderDate'` for the `OrderDate` column.

PATH mode allows you to create highly customized and complex structures. For example, imagine that you are required to create an XML document in the format displayed in Listing 3-14. Here, you will note that there is a root node called `<SalesOrders>`. The next node in the hierarchy is <Orders>. This is a repeating element, with a new occurrence for every order raised by the customer, which is the same as when we explored AUTO mode. The difference is that each sales order has its own hierarchy. First, there is a section for generic order information, stored within a node called <OrderHeader>. This element is the parent element for <CustomerName>, <OrderDate>, and <OrderID>. These values are to be stored as simple elements.

There is also a section for the line details of the order, which are stored in a node called <OrderDetails>. This element contains a repeating child element named <Product>. This repeating element is the parent node for each <ProductName> (StockItemName) and <ProductID> (StockItemID) within the order, as well as the <Price> (unitprice) and <Qty> of each item. These values are all stored as attributes of the <Product> element.

Listing 3-14. Required Format of XML Output

```
<SalesOrders>
  <Order>
    <OrderHeader>
      <CustomerName>Agrita Abele</CustomerName>
      <OrderDate>2016-05-18</OrderDate>
      <OrderID>72637</OrderID>
    </OrderHeader>
    <OrderDetails>
      <Product ProductID="96" ProductName="&quot;The Gu&quot;
      red shirt XML tag t-shirt (Black) XXL" Price="18.00"
      Qty="24" />
      <Product ProductID="107" ProductName="Superhero action
      jacket (Blue) 3XS" Price="25.00" Qty="1" />
      <Product ProductID="138" ProductName="Furry animal socks
      (Pink) S" Price="5.00" Qty="96" />
    </OrderDetails>
  </Order>
```

```xml
<Order>
  <OrderHeader>
    <CustomerName>Agrita Abele</CustomerName>
    <OrderDate>2016-05-18</OrderDate>
    <OrderID>72669</OrderID>
  </OrderHeader>
  <OrderDetails>
    <Product ProductID="147" ProductName="Halloween skull
    mask (Gray) M" Price="18.00" Qty="60" />
    <Product ProductID="206" ProductName="Permanent marker
    black 5mm nib (Black) 5mm" Price="2.70" Qty="84" />
    <Product ProductID="165" ProductName="10 mm Anti static
    bubble wrap (Blue) 10m" Price="26.00" Qty="70" />
    <Product ProductID="3" ProductName="Office cube periscope
    (Black)" Price="18.50" Qty="20" />
  </OrderDetails>
</Order>
<Order>
  <OrderHeader>
    <CustomerName>Agrita Abele</CustomerName>
    <OrderDate>2016-05-18</OrderDate>
    <OrderID>72671</OrderID>
  </OrderHeader>
  <OrderDetails>
    <Product ProductID="105" ProductName="Alien officer
    hoodie (Black) 4XL" Price="35.00" Qty="6" />
    <Product ProductID="209" ProductName="Packing knife with
    metal insert blade (Yellow) 9mm" Price="1.89" Qty="35" />
    <Product ProductID="183" ProductName="Shipping carton
    (Brown) 480x270x320mm" Price="2.74" Qty="150" />
  </OrderDetails>
</Order>
```

```xml
<Order>
  <OrderHeader>
    <CustomerName>Agrita Abele</CustomerName>
    <OrderDate>2016-05-18</OrderDate>
    <OrderID>72713</OrderID>
  </OrderHeader>
  <OrderDetails>
    <Product ProductID="204" ProductName="Tape dispenser
    (Red)" Price="32.00" Qty="20" />
  </OrderDetails>
</Order>
<Order>
  <OrderHeader>
    <CustomerName>Agrita Abele</CustomerName>
    <OrderDate>2016-05-19</OrderDate>
    <OrderID>72770</OrderID>
  </OrderHeader>
  <OrderDetails>
    <Product ProductID="99" ProductName="&quot;The Gu&quot; red
    shirt XML tag t-shirt (Black) 5XL" Price="18.00" Qty="120" />
    <Product ProductID="110" ProductName="Superhero action
    jacket (Blue) S" Price="25.00" Qty="8" />
    <Product ProductID="196" ProductName="Black and orange handle
    with care despatch tape  48mmx100m" Price="4.10" Qty="96" />
    <Product ProductID="181" ProductName="Shipping carton
    (Brown) 356x229x229mm" Price="1.14" Qty="175" />
  </OrderDetails>
</Order>
```

```
<Order>
  <OrderHeader>
    <CustomerName>Agrita Abele</CustomerName>
    <OrderDate>2016-05-19</OrderDate>
    <OrderID>72787</OrderID>
  </OrderHeader>
  <OrderDetails>
    <Product ProductID="37" ProductName="Developer joke mug -
    when your hammer is C++ (Black)" Price="13.00" Qty="2" />
    <Product ProductID="36" ProductName="Developer joke mug -
    when your hammer is C++ (White)" Price="13.00" Qty="9" />
    <Product ProductID="133" ProductName="Furry gorilla with
    big eyes slippers (Black) XL" Price="32.00" Qty="9" />
    <Product ProductID="220" ProductName="Novelty chilli
    chocolates 250g" Price="8.55" Qty="240" />
    <Product ProductID="75" ProductName="Ride on big wheel
    monster truck (Black) 1/12 scale" Price="345.00" Qty="4" />
  </OrderDetails>
</Order>
<Order>
  <OrderHeader>
    <CustomerName>Agrita Abele</CustomerName>
    <OrderDate>2016-05-27</OrderDate>
    <OrderID>73340</OrderID>
  </OrderHeader>
  <OrderDetails>
    <Product ProductID="117" ProductName="Superhero action
    jacket (Blue) 5XL" Price="34.00" Qty="2" />
    <Product ProductID="164" ProductName="32 mm Double sided
    bubble wrap 50m" Price="112.00" Qty="20" />
  </OrderDetails>
</Order>
```

```
<Order>
  <OrderHeader>
    <CustomerName>Agrita Abele</CustomerName>
    <OrderDate>2016-05-27</OrderDate>
    <OrderID>73350</OrderID>
  </OrderHeader>
  <OrderDetails>
    <Product ProductID="21" ProductName="DBA joke mug - you
    might be a DBA if (Black)" Price="13.00" Qty="4" />
    <Product ProductID="33" ProductName="Developer joke mug -
    that's a hardware problem (Black)" Price="13.00" Qty="3" />
    <Product ProductID="142" ProductName="Halloween zombie
    mask (Light Brown) S" Price="18.00" Qty="24" />
    <Product ProductID="205" ProductName="Tape dispenser
    (Blue)" Price="32.00" Qty="90" />
    <Product ProductID="59" ProductName="RC toy sedan car
    with remote control (Red) 1/50 scale" Price="25.00"
    Qty="2" />
  </OrderDetails>
</Order>
<Order>
  <OrderHeader>
    <CustomerName>Agrita Abele</CustomerName>
    <OrderDate>2016-05-27</OrderDate>
    <OrderID>73356</OrderID>
  </OrderHeader>
  <OrderDetails>
    <Product ProductID="225" ProductName="Chocolate sharks
    250g" Price="8.55" Qty="192" />
```

```
   <Product ProductID="74" ProductName="Ride on vintage American
   toy coupe (Black) 1/12 scale" Price="285.00" Qty="10" />
  </OrderDetails>
 </Order>
</SalesOrders>
```

Queries to build XML documents using FOR XML PATH can seem a little complicated at first, but once you understand the principles, they become quite straightforward. Let's examine each requirement and how we can achieve the required shape.

First, we will require a root node called <SalesOrders>, and we will also need to rename the <row> element to <Orders>. This can be achieved in the same way as we did when we were exploring RAW mode, using the optional argument for the <row> element and the ROOT keyword in the FOR XML clause and the root node, as shown in Listing 3-15.

Listing 3-15. Creating a Root and Naming the <row> Element with FOR XML PATH

```
FOR XML PATH('Order'), ROOT ('SalesOrders') ;
```

The next requirement is to create a complex element called <OrderHeader>, which will contain the <CustomerName>, <OrderDate>, and <OrderID> elements. This can be achieved by specifying a path to the element, as well as the element name. As demonstrated in Listing 3-16, when using this technique, the / character denotes a step down the hierarchy.

Listing 3-16. Creating Hierarchy Levels

```
SELECT
        CustomerName 'OrderHeader/CustomerName'
      , OrderDate 'OrderHeader/OrderDate'
      , OrderID 'OrderHeader/OrderID'
```

To create the nested line items, we must use a subquery, which returns the XML data type. For the process to work properly, we must use the TYPE keyword in the FOR XML clause of the subquery. This will cause the results to be returned to the outer query in native XML, as it can be processed server-side. Failure to use this keyword will result in some characters being replaced by control character sequences.

Because we want the values to be stored as attributes of an element called <Product>, we will have to rename the <row> element and prefix our column aliases with the @ symbol. Finally, to ensure that the <Product> elements are nested under an element named <OrderDetails>, we will use OrderDetails as the alias for the column returned by the subquery, as demonstrated in Listing 3-17.

Listing 3-17. OrderDetails Subquery

```
(
        SELECT
                LineItems2.StockItemID '@ProductID'
                , StockItems.StockItemName '@ProductName'
                , LineItems2.UnitPrice '@Price'
                , Quantity '@Qty'
        FROM Sales.OrderLines LineItems2
        INNER JOIN Warehouse.StockItems StockItems
                ON LineItems2.StockItemID = StockItems.Stock
                ItemID
        WHERE LineItems2.OrderID = Base.OrderID
        FOR XML PATH('Product'), TYPE
) 'OrderDetails'
```

Listing 3-18 pulls together the aspects that we have discussed and returns an XML document in the required format.

Listing 3-18. Putting It All Together

```
SELECT
          CustomerName 'OrderHeader/CustomerName'
        , OrderDate 'OrderHeader/OrderDate'
        , OrderID 'OrderHeader/OrderID'
        , (
              SELECT
                        LineItems2.StockItemID '@ProductID'
                      , StockItems.StockItemName '@ProductName'
                      , LineItems2.UnitPrice '@Price'
                      , Quantity '@Qty'
              FROM Sales.OrderLines LineItems2
              INNER JOIN Warehouse.StockItems StockItems
                      ON LineItems2.StockItemID = Stock
                      Items.StockItemID
              WHERE LineItems2.OrderID = Base.OrderID
              FOR XML PATH('Product'), TYPE
          ) 'OrderDetails'
FROM
(
        SELECT DISTINCT
                  Customers.CustomerName
                , SalesOrder.OrderDate
                , SalesOrder.OrderID
        FROM Sales.Orders SalesOrder
        INNER JOIN Sales.OrderLines LineItem
              ON SalesOrder.OrderID = LineItem.OrderID
        INNER JOIN Sales.Customers Customers
              ON Customers.CustomerID = SalesOrder.CustomerID
        WHERE customers.CustomerName = 'Agrita Abele'
) Base
FOR XML PATH('Order'), ROOT ('SalesOrders') ;
```

Using FOR XML EXPLICIT

FOR XML EXPLICIT is the most complex of the FOR XML modes, but it also provides ultimate flexibility. It uses the concept of tags and parents to control nesting. A tag designates a node's position within the hierarchy, and parent indicates the tag of the node that resides above it in the hierarchy. Therefore, the top-level node will have a tag of 1 and a parent of NULL. Each node is specified in a separate query, and the queries are joined using UNION ALL.

For example, imagine that we want to expand the example in Listing 3-18 so that we return an OrderDetails element that has two child elements. The first will contain the name of the salesperson who took the order. The second will be a repeating element, detailing the line items within the order. We could achieve this by using the query in Listing 3-19.

Listing 3-19. Order Details with XML Explicit

```
SELECT
            1 AS Tag
     , 0 AS Parent
     , SalesOrder.OrderID AS
     [OrderDetails!1!SalesOrderID]
     , SalesOrder.OrderDate AS
     [OrderDetails!1!OrderDate]
     , SalesOrder.CustomerID AS
     [OrderDetails!1!CustomerID]
     , NULL AS [SalesPerson!2!SalesPersonName]
     , NULL AS [LineItem!3!LineTotal!ELEMENT]
     , NULL AS [LineItem!3!ProductName!ELEMENT]
```

```
                , NULL AS [LineItem!3!OrderQty!ELEMENT]
FROM   Sales.Orders  SalesOrder
INNER JOIN Sales.Customers Customers
        ON Customers.CustomerID = SalesOrder.CustomerID
WHERE customers.CustomerName = 'Agrita Abele'
UNION ALL
SELECT
                2 AS Tag
            , 1 AS Parent
            , SalesOrder.OrderID
            , NULL
            , NULL
            , People.FullName
            , NULL
            , NULL
            , NULL
FROM   Sales.Orders SalesOrder
INNER JOIN Sales.Customers Customers
        ON Customers.CustomerID = SalesOrder.CustomerID
INNER JOIN Application.People People
        ON People.PersonID = SalesOrder.SalespersonPersonID
WHERE customers.CustomerName = 'Agrita Abele'
UNION ALL
SELECT
                3 AS Tag
            , 1 AS Parent
            , SalesOrder.OrderID
            , NULL
            , NULL
            , People.FullName
            , LineItem.UnitPrice
```

```
                , Product.StockItemName
                , LineItem.Quantity
FROM     Sales.Orders SalesOrder
INNER JOIN Sales.OrderLines LineItem
           ON    SalesOrder.OrderID = LineItem.OrderID
INNER JOIN Sales.Customers Customers
        ON Customers.CustomerID = SalesOrder.CustomerID
INNER JOIN Warehouse.StockItems Product
        ON Product.StockItemID = LineItem.StockItemID
INNER JOIN Application.People People
        ON People.PersonID = SalesOrder.SalespersonPersonID
WHERE customers.CustomerName = 'Agrita Abele'
ORDER BY
                [OrderDetails!1!SalesOrderID]
            , [SalesPerson!2!SalesPersonName]
            , [LineItem!3!LineTotal!ELEMENT]
FOR XML EXPLICIT, ROOT('SalesOrders') ;
```

There are various things that we should note about the query in Listing 3-19. First, each complex node is in its own query, and these queries are connected by using UNION ALL. Just like every use of UNION ALL, each query must have the same number of columns. Therefore, NULL values are used when a node does not exist within the complex node being defined by the query. Also, note that the OrderID column is used in all three queries. This column is used to define which salespeople, and line details should be ordered under each sales order.

Because the SalesPerson and LineItem nodes are siblings, both the second and third queries have their parent configured as 1, which is the tag of the first query. This means that both will be nested under the OrderDetails node, at the same level of the hierarchy. The query defining the OrderDetails node has its parent configured as NULL. This denotes that it is at the top of the hierarchy, with the exception of the root node, which is defined in the FOR XML clause.

As with other UNION ALL queries, where column names are derived from the first query, the node names are taken from the first query. If you examine the column aliases in the first query, you will clearly see how the structure of the node names is defined. The name parts are separated with a !. The first name part defines the name of the complex node. The second part describes the ID of the tag that is being named. The third part of the name defines the name of the node that will store the data within the column. By default, FOR XML EXPLICIT is attribute-centric. Therefore, if you require a node to be an element, you must add a fourth part to the name, known as the ELEMENT directive.

The query in Listing 3-19 produces the XML document in Listing 3-20.

Listing 3-20. FOR XML EXPLICIT Results

```
<SalesOrders>
  <OrderDetails SalesOrderID="72637" OrderDate="2016-05-18"
  CustomerID="1061">
    <SalesPerson SalesPersonName="Taj Shand" />
    <LineItem>
      <LineTotal>5.00</LineTotal>
      <ProductName>Furry animal socks (Pink) S</ProductName>
      <OrderQty>96</OrderQty>
    </LineItem>
    <LineItem>
      <LineTotal>18.00</LineTotal>
      <ProductName>"The Gu" red shirt XML tag t-shirt (Black)
      XXL</ProductName>
      <OrderQty>24</OrderQty>
    </LineItem>
    <LineItem>
```

```
    <LineTotal>25.00</LineTotal>
    <ProductName>Superhero action jacket (Blue) 3XS</ProductName>
    <OrderQty>1</OrderQty>
  </LineItem>
</OrderDetails>
<OrderDetails SalesOrderID="72669" OrderDate="2016-05-18"
CustomerID="1061">
  <SalesPerson SalesPersonName="Hudson Onslow" />
  <LineItem>
    <LineTotal>2.70</LineTotal>
    <ProductName>Permanent marker black 5mm nib (Black) 5mm
    </ProductName>
    <OrderQty>84</OrderQty>
  </LineItem>
  <LineItem>
    <LineTotal>18.00</LineTotal>
    <ProductName>Halloween skull mask (Gray) M</ProductName>
    <OrderQty>60</OrderQty>
  </LineItem>
  <LineItem>
    <LineTotal>18.50</LineTotal>
    <ProductName>Office cube periscope (Black)</ProductName>
    <OrderQty>20</OrderQty>
  </LineItem>
  <LineItem>
    <LineTotal>26.00</LineTotal>
    <ProductName>10 mm Anti static bubble wrap (Blue) 10m
    </ProductName>
    <OrderQty>70</OrderQty>
  </LineItem>
</OrderDetails>
```

```xml
<OrderDetails SalesOrderID="72671" OrderDate="2016-05-18"
CustomerID="1061">
  <SalesPerson SalesPersonName="Hudson Hollinworth" />
  <LineItem>
    <LineTotal>1.89</LineTotal>
    <ProductName>Packing knife with metal insert blade
    (Yellow) 9mm</ProductName>
    <OrderQty>35</OrderQty>
  </LineItem>
  <LineItem>
    <LineTotal>2.74</LineTotal>
    <ProductName>Shipping carton (Brown) 480x270x320mm
    </ProductName>
    <OrderQty>150</OrderQty>
  </LineItem>
  <LineItem>
    <LineTotal>35.00</LineTotal>
    <ProductName>Alien officer hoodie (Black) 4XL</ProductName>
    <OrderQty>6</OrderQty>
  </LineItem>
</OrderDetails>
<OrderDetails SalesOrderID="72713" OrderDate="2016-05-18"
CustomerID="1061">
  <SalesPerson SalesPersonName="Hudson Onslow" />
  <LineItem>
    <LineTotal>32.00</LineTotal>
    <ProductName>Tape dispenser (Red)</ProductName>
    <OrderQty>20</OrderQty>
  </LineItem>
</OrderDetails>
```

```
<OrderDetails SalesOrderID="72770" OrderDate="2016-05-19"
CustomerID="1061">
  <SalesPerson SalesPersonName="Hudson Onslow" />
  <LineItem>
    <LineTotal>1.14</LineTotal>
    <ProductName>Shipping carton (Brown) 356x229x229mm
    </ProductName>
    <OrderQty>175</OrderQty>
  </LineItem>
  <LineItem>
    <LineTotal>4.10</LineTotal>
    <ProductName>Black and orange handle with care despatch
    tape  48mmx100m</ProductName>
    <OrderQty>96</OrderQty>
  </LineItem>
  <LineItem>
    <LineTotal>18.00</LineTotal>
    <ProductName>"The Gu" red shirt XML tag t-shirt (Black)
    5XL</ProductName>
    <OrderQty>120</OrderQty>
  </LineItem>
  <LineItem>
    <LineTotal>25.00</LineTotal>
    <ProductName>Superhero action jacket (Blue) S
    </ProductName>
    <OrderQty>8</OrderQty>
  </LineItem>
</OrderDetails>
```

```
<OrderDetails SalesOrderID="72787" OrderDate="2016-05-19"
CustomerID="1061">
  <SalesPerson SalesPersonName="Jack Potter" />
  <LineItem>
    <LineTotal>8.55</LineTotal>
    <ProductName>Novelty chilli chocolates 250g</ProductName>
    <OrderQty>240</OrderQty>
  </LineItem>
  <LineItem>
    <LineTotal>13.00</LineTotal>
    <ProductName>Developer joke mug - when your hammer is
    C++ (White)</ProductName>
    <OrderQty>9</OrderQty>
  </LineItem>
  <LineItem>
    <LineTotal>13.00</LineTotal>
    <ProductName>Developer joke mug - when your hammer is
    C++ (Black)</ProductName>
    <OrderQty>2</OrderQty>
  </LineItem>
  <LineItem>
    <LineTotal>32.00</LineTotal>
    <ProductName>Furry gorilla with big eyes slippers (Black)
    XL</ProductName>
    <OrderQty>9</OrderQty>
  </LineItem>
  <LineItem>
    <LineTotal>345.00</LineTotal>
```

```xml
    <ProductName>Ride on big wheel monster truck (Black) 1/12
    scale</ProductName>
    <OrderQty>4</OrderQty>
  </LineItem>
</OrderDetails>
<OrderDetails SalesOrderID="73340" OrderDate="2016-05-27"
CustomerID="1061">
  <SalesPerson SalesPersonName="Taj Shand" />
  <LineItem>
    <LineTotal>34.00</LineTotal>
    <ProductName>Superhero action jacket (Blue) 5XL
    </ProductName>
    <OrderQty>2</OrderQty>
  </LineItem>
  <LineItem>
    <LineTotal>112.00</LineTotal>
    <ProductName>32 mm Double sided bubble wrap 50m
    </ProductName>
    <OrderQty>20</OrderQty>
  </LineItem>
</OrderDetails>
<OrderDetails SalesOrderID="73350" OrderDate="2016-05-27"
CustomerID="1061">
  <SalesPerson SalesPersonName="Sophia Hinton" />
  <LineItem>
    <LineTotal>13.00</LineTotal>
    <ProductName>DBA joke mug - you might be a DBA if
    (Black)</ProductName>
    <OrderQty>4</OrderQty>
  </LineItem>
```

```
    <LineItem>
      <LineTotal>13.00</LineTotal>
      <ProductName>Developer joke mug - that's a hardware
      problem (Black)</ProductName>
      <OrderQty>3</OrderQty>
    </LineItem>
    <LineItem>
      <LineTotal>18.00</LineTotal>
      <ProductName>Halloween zombie mask (Light Brown) S
      </ProductName>
      <OrderQty>24</OrderQty>
    </LineItem>
    <LineItem>
      <LineTotal>25.00</LineTotal>
      <ProductName>RC toy sedan car with remote control (Red)
      1/50 scale</ProductName>
      <OrderQty>2</OrderQty>
    </LineItem>
    <LineItem>
      <LineTotal>32.00</LineTotal>
      <ProductName>Tape dispenser (Blue)</ProductName>
      <OrderQty>90</OrderQty>
    </LineItem>
  </OrderDetails>
  <OrderDetails SalesOrderID="73356" OrderDate="2016-05-27"
  CustomerID="1061">
    <SalesPerson SalesPersonName="Anthony Grosse" />
    <LineItem>
      <LineTotal>8.55</LineTotal>
      <ProductName>Chocolate sharks 250g</ProductName>
      <OrderQty>192</OrderQty>
    </LineItem>
```

```
  <LineItem>
    <LineTotal>285.00</LineTotal>
    <ProductName>Ride on vintage American toy coupe (Black)
    1/12 scale</ProductName>
    <OrderQty>10</OrderQty>
  </LineItem>
  </OrderDetails>
</SalesOrders>
```

Summary

The FOR XML clause can be used to construct XML data from a T-SQL query. The FOR XML clause can be used in four modes: RAW, AUTO, PATH, and EXPLICIT.

When used in RAW mode, FOR XML will produce a flat XML instance, with no nesting. It is very simple to use and allows for the XML instance to be either attribute-centric or element-centric. It can also produce well-formed XML, by adding a root node. It provides very little control over formatting, however.

FOR XML AUTO is very simple to use and allows the developer to create nested XML instances. Just as with FOR XML RAW, FOR XML AUTO can produce either element-centric or attribute-centric documents, which can be well-formatted with the addition of a root node. Data within the XML document will be nested automatically, based on table joins. Nodes will derive their names from table aliases.

When used in PATH mode, FOR XML provides much more granular control over the layout of the XML document. Each column can be defined as either an element or an attribute, by including or omitting the @ prefix. Hierarchical position can be defined through column aliases, and complex nesting requirements can be achieved through subqueries.

111

FOR XML EXPLICIT is the most complex of the FOR XML modes but also the most powerful. It is implemented by defining each complex node in a separate query, with the queries joined by using the UNION ALL clause. Hierarchical positioning is defined through tag and parent columns, which are always the first and second columns, respectively, in the SELECT list. Column aliases allow for the declaration of node names and define if each node should be element-centric or attribute-centric.

CHAPTER 4

Querying and Shredding XML

To allow developers to query and navigate XML documents from within SQL Server, the XQuery language can be combined with T-SQL queries. In this chapter, I will discuss how to use XQuery to filter, extract, and modify XML. I will also discuss shredding XML, which is the process of converting XML data into relational results sets. Finally, an overview of how to bind an XSD schema to a column of data type XML is provided.

Querying XML

XQuery is a language for querying XML, in the same way that SQL is a language for querying relational data. The language is built on XPath but has been enhanced for better iteration and sorting. It also allows for the construction of XML. The XQuery standard is developed by the W3C (World Wide Web Consortium), in conjunction with Microsoft and other major relational database management system (RDBMS) vendors.

XQuery in SQL Server supports five methods against the XML data type. An overview of these methods can be found in Table 4-1, and each of the methods will be demonstrated throughout this chapter. XQuery also supports the use of XSD schemas, to help interact with complex documents and FLWOR (pronounced flower) statements. FLWOR is an acronym of for, let, where, order by, and return.

© Peter A. Carter 2018
P. A. Carter, *SQL Server Advanced Data Types*,
https://doi.org/10.1007/978-1-4842-3901-8_4

Table 4-1. *XQuery Methods*

Method	Description
exist()	Checks for the existence of a node with a specified value within an XML document. It returns 1 if the node exists with the specified value and 0 if it does not.
modify()	Performs data modification statements against an XML document. Acceptable DML actions are insert, delete, and replace value of.
nodes()	Returns a row set that contains copies of original XML instances. It is used for shredding XML into a relational result set.
query()	This returns a subset of an XML document, in XML format.
value()	This returns a single scalar value from an XML document, mapped to an SQL Server data type.

Tip   The structure and benefits of XSD schemas are explained in Chapter 2.

for statements allow you to iterate through a sequence of nodes. let statements bind a sequence to a variable. where statements filter nodes based on a Boolean expression. order by statements order nodes before they are returned. return statements specify what should be returned.

To demonstrate the use of the XQuery methods in this chapter, we will create a table in the WideWorldImporters database, called Sales. CustomerOrderSummary. This table can be created using the script in Listing 4-1.

Listing 4-1. Creating the Sales.CustomerOrderSummary Table

```
USE WideWorldImporters
GO

CREATE TABLE Sales.CustomerOrderSummary
(
        ID INT NOT NULL IDENTITY,
        CustomerID INT NOT NULL,
        OrderSummary XML
) ;

INSERT INTO Sales.CustomerOrderSummary (CustomerID,
OrderSummary)
SELECT
        CustomerID,
        (
                SELECT
                        CustomerName 'OrderHeader/CustomerName'
                        , OrderDate 'OrderHeader/OrderDate'
                        , OrderID 'OrderHeader/OrderID'
                        , (
                                SELECT
                                        LineItems2.StockItemID
                                        '@ProductID'
                                        , StockItems.StockItem
                                        Name '@ProductName'
                                        , LineItems2.UnitPrice
                                        '@Price'
                                        , Quantity '@Qty'
                                FROM Sales.OrderLines LineItems2
                                INNER JOIN Warehouse.StockItems
                                StockItems
```

```
                                      ON LineItems2.StockItemID
                                         = StockItems.StockItemID
                              WHERE LineItems2.OrderID =
                              Base.OrderID
                              FOR XML PATH('Product'), TYPE
                        ) 'OrderDetails'
            FROM
            (
                        SELECT DISTINCT
                                Customers.CustomerName
                              , SalesOrder.OrderDate
                              , SalesOrder.OrderID
                        FROM Sales.Orders SalesOrder
                        INNER JOIN Sales.OrderLines LineItem
                              ON SalesOrder.OrderID =
                              LineItem.OrderID
                        INNER JOIN Sales.Customers Customers
                              ON Customers.CustomerID =
                              SalesOrder.CustomerID
                        WHERE customers.CustomerID = OuterCust.
                        CustomerID
                  ) Base
                  FOR XML PATH('Order'), ROOT ('SalesOrders'), TYPE
            ) AS OrderSummary
FROM Sales.Customers OuterCust ;
```

Using exist()

The exist() method is used to check for the existence of a node with a specified value. For example, please consider the script in Listing 4-2. The query will programmatically check to see if the XML document containing sales order details contains the Chocolate sharks 250g product. The first portion of the XQuery defines the path to the node to be evaluated, in this case, the StockItemName attribute. We have defined that the node is an attribute, by prefixing the node name with the @ symbol. We then specify eq as the comparison operator, before supplying the value that we want to validate the node against. If the criteria are met, exist() will return 1. If the criteria are not met, it will return 0.

Listing 4-2. Checking for the Existence of a Value

```
DECLARE @SalesOrders XML

SET @SalesOrders =
'<SalesOrder OrderDate="2016-05-27" OrderID="73356">
        <Customers CustomerName="Agrita Abele">
              <Product StockItemName="Chocolate sharks 250g">
                <LineItem Quantity="192" UnitPrice="8.55" />
              </Product>
        </Customers>
      </SalesOrder>' ;

SELECT @SalesOrders.exist('SalesOrder/Customers/Product[
(@StockItemName) eq "Chocolate sharks 250g"]') ;
```

The results of this script are displayed in Figure 4-1.

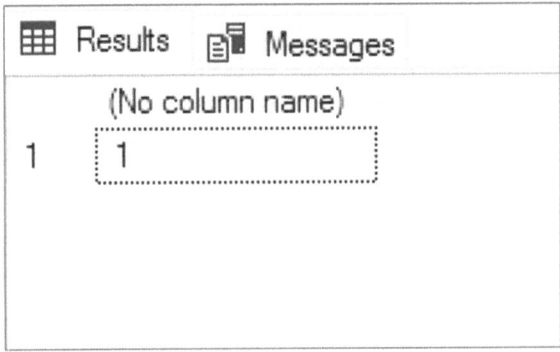

Figure 4-1. *Results of checking for the existence of a value*

You can see how the exist() method could easily be used in a WHERE clause, against a column of data type XML. For example, consider the script in Listing 4-3, which uses the exist() method in a WHERE clause against the Sales.CustomerOrderSummary table in the WideWorldImporters database, to return just the order summary for Tailspin Toys (Absecon, NJ).

You will notice that because we are evaluating the value of an element, as opposed to an attribute, we have used the text() method to extract the value. The [1] denotes that a singleton value will be returned.

Listing 4-3. Filtering a Table Using the exist() Method

```
SELECT
        CustomerID
    , OrderSummary
FROM WideWorldImporters.Sales.CustomerOrderSummary
WHERE OrderSummary.exist('SalesOrders/Order/OrderHeader/
CustomerName[(text()[1]) eq "Tailspin Toys (Absecon, NJ)"]') = 1 ;
```

Using value( )

The value() method is used to extract a single, scalar value from an XML document and map it to an SQL Server data type. For example, consider the script in Listing 4-4. The script uses the same XML document as Listing 4-1 but this time extracts the customer name from the document. In the same way as when we used the exist() method, we will have to use the @ symbol to prefix an attribute. We also must denote that a singleton value will be returned.

Listing 4-4. Using the value() Method

```
DECLARE @SalesOrders XML ;

SET @SalesOrders =
'<SalesOrder OrderDate="2016-05-27" OrderID="73356">
        <Customers CustomerName="Agrita Abele">
            <Product StockItemName="Chocolate sharks 250g">
                <LineItem Quantity="192" UnitPrice="8.55" />
            </Product>
        </Customers>
    </SalesOrder>' ;

SELECT @SalesOrders.value('(/SalesOrder/Customers/
@CustomerName)[1]', 'nvarchar(100)') AS CustomerName ;
```

The results of this script are illustrated in Figure 4-2.

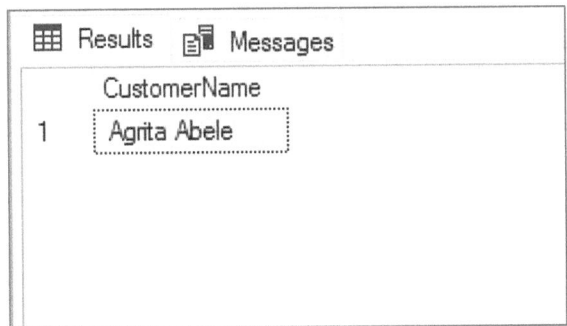

Figure 4-2. *Results of using the value() method*

The value() method can also be used against a table, to extract values from each row. For example, the script in Listing 4-5 can be used to extract the customer name from each row in the Sales.CustomerOrderSummary table.

119

Listing 4-5. Using the value() Method Against a Table

```
USE WideWorldImporters
GO

SELECT
    CustomerID
  , OrderSummary
  , OrderSummary.value('(/SalesOrders/Order/OrderHeader/
    CustomerName)[1]', 'nvarchar(100)') AS CustomerName
FROM Sales.CustomerOrderSummary ;
```

Partial results of this query can be found in Figure 4-3.

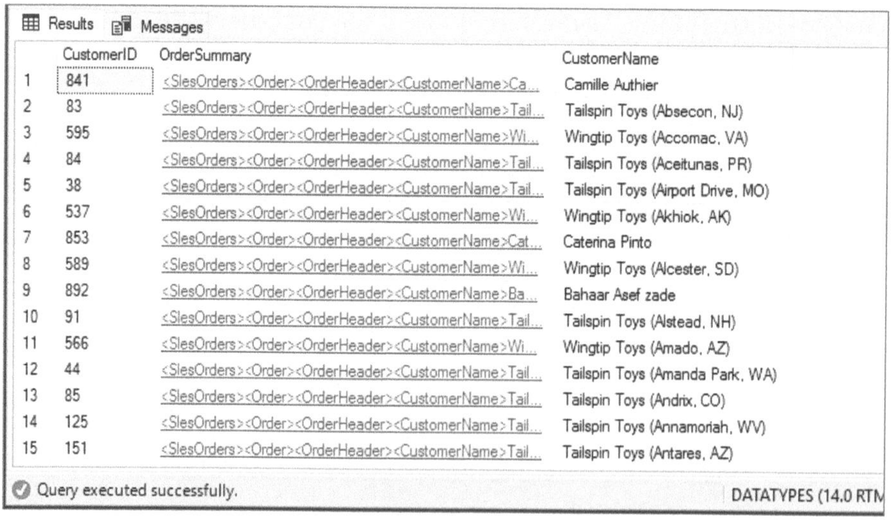

Figure 4-3. *Results of using the value() method against a table*

The value() method can also be used in the WHERE clause of a query. For example, the query in Listing 4-6 is functionally equivalent to the query in Listing 4-5. It has simply been rewritten using the value() method instead of the exist() method.

Listing 4-6. Filtering a Table Using the `value()` Method

```
USE WideWorldImporters
GO

SELECT
        CustomerID
    , OrderSummary
FROM WideWorldImporters.Sales.CustomerOrderSummary
WHERE OrderSummary.value('(/SalesOrders/Order/OrderHeader/
CustomerName)[1]', 'nvarchar(100)') = 'Tailspin Toys (Absecon, NJ)' ;
```

Using query( )

The query() method is used to return an untyped XML document from an XML document. For example, consider the script in Listing 4-7. The query will extract the product details from the XML document in an XML format.

Listing 4-7. Extracting Product Details

```
DECLARE @SalesOrders XML ;

SET @SalesOrders =
'<SalesOrder OrderDate="2016-05-27" OrderID="73356">
        <Customers CustomerName="Agrita Abele">
            <Product StockItemName="Chocolate sharks 250g">
                <LineItem Quantity="192" UnitPrice="8.55" />
            </Product>
        </Customers>
    </SalesOrder>' ;

SELECT @SalesOrders.query('/SalesOrder/Customers/Product') AS
ProductDetails ;
```

The results of this query can be seen in Figure 4-4.

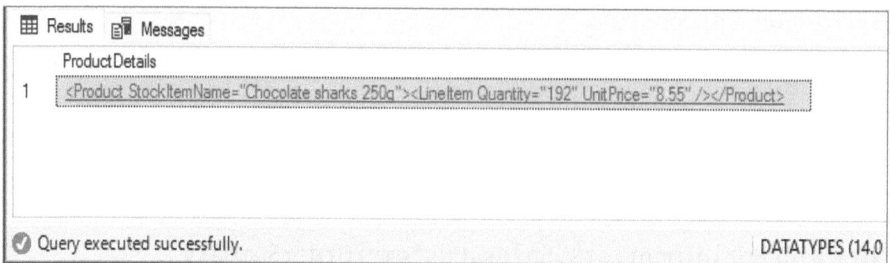

Figure 4-4. Results of extracting product details

To see how the query() method could be used when querying a table, consider the script in Listing 4-8. This query uses all of the XQuery methods that have been discussed so far. The value() method is used to extract the customer's name and order ID, while the query() method is used to extract details of the products that were ordered. The table is filtered using the exist() method.

Listing 4-8. Using query(), value(), and exist() Against a Table

```
USE WideWorldImporters
GO

SELECT
        OrderSummary
        , OrderSummary.value('(/SalesOrders/Order/OrderHeader/
        CustomerName)[1]', 'nvarchar(100)') AS CustomerName
        , OrderSummary.value('(/SalesOrders/Order/OrderHeader/
        OrderID)[1]', 'int') AS OrderID
        , OrderSummary.query('/SalesOrders/Order/OrderDetails/
        Product') AS ProductsOrdered
FROM Sales.CustomerOrderSummary
WHERE OrderSummary.exist('SalesOrders/Order/OrderHeader/
CustomerName[(text()[1]) eq "Tailspin Toys (Absecon, NJ)"]') = 1 ;
```

This query returns the results shown in Figure 4-5.

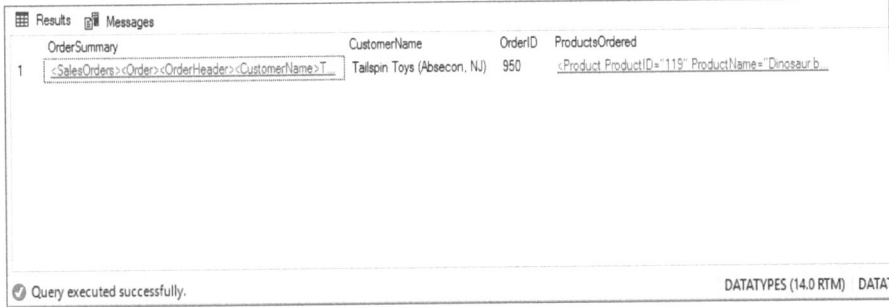

Figure 4-5. *Results of using* query()*,* value()*, and* exist() *against a table*

Using Relational Values in XQuery

Relational values from T-SQL variables and columns can also be passed into XQuery expressions. They can be used for filtering or even constructing data, but they are read-only. Therefore, the XQuery expression cannot be used to modify the relational variable or column value.

To see this functionality in action, consider the query in Listing 4-9. The query is functionally equivalent to the query in Listing 4-7. This time, however, instead of using a hard-coded filter for the customer name, we pass this in from a T-SQL variable. Queries that use T-SQL variables or columns from tables are known as cross-domain queries.

Listing 4-9. Parameterizing an exist() Method

```
USE WideWorldImporters
GO

DECLARE @CustomerName NVARCHAR(100) ;

SET @CustomerName = 'Tailspin Toys (Absecon, NJ)' ;

SELECT
```

```
        OrderSummary
     , OrderSummary.value('(/SalesOrders/Order/OrderHeader/
     CustomerName)[1]', 'nvarchar(100)') AS CustomerName
       , OrderSummary.value('(/SalesOrders/Order/OrderHeader/
       OrderID)[1]', 'int') AS OrderID
       , OrderSummary.query('/SalesOrders/Order/OrderDetails/
       Product') AS ProductsOrdered
FROM Sales.CustomerOrderSummary
WHERE OrderSummary.exist('SalesOrders/Order/OrderHeader/
CustomerName[(text()[1]) eq sql:variable("@CustomerName") ]') = 1 ;
```

T-SQL variables can also be used in the construction of XML. For example, the script in Listing 4-10 generates a new column in the result set, which contains an XML fragment. This fragment has an element called CustomerDetails. Within this element, you will notice an attribute called GoldCustomer. This is a flag that is configured from a T-SQL variable. Note that when used inside the query() method, we have enclosed the sql:variable statement inside double quotes and curly brackets.

Listing 4-10. Constructing an XML Fragment and Passing a Value from a T-SQL Variable

```
USE WideWorldImporters
GO

DECLARE @Gold NVARCHAR(3)

DECLARE @CustomerName NVARCHAR(100)

SET @Gold = 'Yes'

SET @CustomerName = 'Tailspin Toys (Absecon, NJ)'
```

```
SELECT
    OrderSummary
    , OrderSummary.value('(/SalesOrders/Order/OrderHeader/
    CustomerName)[1]', 'nvarchar(100)') AS CustomerName
    , OrderSummary.value('(/SalesOrders/Order/OrderHeader/
    OrderID)[1]', 'int') AS OrderID
    , OrderSummary.query('/SalesOrders/Order/OrderDetails/
    Product') AS ProductsOrdered
    , OrderSummary.query('<CustomerDetails>GoldCustomer =
    "{ sql:variable("@Gold") }"  </CustomerDetails>') AS
    CustomerDetails
FROM Sales.CustomerOrderSummary
WHERE OrderSummary.exist('SalesOrders/Order/OrderHeader/
CustomerName[(text()[1]) eq sql:variable("@CustomerName") ]') = 1 ;
```

The results of this query can be found in Figure 4-6. The resultant XML
fragment can be found in the CustomerDetails column.

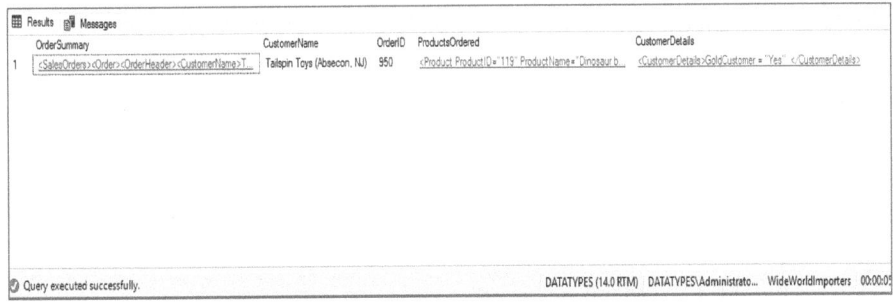

Figure 4-6. *Results of constructing an XML fragment and passing a*
value from a T-SQL variable

When the XQuery expression is run against an XML column within a table, relational data, stored in other columns, can also be passed to the XQuery expression. For example, the script in Listing 4-11 expands the generated CustomerDetails XML fragment to include the Customer ID from the CustomerID column of the Sales.CustomerOrderSummary table.

Listing 4-11. Constructing an XML Fragment Using a Relational Column

```
USE WideWorldImporters
GO

DECLARE @Gold NVARCHAR(3)

DECLARE @CustomerName NVARCHAR(100)

SET @Gold = 'Yes'

SET @CustomerName = 'Tailspin Toys (Absecon, NJ)'

SELECT
    OrderSummary
        , OrderSummary.value('(/SalesOrders/Order/OrderHeader/
        CustomerName)[1]', 'nvarchar(100)') AS CustomerName
        , OrderSummary.value('(/SalesOrders/Order/OrderHeader/
        OrderID)[1]', 'int') AS OrderID
        , OrderSummary.query('/SalesOrders/Order/OrderDetails/
        Product') AS ProductsOrdered
        , OrderSummary.query('<CustomerDetails> CustomerID =
        "{ sql:column("CustomerID") }" GoldCustomer =
        "{ sql:variable("@Gold") }"  </CustomerDetails>')
        As CustomerDetails
FROM Sales.CustomerOrderSummary
WHERE OrderSummary.exist('SalesOrders/Order/OrderHeader/
CustomerName[(text()[1]) eq sql:variable("@CustomerName") ]') = 1 ;
```

The results of this query can be seen in Figure 4-7. Once again, pay attention to the CustomerDetails column, to see the resultant XML fragment.

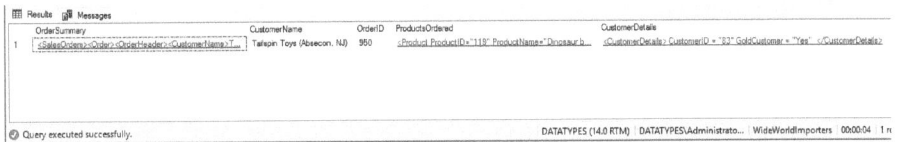

Figure 4-7. *Results of constructing an XML fragment using a relational column*

FLWOR

As previously mentioned, FLWOR stands for for, let, where, order by, and return. These statements provide granular control, allowing a developer to navigate to, iterate over, filter, and present XML nodes exactly as required.

The for statement binds a variable to an input sequence. The let statement is used to assign an XQuery expression to a variable, for use within an iteration of FOR. The expression can return either atomic values or a sequence of nodes. The let statement is optional. The where statement is also optional but can be used to filter the results that are returned. The order by statement can be used optionally to order the results of the FLWOR statement. The mandatory return statement specifies what data will be returned.

For example, consider the XML document in Listing 4-12. This XML document contains the first two orders from the XML document returned by the OrderSummary column in Listing 4-11.

Listing 4-12. XML Document for FLWOR Examples

```
DECLARE @XML XML = N'<SalesOrders>
  <Order>
    <OrderHeader>
      <CustomerName>Tailspin Toys (Absecon, NJ)</CustomerName>
      <OrderDate>2013-01-17</OrderDate>
      <OrderID>950</OrderID>
    </OrderHeader>
    <OrderDetails>
      <Product ProductID="119" ProductName="Dinosaur battery-
      powered slippers (Green) M" Price="32.00" Qty="2" />
      <Product ProductID="61" ProductName="RC toy sedan car with
      remote control (Green) 1/50 scale" Price="25.00" Qty="2" />
      <Product ProductID="194" ProductName="Black and orange glass
      with care despatch tape  48mmx100m" Price="4.10" Qty="216" />
      <Product ProductID="104" ProductName="Alien officer
      hoodie (Black) 3XL" Price="35.00" Qty="2" />
    </OrderDetails>
  </Order>
  <Order>
    <OrderHeader>
      <CustomerName>Tailspin Toys (Absecon, NJ)</CustomerName>
      <OrderDate>2013-01-29</OrderDate>
      <OrderID>1452</OrderID>
    </OrderHeader>
    <OrderDetails>
      <Product ProductID="33" ProductName="Developer joke mug -
      that's a hardware problem (Black)" Price="13.00" Qty="9" />
```

```
    <Product ProductID="121" ProductName="Dinosaur battery-
    powered slippers (Green) XL" Price="32.00" Qty="1" />
  </OrderDetails>
 </Order>
<SalesOrders>'
```

If we wanted to iterate over each Product element within the second order, we could use the FOR statement as follows in Listing 4-13.

Note that we use an internal variable, which we name $product, and the in keyword to designate the path to the ProductName attribute. This approach and syntax will be familiar to those of you who have worked with foreach loops in languages such as PowerShell.

The return statement is then used to append the ProductName attribute's value to the end of the $product string. Note that we use [2] in square brackets, to denote that we are interested in the second order, which will be a singleton element (albeit a complex element containing multiple other elements).

Caution   The following code examples in this section expect a variable called XML to be declared that contains the XML document in Listing 4-12. For space reasons, this variable is not explicitly declared or set within each code example.

Listing 4-13. Using for to Iterate over Product Elements

```
SELECT @XML.query('
        for $product in /SalesOrders/Order[2]/OrderDetails/
        Product/@ProductName
        return string($product)
');
```

The results of this query are illustrated in Figure 4-8.

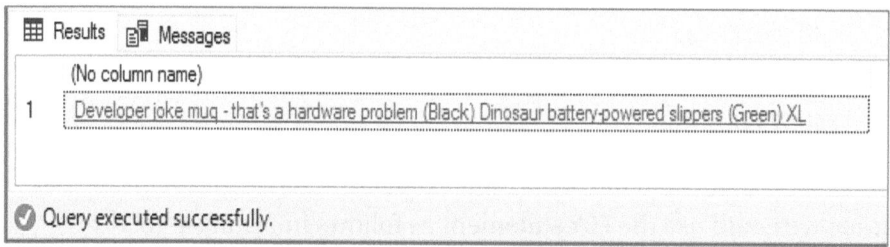

Figure 4-8. *Results of using* for *to iterate over product elements*

The query in Listing 4-14 uses a let statement, instead of a for iteration, to retrieve the name of the first product, within the first order, within the XML document. The return statement requires a singleton value, and as let simply assigns a value, as opposed to iterating over multiple values, we cannot return multiple products.

Listing 4-14. Using let to Find a Product Name

```
SELECT @XML.query('
        let $product := /SalesOrders/Order[1]/OrderDetails/
        Product/@ProductName
     return string($product[1])
') ;
```

The results of this query can be found in Figure 4-9.

⊞ Results	🗐 Messages
(No column name)
1	Dinosaur battery-powered slippers (Green) M
✓ Query executed successfully.

Figure 4-9. *Results of using* let *to find a product name*

130

The query in Listing 4-15 combines both a for statement and a let statement to construct a new XML document containing the customer name and product name for each product sold.

Listing 4-15. Combining for and let

```
SELECT @XML.query('
    for $product in /SalesOrders/Order/OrderDetails/Product/
    @ProductName
        let $customer := /SalesOrders/Order/OrderHeader/
        CustomerName
        return
        <Customer>
          {$customer[1]}
        <OrderDetails>
          {$product}
        </OrderDetails>
        </Customer>
') ;
```

The resultant XML document can be found in Listing 4-16.

Listing 4-16. Results of Combining for and let

```
<Customer>
  <CustomerName>Tailspin Toys (Absecon, NJ)</CustomerName>
  <OrderDetails ProductName="Dinosaur battery-powered slippers
  (Green) M" />
</Customer>
<Customer>
  <CustomerName>Tailspin Toys (Absecon, NJ)</CustomerName>
  <OrderDetails ProductName="RC toy sedan car with remote
  control (Green) 1/50 scale" />
</Customer>
```

```
<Customer>
  <CustomerName>Tailspin Toys (Absecon, NJ)</CustomerName>
  <OrderDetails ProductName="Black and orange glass with care
  despatch tape  48mmx100m" />
</Customer>
<Customer>
  <CustomerName>Tailspin Toys (Absecon, NJ)</CustomerName>
  <OrderDetails ProductName="Alien officer hoodie (Black) 3XL" />
</Customer>
<Customer>
  <CustomerName>Tailspin Toys (Absecon, NJ)</CustomerName>
  <OrderDetails ProductName="Developer joke mug - that's a
  hardware problem (Black)" />
</Customer>
<Customer>
  <CustomerName>Tailspin Toys (Absecon, NJ)</CustomerName>
  <OrderDetails ProductName="Dinosaur battery-powered slippers
  (Green) XL" />
</Customer>
```

The query in Listing 4-17 enhances the query in Listing 4-15, to add a where statement, which will filter the products, so that only the dinosaur slippers are returned. The query also uses an order by statement, to guarantee that the order of the results is by product name.

Listing 4-17. Using where and order by

```
SELECT @XML.query('
    for $product in /SalesOrders/Order/OrderDetails/Product/
    @ProductName
        let $customer := /SalesOrders/Order/OrderHeader/
        CustomerName
```

```
     where $product = "Dinosaur battery-powered slippers
     (Green) M"
       or $product = "Dinosaur battery-powered slippers
       (Green) XL"
     order by $product
    return
    <Customer>
      {$customer[1]}
    <OrderDetails>
      {$product}
    </OrderDetails>
    </Customer>
') ;
```

Modifying XML Data

XML data can be modified using XQuery's modify method. When using
modify, a developer has three options. You can use the insert option, the
delete option, or the replace value of option. The replace value of
option replaces an existing value within an XML document.

To understand how the insert option works, consider the script in
Listing 4-18. The script populates a variable with an empty order. The
modify method is then used to add an order line to the sales order.

Listing 4-18. Using the modify Insert

```
DECLARE @SalesOrder xml;
SET @SalesOrder = '
<Order>
  <OrderHeader>
    <CustomerName>Camille Authier</CustomerName>
    <OrderDate>2013-01-02</OrderDate>
```

```
   <OrderID>121</OrderID>
 </OrderHeader>
 <OrderDetails>
 </OrderDetails>
</Order>'  ;

SET @SalesOrder.modify('
insert <Product ProductID="22" ProductName="DBA joke mug - it
depends (White)" Price="13" Qty="6" />
into (/Order/OrderDetails)[1]') ;

SELECT @SalesOrder ;
```

The results of running this query can be seen in Listing 4-19.

Listing 4-19. Results of Using the modify Insert

```
<Order>
  <OrderHeader>
    <CustomerName>Camille Authier</CustomerName>
    <OrderDate>2013-01-02</OrderDate>
    <OrderID>121</OrderID>
  </OrderHeader>
  <OrderDetails>
    <Product ProductID="22" ProductName="DBA joke mug - it
    depends (White)" Price="13" Qty="6" />
  </OrderDetails>
</Order>
```

If Product elements already existed within the OrderDetails element, however, you could gain granular control over where you would like the element to be inserted by using the as first, as last, before, or after options. For example, the query in Listing 4-20 will insert the new Product element as the first element in the OrderDetails element.

Listing 4-20. Inserting an Element As First

```
DECLARE @SalesOrder xml;
SET @SalesOrder = '
<Order>
  <OrderHeader>
    <CustomerName>Camille Authier</CustomerName>
    <OrderDate>2013-01-02</OrderDate>
    <OrderID>121</OrderID>
  </OrderHeader>
  <OrderDetails>
    <Product ProductID="22" ProductName="DBA joke mug - it
    depends (White)" Price="13" Qty="6" />
  </OrderDetails>
</Order>'  ;

SET @SalesOrder.modify('
insert <Product ProductID="2" ProductName="USB rocket launcher
(Gray)" Price="25" Qty="9" /> as first
into (/Order/OrderDetails)[1]') ;

SELECT @SalesOrder ;
```

The results of this query can be seen in Listing 4-21.

Listing 4-21. Results of Inserting an Element As First

```
<Order>
  <OrderHeader>
    <CustomerName>Camille Authier</CustomerName>
    <OrderDate>2013-01-02</OrderDate>
    <OrderID>121</OrderID>
  </OrderHeader>
```

```
<OrderDetails>
  <Product ProductID="2" ProductName="USB rocket launcher
  (Gray)" Price="25" Qty="9" />
  <Product ProductID="22" ProductName="DBA joke mug - it
  depends (White)" Price="13" Qty="6" />
</OrderDetails>
</Order>
```

Alternatively, the query in Listing 4-22 demonstrates how you can insert an element after another, specific element. In this case, we will insert the Superhero Action Jacket after the USB Rocket Launcher.

Listing 4-22. Inserting an Element After Another Element

```
DECLARE @SalesOrder xml;
SET @SalesOrder = '
<Order>
  <OrderHeader>
    <CustomerName>Camille Authier</CustomerName>
    <OrderDate>2013-01-02</OrderDate>
    <OrderID>121</OrderID>
  </OrderHeader>
  <OrderDetails>
    <Product ProductID="2" ProductName="USB rocket launcher
    (Gray)" Price="25" Qty="9" />
    <Product ProductID="22" ProductName="DBA joke mug - it
    depends (White)" Price="13" Qty="6" />
  </OrderDetails>
</Order>'  ;

DECLARE @ProductName NVARCHAR(200) ;

SET @ProductName = 'USB rocket launcher (Gray)' ;
```

```
SET @SalesOrder.modify('
insert <Product ProductID="111" ProductName="Superhero action
jacket (Blue) M" Price="30" Qty="10" />
after (/Order/OrderDetails/Product[@ProductName =
sql:variable("@ProductName")])[1]') ;

SELECT @SalesOrder ;
```

This query uses `sql:variable` to pass the product's name from an T-SQL variable, using the techniques you learned in the "Using Relational Values in XQuery" section of this chapter. The results of the query can be seen in Listing 4-23.

Listing 4-23. Results of Inserting an Element After Another Element

```
<Order>
  <OrderHeader>
    <CustomerName>Camille Authier</CustomerName>
    <OrderDate>2013-01-02</OrderDate>
    <OrderID>121</OrderID>
  </OrderHeader>
  <OrderDetails>
    <Product ProductID="2" ProductName="USB rocket launcher
    (Gray)" Price="25" Qty="9" />
    <Product ProductID="111" ProductName="Superhero action
    jacket (Blue) M" Price="30" Qty="10" />
    <Product ProductID="22" ProductName="DBA joke mug - it
    depends (White)" Price="13" Qty="6" />
  </OrderDetails>
</Order>
```

The delete option can be used to remove nodes from an XML document. For example, consider the script in Listing 4-24. Here, we take the XML document produced by the query in Listing 4-22 and remove the last order line that we added to the document.

Listing 4-24. Using the delete Option

```
DECLARE @SalesOrder xml;
SET @SalesOrder = '
<Order>
  <OrderHeader>
    <CustomerName>Camille Authier</CustomerName>
    <OrderDate>2013-01-02</OrderDate>
    <OrderID>121</OrderID>
  </OrderHeader>
  <OrderDetails>
    <Product ProductID="2" ProductName="USB rocket launcher
    (Gray)" Price="25" Qty="9" />
    <Product ProductID="111" ProductName="Superhero action
    jacket (Blue) M" Price="30" Qty="10" />
    <Product ProductID="22" ProductName="DBA joke mug - it
    depends (White)" Price="13" Qty="6" />
  </OrderDetails>
</Order>'   ;

DECLARE @ProductName NVARCHAR(200) ;

SET @ProductName = 'Superhero action jacket (Blue) M' ;

SET @SalesOrder.modify('
delete (/Order/OrderDetails/Product[@ProductName =
sql:variable("@ProductName")])[1]') ;

SELECT @SalesOrder ;
```

You can see the resultant XML document in Listing 4-25.

Listing 4-25. Results of Using the `delete` Option

```
<Order>
  <OrderHeader>
    <CustomerName>Camille Authier</CustomerName>
    <OrderDate>2013-01-02</OrderDate>
    <OrderID>121</OrderID>
  </OrderHeader>
  <OrderDetails>
    <Product ProductID="2" ProductName="USB rocket launcher
    (Gray)" Price="25" Qty="9" />
    <Product ProductID="22" ProductName="DBA joke mug - it
    depends (White)" Price="13" Qty="6" />
  </OrderDetails>
</Order>
```

The `replace` value of `option` performs an update on an existing node. For example, the script in Listing 4-26 updates the quantity of DBA Joke Mugs ordered from six to ten. Once again, we bind SQL variables to allow us to pass in the `ProductName` that we wish to update and the new quantity. Note that we use `replace value of` to define the node that should be updated and `with` to define the new value.

Listing 4-26. Using `replace value of`

```
DECLARE @SalesOrder xml;
SET @SalesOrder = '
<Order>
  <OrderHeader>
    <CustomerName>Camille Authier</CustomerName>
```

```
    <OrderDate>2013-01-02</OrderDate>
    <OrderID>121</OrderID>
  </OrderHeader>
  <OrderDetails>
    <Product ProductID="2" ProductName="USB rocket launcher
    (Gray)" Price="25" Qty="9" />
    <Product ProductID="22" ProductName="DBA joke mug - it
    depends (White)" Price="13" Qty="6" />
  </OrderDetails>
</Order>'  ;

DECLARE @ProductName NVARCHAR(200) ;

SET @ProductName = 'DBA joke mug - it depends (White)' ;

DECLARE @Quantity INT ;

SET @Quantity = 10

SET @SalesOrder.modify('
replace value of (/Order/OrderDetails/Product[@Product
Name = sql:variable("@ProductName")]/@Qty)[1]
with "10"
') ;

SELECT @SalesOrder ;
```

The results of this query can be seen in Listing 4-27.

Listing 4-27. Results of Using `replace value of`

```
<Order>
  <OrderHeader>
    <CustomerName>Camille Authier</CustomerName>
    <OrderDate>2013-01-02</OrderDate>
    <OrderID>121</OrderID>
  </OrderHeader>
  <OrderDetails>
    <Product ProductID="2" ProductName="USB rocket launcher
    (Gray)" Price="25" Qty="9" />
    <Product ProductID="22" ProductName="DBA joke mug - it
    depends (White)" Price="13" Qty="10" />
  </OrderDetails>
</Order>
```

Shredding XML

Shredding XML is the process of taking an XML result set and converting it to a relational result set. In SQL Server, there are two ways to achieve this: the OPENXML() function and the nodes() XQuery method.

Shredding XML with OPENXML()

OPENXML() is a function that takes an XML document and converts it to a relational result set. It accepts the parameters detailed in Table 4-2.

Table 4-2. *OPENXML ( ) Parameters*

Parameter	Description
idoc	A pointer to an internal representation of the XML document
rowpattern	The path to the lowest level of the XML document that should be converted to rows
flags	An optional parameter that specifies the mapping between the XML data and relational result set. The possible values are detailed in Table 4-3.

Table 4-3 details the valid flags values that can be passed to OPENXML().

Table 4-3. *Flags Values*

Value	Description
0	Defaults to attribute-centric mapping
1	Use attribute-centric mapping, unless XML_ELEMENTS is specified. If XML_ELEMENTS is specified, attributes will be mapped first, followed by elements.
2	Element-centric mapping, unless XML_ATTRIBUTES is specified. If XML_ATTRIBUTES is specified, elements will be mapped first, followed by attributes.
8	XML_ATTRIBUTES and XML_ELEMENTS, combined with a logical OR

In addition to the function's parameters, a WITH clause can also be specified, which defines the schema of the result set to be returned. While the WITH clause is optional, not specifying the schema will cause an edge table to be returned. The schema is used to specify a relation column name, a relational data type, and the path to the relevant node.

Note   The flags will be overridden by specific mapping in the
WITH clause.

A limitation of the OPENXML() function is that it does not parse an XML
document itself. Instead, you must parse the document before calling
the function. This can be achieved using the sp_xml:preparedocument
system stored procedure. This procedure parses an XML document, using
the MSXML parser, and creates a handle to the parsed version of the
document that is ready for consumption.

After the OPENXML() function has completed, you should use the
sp_xml:removedocument system stored procedure to remove the parsed
document from memory. It is important to remember to tear down the
parsed document, or you could start running into memory issues, if the
sp_xml:preparedocument procedure is called frequently.

To see the OPENXML() function in action, see the script in Listing 4-28.
This script passes a sales orders document into a variable, before using
OPENXML() to shred the data.

Tip   The structure of the XML document has been changed from
previous examples in this chapter, to allow a broader demonstration
of the navigation of an XML document with OPENXML().

Listing 4-28. Using OPENXML()

```
DECLARE @SalesOrder XML ;
DECLARE @ParseDoc INT ;

SET @SalesOrder = '
<SalesOrders>
  <Order>
```

```
      <OrderDate>2013-01-02</OrderDate>
      <OrderHeader>
        <CustomerName>Camille Authier</CustomerName>
      </OrderHeader>
      <OrderDetails>
        <Product ProductID="45" ProductName="Developer joke
        mug - there are 10 types of people in the world (Black)"
        Price="13" Qty="7" />
        <Product ProductID="58" ProductName="RC toy sedan car with
        remote control (Black) 1/50 scale" Price="25" Qty="4" />
      </OrderDetails>
    </Order>
    <Order>
      <OrderDate>2013-01-02</OrderDate>
      <OrderHeader>
        <CustomerName>Camille Authier</CustomerName>
          </OrderHeader>
      <OrderDetails OrderID = "122">
        <Product ProductID="22" ProductName="DBA joke mug - it
        depends (White)" Price="13" Qty="6" />
        <Product ProductID="2" ProductName="USB rocket launcher
        (Gray)" Price="25" Qty="9" />
        <Product ProductID="111" ProductName="Superhero action
        jacket (Blue) M" Price="30" Qty="10" />
        <Product ProductID="116" ProductName="Superhero action
        jacket (Blue) 4XL" Price="34" Qty="4" />
      </OrderDetails>
    </Order>
</SalesOrders>' ;

EXEC sp_xml:preparedocument @ParseDoc OUTPUT, @SalesOrder ;
SELECT *
```

```
FROM OPENXML(@ParseDoc, '/SalesOrders/Order/OrderDetails/Product')
WITH (
                    ProductID        INT              '@ProductID',
    ProductName     NVARCHAR(200)    '@ProductName',
    Quantity        INT                          '@Qty',
    OrderID         INT                    '../@OrderID',
    OrderDate       DATE               '../../OrderDate',
    CustomerName  NVARCHAR(200)  '../../OrderHeader/CustomerName'
) ;
```

```
EXEC sp_xml:removedocument @ParseDoc ;
```

When you examine the WITH clause of the OPENXML() statement of this script, you will see that we first specify the relational column name. By looking at the Quantity mapping, you will see that the relational names do not have to match the names of the XML nodes. We then specify a relational data type for the resultant value, before specifying a path to the node that we wish to retrieve. This is the most interesting aspect of the query. You will notice that we have used the rowpattern parameter of the OPENXML() function to map down to the Product element, as the lowest level. This means that the Product element is the starting point for our paths. The ProductID, ProductName, and Quantity attributes are all attributes of the Product element. Therefore, we prefix these with the @ symbol, to designate that they are attributes, but no other path mapping is required. The OrderID attribute is an attribute of the OrderDetails element. Because the OrderDetails element is one level above the Product element, we use the ../ syntax, to specify that we must navigate up one level. The OrderDate element is two levels above the Product element; therefore, we use ../ twice, to indicate we should move two levels up the hierarchy. Also, note that because OrderDate is an element, not an attribute, we have not prefixed the node with an @ symbol. Finally, to map to the CustomerName element, we first must navigate two levels up the hierarchy, using the ../ syntax. We then must drop down into a sibling node (OrderHeader), to retrieve the CustomerName element.

The results of the query can be found in Figure 4-10. Note that NULL values have been returned for OrderID against two of the products. This is because no OrderID element was specified against the second sales order.

	ProductID	ProductName	Quantity	OrderID	OrderDate	CustomerName
1	45	Developer joke mug - there are 10 types of peop...	7	NULL	2013-01-02	Camille Authier
2	58	RC toy sedan car with remote control (Black) 1/...	4	NULL	2013-01-02	Camille Authier
3	22	DBA joke mug - it depends (White)	6	122	2013-01-02	Camille Authier
4	2	USB rocket launcher (Gray)	9	122	2013-01-02	Camille Authier
5	111	Superhero action jacket (Blue) M	10	122	2013-01-02	Camille Authier
6	116	Superhero action jacket (Blue) 4XL	4	122	2013-01-02	Camille Authier

Figure 4-10. *Results of using OPENXML()*

Shredding XML with Nodes

If you want to shred the data from a column instead of using a variable, you can avoid the need for iterative logic by shredding the data with XQuery. Specifically, the nodes() method can be used to identify the nodes that should be mapped to relational columns. This can be combined with the value() method, to extract the data from the nodes. For example, consider the query in Listing 4-29. This query is functionally equivalent to the query in Listing 4-28 but uses the nodes() method instead of OPENXML().

Listing 4-29. Using nodes() to Shred XML

```
DECLARE @SalesOrder XML ;

SET @SalesOrder = '
<SalesOrders>
  <Order>
    <OrderDate>2013-01-02</OrderDate>
    <OrderHeader>
      <CustomerName>Camille Authier</CustomerName>
        </OrderHeader>
    <OrderDetails>
      <Product ProductID="45" ProductName="Developer joke
      mug - there are 10 types of people in the world (Black)"
      Price="13" Qty="7" />
      <Product ProductID="58" ProductName="RC toy sedan car with
      remote control (Black) 1/50 scale" Price="25" Qty="4" />
    </OrderDetails>
  </Order>
  <Order>
    <OrderDate>2013-01-02</OrderDate>
    <OrderHeader>
      <CustomerName>Camille Authier</CustomerName>
        </OrderHeader>
    <OrderDetails OrderID = "122">
      <Product ProductID="22" ProductName="DBA joke mug - it
      depends (White)" Price="13" Qty="6" />
      <Product ProductID="2" ProductName="USB rocket launcher
      (Gray)" Price="25" Qty="9" />
      <Product ProductID="111" ProductName="Superhero action
      jacket (Blue) M" Price="30" Qty="10" />
```

```
        <Product ProductID="116" ProductName="Superhero action
jacket (Blue) 4XL" Price="34" Qty="4" />
    </OrderDetails>
  </Order>
</SalesOrders>' ;

SELECT
            TempCol.value('@ProductID', 'INT') AS ProductID
          , TempCol.value('@ProductName', 'NVARCHAR(70)') AS
          ProductName
          , TempCol.value('@Qty', 'INT') AS Quantity
          , TempCol.value('../@OrderID', 'INT') AS OrderID
          , TempCol.value('../../OrderDate[1]', 'NVARCHAR(10)')
          AS OorderDate
          , TempCol.value('../../OrderHeader[1]/CustomerName[1]',
          'NVARCHAR(15)') AS CustomerName
FROM @SalesOrder.nodes('SalesOrders/Order/OrderDetails/
Product') TempTable(TempCol) ;
```

When reviewing this script, you should pay particular attention to the FROM clause. Here, we pass an XQuery expression into the nodes() method, to define the grain. We then define arbitrary names for a table and column, which will contain the intermediate results set.

The nodes() method can also be used in conjunction with the query() method, to shred an XML document into smaller XML documents. For example, consider the query in Listing 4-30. This query extracts the Product elements from the XML document, in XML format.

Listing 4-30. Using the nodes() Method with the query() Method

```
DECLARE @SalesOrder XML ;

SET @SalesOrder = '
<SalesOrders>
  <Order>
    <OrderDate>2013-01-02</OrderDate>
    <OrderHeader>
      <CustomerName>Camille Authier</CustomerName>
        </OrderHeader>
    <OrderDetails>
      <Product ProductID="45" ProductName="Developer joke
      mug - there are 10 types of people in the world (Black)"
      Price="13" Qty="7" />
      <Product ProductID="58" ProductName="RC toy sedan car
      with remote control (Black) 1/50 scale" Price="25"
      Qty="4" />
    </OrderDetails>
  </Order>
  <Order>
    <OrderDate>2013-01-02</OrderDate>
    <OrderHeader>
      <CustomerName>Camille Authier</CustomerName>
        </OrderHeader>
    <OrderDetails OrderID = "122">
      <Product ProductID="22" ProductName="DBA joke mug - it
      depends (White)" Price="13" Qty="6" />
      <Product ProductID="2" ProductName="USB rocket launcher
      (Gray)" Price="25" Qty="9" />
      <Product ProductID="111" ProductName="Superhero action
      jacket (Blue) M" Price="30" Qty="10" />
```

```
    <Product ProductID="116" ProductName="Superhero action
    jacket (Blue) 4XL" Price="34" Qty="4" />
  </OrderDetails>
 </Order>
</SalesOrders>' ;
```

```
SELECT
        TempCol.query('.') AS Product
FROM @SalesOrder.nodes('SalesOrders/Order/OrderDetails/
Product') TempTable(TempCol) ;
```

The results of this query can be seen in Figure 4-11.

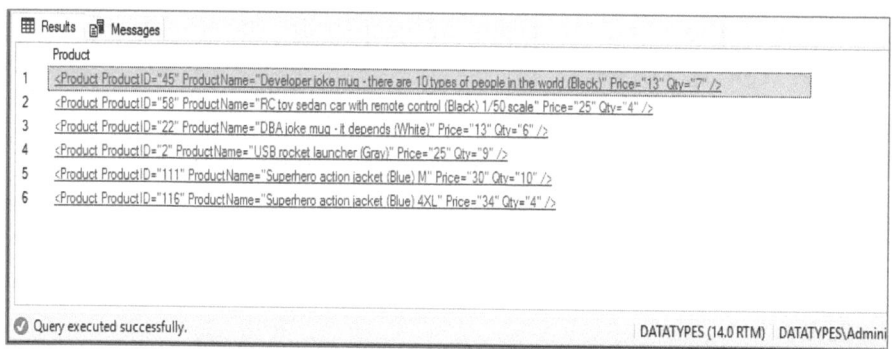

Figure 4-11. *Results of using the nodes() method with the query()
method*

The biggest benefit of the nodes() method over OPENXML() is its
ease of use against a table. The CROSS APPLY operator can be used to
apply the nodes() method to multiple rows within a table. The query in
Listing 4-31 demonstrates this, by calling the nodes() method against the
OrderSummary column in the Sales.CustomerOrderSummary table. The
query will return one row for every product on every sales order placed by
a customer with the CustomerID of 814. The results are then ordered by
the quantity of each product.

Listing 4-31. Using the nodes() Method Against a Table

```
USE WideWorldImporters
GO

SELECT
      CustomerID
        , TempCol.value('@Qty', 'INT') AS Quantity
        , TempCol.value('@ProductName', 'NVARCHAR(70)') AS
        ProductName
        , TempCol.query('.') AS Product
FROM Sales.CustomerOrderSummary
CROSS APPLY OrderSummary.nodes('SalesOrders/Order/OrderDetails/
Product') TempTable(TempCol)
WHERE CustomerID = 841
ORDER BY TempCol.value('@Qty', 'INT') DESC ;
```

Partial results of this query can be seen in Figure 4-12.

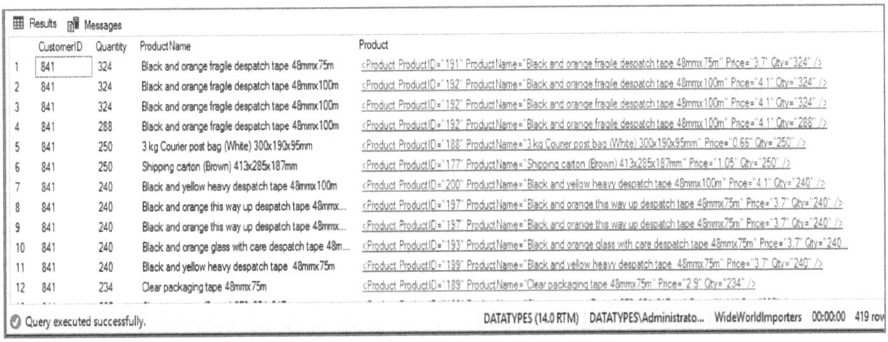
Results Messages

	CustomerID	Quantity	ProductName	Product
1	841	324	Black and orange fragile despatch tape 48mmx75m	<Product ProductID="191" ProductName="Black and orange fragile despatch tape 48mmx75m" Price="3.7" Qty="324" />
2	841	324	Black and orange fragile despatch tape 48mmx100m	<Product ProductID="192" ProductName="Black and orange fragile despatch tape 48mmx100m" Price="4.1" Qty="324" />
3	841	324	Black and orange fragile despatch tape 48mmx100m	<Product ProductID="192" ProductName="Black and orange fragile despatch tape 48mmx100m" Price="4.1" Qty="324" />
4	841	288	Black and orange fragile despatch tape 48mmx100m	<Product ProductID="192" ProductName="Black and orange fragile despatch tape 48mmx100m" Price="4.1" Qty="288" />
5	841	250	3 kg Courier post bag (White) 300x190x95mm	<Product ProductID="188" ProductName="3 kg Courier post bag (White) 300x190x95mm" Price="0.66" Qty="250" />
6	841	250	Shipping carton (Brown) 413x285x187mm	<Product ProductID="177" ProductName="Shipping carton (Brown) 413x285x187mm" Price="1.05" Qty="250" />
7	841	240	Black and yellow heavy despatch tape 48mmx100m	<Product ProductID="200" ProductName="Black and yellow heavy despatch tape 48mmx100m" Price="4.1" Qty="240" />
8	841	240	Black and orange this way up despatch tape 48mmx...	<Product ProductID="197" ProductName="Black and orange this way up despatch tape 48mmx75m" Price="3.7" Qty="240" />
9	841	240	Black and orange this way up despatch tape 48mmx...	<Product ProductID="197" ProductName="Black and orange this way up despatch tape 48mmx75m" Price="3.7" Qty="240" />
10	841	240	Black and orange glass with care despatch tape 48m...	<Product ProductID="193" ProductName="Black and orange glass with care despatch tape 48mmx75m" Price="3.7" Qty="240...
11	841	240	Black and yellow heavy despatch tape 48mmx75m	<Product ProductID="199" ProductName="Black and yellow heavy despatch tape 48mmx75m" Price="3.7" Qty="240" />
12	841	234	Clear packaging tape 48mmx75m	<Product ProductID="189" ProductName="Clear packaging tape 48mmx75m" Price="2.9" Qty="234" />

Query executed successfully. DATATYPES (14.0 RTM) DATATYPES\Administrato... WideWorldImporters 00:00:00 419 row

Figure 4-12. *Results of using the nodes() method against a table*

Using Schemas

As discussed in Chapter 3, an XML document can be bound to a schema, to ensure that its structure meets the client contract. In SQL Server, we can define an XSD schema by creating an XML SCHEMA COLLECTION. To demonstrate this, imagine that we wanted to bind our OrderSummary column, in the Sales.CustomerOrderSummary table, to a schema. The first step would be to create the XSD SCHEMA COLLECTION. We could achieve this using the code in Listing 4-32.

Listing 4-32. Creating an XML SCHEMA COLLECTION

```
USE WideWorldImporters
GO

CREATE XML SCHEMA COLLECTION OrderSummary AS
N'<?xml version="1.0" encoding="utf-16"?>
<xs:schema attributeFormDefault="unqualified"
elementFormDefault="qualified" xmlns:xs="http://www.
w3.org/2001/XMLSchema">
  <xs:element name="SalesOrders">
    <xs:complexType>
      <xs:sequence>
        <xs:element maxOccurs="unbounded" name="Order">
          <xs:complexType>
            <xs:sequence>
              <xs:element name="OrderHeader">
                <xs:complexType>
                  <xs:sequence>
                    <xs:element name="CustomerName"
                    type="xs:string" />
                    <xs:element name="OrderDate" type="xs:date" />
```

```
                <xs:element name="OrderID"
                type="xs:unsignedInt" />
              </xs:sequence>
            </xs:complexType>
          </xs:element>
          <xs:element name="OrderDetails">
            <xs:complexType>
              <xs:sequence>
                <xs:element maxOccurs="unbounded"
                name="Product">
                  <xs:complexType>
                    <xs:attribute name="ProductID"
                    type="xs:unsignedByte" use="required" />
                    <xs:attribute name="ProductName"
                    type="xs:string" use="required" />
                    <xs:attribute name="Price"
                    type="xs:decimal" use="required" />
                    <xs:attribute name="Qty"
                    type="xs:unsignedShort" use="required" />
                  </xs:complexType>
                </xs:element>
              </xs:sequence>
            </xs:complexType>
          </xs:element>
        </xs:sequence>
      </xs:complexType>
    </xs:element>
  </xs:sequence>
</xs:complexType>
</xs:element>
</xs:schema>' ;
```

153

> **Tip**   Because the schema does not specify a namespace, it will be
> associated with the default empty string namespace. A namespace
> can be added to the schema, using the `<xs:schema>` attribute
> `xmlns:ns=http://your-namespace`.

We could bind our schema to the OrderSummary column by using the
query in Listing 4-33.

Listing 4-33. Binding a Schema to a Column

```
ALTER TABLE Sales.CustomerOrderSummary
        ALTER COLUMN OrderSummary XML(OrderSummary) ;
```

We can also reference a schema when constructing or querying XML
data. The FOR XML clause includes a WITH XMLNAMESPACES option that can
be used to specify the target namespace of the resultant XML document,
and XQuery methods, such as query, can begin with a declare namespace
statement.

> **Tip**   A full discussion of the use of namespaces is beyond the scope
> of this book. However, examples of using WITH XMLNAMESPACES
> can be found at `https://docs.microsoft.com/en-us/sql/t-`
> `sql/xml/with-xmlnamespaces?view=sql-server-2017`,
> and examples of using a namespace with the query method can be
> found at `https://docs.microsoft.com/en-us/sql/t-sql/`
> `xml/value-method-xml-data-type?view=sql-server-2017`.

Summary

XQuery is a language that can be used to query XML data when it is stored in SQL Server columns and variables. The exist() method can be used to check for the existence of a node or a node containing a specific value. The value() method can be used to extract a scalar value from an XML document, and the query() method can be used to return a subset of an XML document still in XML format.

FLWOR statements can be used to help navigate and iterate an XML document. The for statement binds a variable to an input sequence. The let statement is used to assign an XQuery expression to a variable. The where statement can be used to filter the results that are returned. The order by statement can optionally be used to order the results of the FLWOR statement. The return statement specifies what data will be returned.

T-SQL variables and columns can be passed into XQuery statements. When this technique is adopted, it is known as a cross-domain query. It allows for values to easily be bound to XQuery statements, helping to simplify logic and reduce duplicate code.

XML data can be modified by using the modify() method. This method allows developers to use one of three options: insert, replace value of, or delete. When inserting data, there are further options that developers can take advantage of, to give them granular control over where the insert occurs. For example, you can choose to insert first, last, after a node, or before a node.

XML data can be converted into relational data (that is, shredded) by using either the OPENXML() function or the nodes() XQuery method. When the OPENXML() function is used, the XML document to be shredded must first be parsed. This can be achieved with the sys.sp_ xml:preparedocument system-stored procedure. Once the document has been shredded, the parse tree should be removed from memory, by using the sys.sp_xml:removedocument system-stored procedure.

When the nodes() XQuery method is used to shred data, it can be used in conjunction with either the value() method, which will shred the data into relational results, or the query() method, which will shred the data into smaller XML documents. You can also use nodes() with a combination of both value() and query(). The biggest advantage of the nodes() method is the ease with which it can be applied to a column, using the CROSS APPLY operator.

CHAPTER 5

XML Indexes

As discussed in Chapters 3 and 4, SQL Server allows you to store data in tables, in a native XML format, using the XML data type. Like other large object types, it can store up to a maximum of 2GB per tuple. Although standard operators such as = and LIKE can be used against XML columns, you also have the option of using XQuery expressions (discussed in this chapter). They can be rather inefficient, however, unless you create XML indexes.

XML indexes will outperform full-text indexes for most queries against XML columns. SQL Server offers support for primary XML indexes and three types of secondary XML indexes: PATH, VALUE, and PROPERTY. Each of these indexes will be discussed in the following sections. First, however, I will briefly discuss clustered indexes, as a clustered index must exist on the table before you can create an XML index.

Preparing the Environment

Because the WideWorldImporters database has no tables that contain native XML columns, we will create an OrderSummary table, for demonstrations within this chapter. The table will contain three columns: an IDENTITY column (named ID), a CustomerID column, and an XML column (called OrderSummary), which will contain a summary of all orders that a customer has placed. The table can be created and populated using the script in Listing 5-1.

© Peter A. Carter 2018
P. A. Carter, *SQL Server Advanced Data Types*,
https://doi.org/10.1007/978-1-4842-3901-8_5

Listing 5-1. Creating an OrderSummary Table

```
USE WideWorldImporters
GO

CREATE TABLE Sales.OrderSummary
(
        ID            INT          NOT NULL          IDENTITY,
        CustomerID    INT          NOT NULL,
        OrderSummary       XML
) ;

INSERT INTO Sales.OrderSummary (CustomerID, OrderSummary)
SELECT
        CustomerID,
        (
                SELECT
                        CustomerName 'OrderHeader/CustomerName'
                        , OrderDate 'OrderHeader/OrderDate'
                        , OrderID 'OrderHeader/OrderID'
                        , (
                                SELECT
                                        LineItems2.StockItemID
                                        '@ProductID'
                                        , StockItems.StockI
                                        temName '@ProductName'
                                        , LineItems2.UnitPrice
                                        '@Price'
                                        , Quantity '@Qty'
                                FROM Sales.OrderLines LineItems2
                                INNER JOIN Warehouse.StockItems
                                StockItems
```

```
                                ON LineItems2.StockItemID
                                = StockItems.StockItemID
                        WHERE LineItems2.OrderID =
                        Base.OrderID
                        FOR XML PATH('Product'), TYPE
                    ) 'OrderDetails'
            FROM
            (
                    SELECT DISTINCT
                            Customers.CustomerName
                          , SalesOrder.OrderDate
                          , SalesOrder.OrderID
                    FROM Sales.Orders SalesOrder
                    INNER JOIN Sales.OrderLines LineItem
                            ON SalesOrder.OrderID =
                            LineItem.OrderID
                    INNER JOIN Sales.Customers Customers
                            ON Customers.CustomerID =
                            SalesOrder.CustomerID
                    WHERE customers.CustomerID = OuterCust.
                    CustomerID
                ) Base
                FOR XML PATH('Order'), ROOT ('SalesOrders'), TYPE
            ) AS OrderSummary
FROM Sales.Customers OuterCust ;
```

Clustered Indexes

A clustered index causes the data pages of a table to be logically stored
in the order of the clustered index key. The clustered index key can be a
single column or a set of columns. This is often the table's primary key, but

this is not enforced, and there are some circumstances in which you would want to use a different column. This will be discussed in more detail later in this chapter.

Tables Without a Clustered Index

When a table exists without a clustered index, it is known as a heap. A heap consists of an IAM (index allocation map) page (or pages) and a series of data pages that are not linked together or stored in order. The only way SQL Server can determine the pages of the table is by reading the IAM page(or pages). When a table is stored as a heap, every time the table is accessed, SQL Server must read every single page in the table, even if you only want to return one row. The diagram in Figure 5-1 illustrates how a heap is structured.

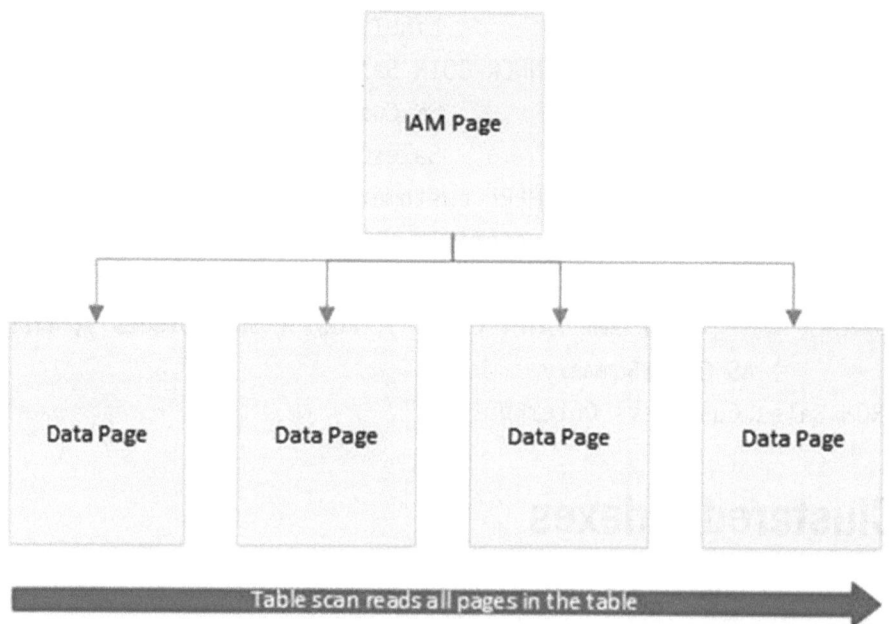

Figure 5-1. *Heap structure*

When data is stored on a heap, SQL Server must maintain a unique identifier for each row. It does this by creating a RID (row identifier). Even if a table has nonclustered indexes, it is still stored as a heap, unless there is a clustered index. When nonclustered indexes are created on a heap, the RID is used as a pointer, so that nonclustered indexes can link back to the correct row in the base table. Nonclustered indexes store the RID with a format of FileID: Page ID: Slot Number.

Tables with a Clustered Index

When you create a clustered index on a table, a B-Tree (balanced tree) structure is created. This allows for more efficient search operations to be performed, by creating a tiered set of pointers to the data, as illustrated in Figure 5-2. The page at the top level of this hierarchy is called the root node. The bottom level of the structure is called the leaf level, and with a clustered index, the leaf level consists of the actual data pages of the table. There can be one or more intermediate levels of B-Tree structures, depending on the size of the table.

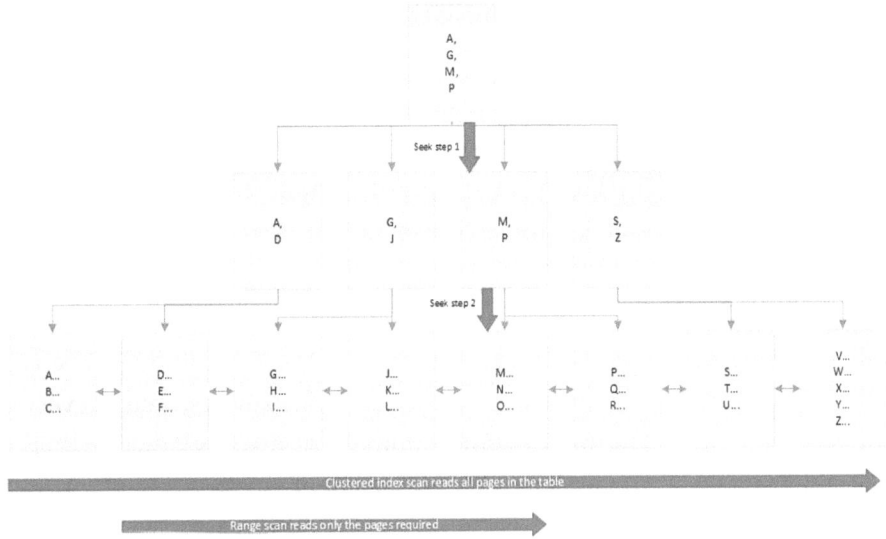

Figure 5-2. *Clustered index structure*

The diagram in Figure 5-2 shows that while the leaf level is the data itself, the levels above contain pointers to the pages below them in the tree. This allows for SQL Server to perform a seek operation. This is a very efficient method of returning a small number of rows. It works by navigating its way down the B-Tree, using the pointers to find the row(s) it requires. We can see that, if required, SQL Server can still scan all pages of the table, in order to retrieve the required rows. This is known as a Clustered Index Scan. Alternatively, SQL Server may decide to combine these two methods, to perform a range scan. Here, SQL Server will seek the first value of the required range and then scan the leaf level, until it encounters the first value that is not required. SQL Server can do this because the table is ordered by the index key, meaning that it can guarantee that there will be no other matching values later in the table.

Clustering the Primary Key

The primary key of a table is often the natural choice for the clustered index. In fact, by default, unless you specify otherwise, or unless a clustered index already exists on the table, creating a primary key will automatically generate a clustered index on that key. There are circumstances in which the primary key is not the correct choice for the clustered index. An example of this that I have witnessed is a third-party application that required the primary key of the table to be a GUID. A GUID (globally unique identifier) is used to guarantee uniqueness across the entire network.

This introduces two major problems if the clustered index were to be built on the primary key. The first is size. A GUID is 16 bytes long. When a table has nonclustered indexes, the clustered index key is stored in every nonclustered index. For unique nonclustered indexes, it is stored for every row at the leaf level, and for non-unique nonclustered indexes, it is also stored at every row in the root and intermediate levels of the index as well.

When you multiply 16 bytes by millions of rows, this will drastically increase the size of the indexes, making them less efficient.

The second issue is that when a GUID is generated, it is a random value. Because the data in your table is stored in the order of the clustered index key, for good performance, you need the values of this key to be generated in sequential order. Generating random values for your clustered index key will result in the index becoming more and more fragmented every time you insert a new row. Fragmentation will be discussed later in this chapter.

There is a workaround for the second issue, however. SQL Server has a function called NEWSEQUENTIALID() that will always generate a GUID value higher than previous values generated on the server. Therefore, if you use this function in the Default constraint of your primary key, you can enforce sequential inserts.

Caution   After the server has been restarted, NEWSEQUENTIALID() can start with a lower value. This may lead to fragmentation.

If the primary key must be a GUID, or another wide column, such as National Insurance Number, or a set of columns forming a natural key, such as Customer ID, Order Date, and Product ID, it is highly recommended that you create an additional column in your table. This column could be an INT or BIGINT, depending on the number of rows you expect the table to have, and could use either the IDENTITY property or a SEQUENCE to create a narrow, sequential key that can be used for your clustered index. I recommend ensuring a narrow key, as it will be included in all nonclustered indexes on the table. It will also use less memory when joining tables.

Caution   If you intend to use XML indexes, the clustered index must be created on the primary key.

Performance Considerations for Clustered Indexes

Because an IAM page lists the extents of a heap table in the order in which they are stored in the data file, as opposed to the order of the index key, a table scan of a heap may prove to be slightly faster than a clustered index scan, unless the clustered index has 0% fragmentation, which is rare.

Inserts into a clustered index may be faster than inserts into a heap, when the clustered index key is ever-increasing. This is especially true when there are multiple inserts happening in parallel, because a heap will experience more contention on system pages (GAM/SGAM/PFS) when the database engine is looking for spaces to place the new data. If the clustered index key is not ever-increasing, however, then inserts will lead to page splits and fragmentation. The knock-on effect is that inserts would be slower than they would be into a heap. A large insert into a heap may also be faster, if you take out a table lock and take advantage of minimally logged inserts. This is because of reduced IO to the transaction log.

Updates that cause a row to relocate, due to a change in size, will be faster when performed against a clustered index, as opposed to a heap. This is, for the same reason as mentioned above for insert operations, where there will be more contention against the system pages. When updated, rows may change in size, for reasons such as updating a VARCHAR column with a longer string. If the update to the row can be made in place (without relocating the row), there is likely to be little difference in performance. Deletes may also be slightly faster into a clustered index than into a heap, but the difference will be less noticeable than for update operations.

Creating a Clustered Index

With SSMS (SQL Server Management Studio), we can create a clustered index on the ID column of the OrderSummary table, by expanding Databases ➤ WideWorldImporters ➤ Tables ➤ Sales.OrderSummary in Object Explorer, right-clicking the Indexes node, and selecting New index ➤ Clustered index. This will cause the New Index dialog box to be invoked, as shown in Figure 5-3.

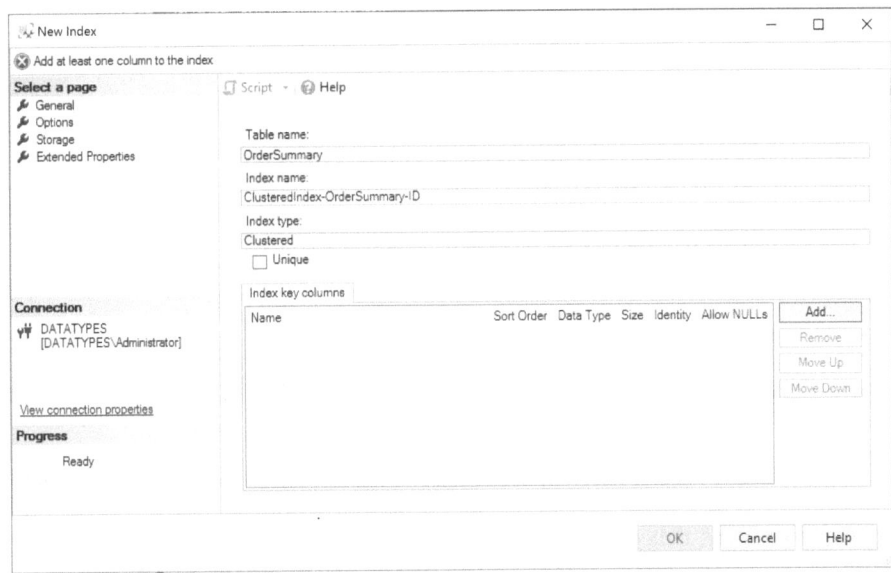

Figure 5-3. *New Index dialog box*

Caution   If you plan to follow later demonstrations in this chapter, do not execute the steps illustrated in Figures 5-3 and 5-4. Also, avoid executing the script in Listing 5-2. If you do create the index, you will have to drop it before running further examples.

On the General page of the dialog box, give the index a descriptive name, then use the Add button, to select the column(s) that the index will be built on, as shown in Figure 5-4.

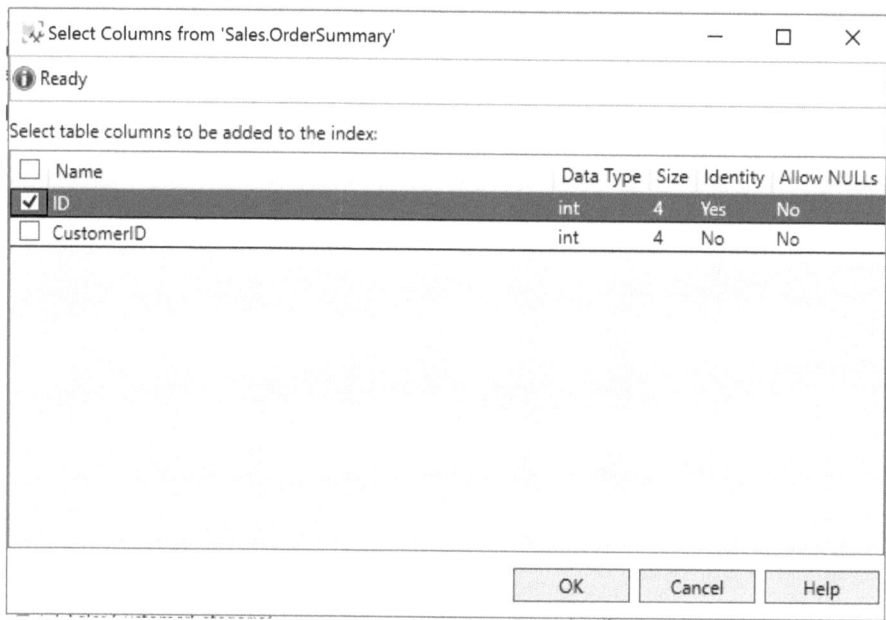

Figure 5-4. *Add columns dialog box*

Alternatively, this clustered index could be created using the script in Listing 5-2.

Listing 5-2. Creating a Clustered Index

```
USE WideWorldImporters
GO

CREATE CLUSTERED INDEX [ClusteredIndex-OrderSummary-ID] ON
Sales.OrderSummary (ID) ;
GO
```

Note   Advanced options for creating clustered indexes are beyond the scope of this book, but further information can be found in *Pro SQL Server Administration* (Apress, 2015), available at www.apress. com/gb/book/9781484207116.

Because our XML indexes require the clustered index to be built on a primary key, instead of executing the preceding script, we should instead run the script in Listing 5-3. This script will create a primary key on the ID column and then a clustered index on the primary key.

Listing 5-3. Creating a Primary Key and Clustered Index

```
USE WideWorldImporters
GO

ALTER TABLE Sales.OrderSummary ADD CONSTRAINT
        PK_OrderSummary PRIMARY KEY CLUSTERED (ID) ;
```

Primary XML Indexes

A primary XML index is actually a multicolumn clustered index on an internal system table called the Node table. This table stores a shredded representation on the XML objects within an XML column, along with the clustered index key of the base table. This means that a table must have a clustered index before a primary XML index can be created. Additionally, the clustered index must be created on the primary key and must consist of 32 columns or less.

The system table stores enough information that the scalar or XML subtrees required by a query can be reconstructed from the index itself. This information includes the node ID and name, the tag name and URI, a tokenized version of the node's data type, the first position of the node value in the document, pointers to the long node value and binary value, the nullability of the node, and the value of the base table's clustered index key for the corresponding row.

Primary XML indexes can provide a performance improvement when a query must shred scalar values from an XML document (or documents) or return a subset of nodes from an XML document (or documents).

Creating Primary XML Indexes

To create a primary XML index using SSMS, drill through Databases ➤ WideWorldImporters ➤ Tables ➤ Sales.OrderSummary in Object Explore. Then select New Index ➤ Primary XML Index from the context menu of indexes. This will cause the General page of the New Index dialog box to be displayed. This is shown in Figure 5-5.

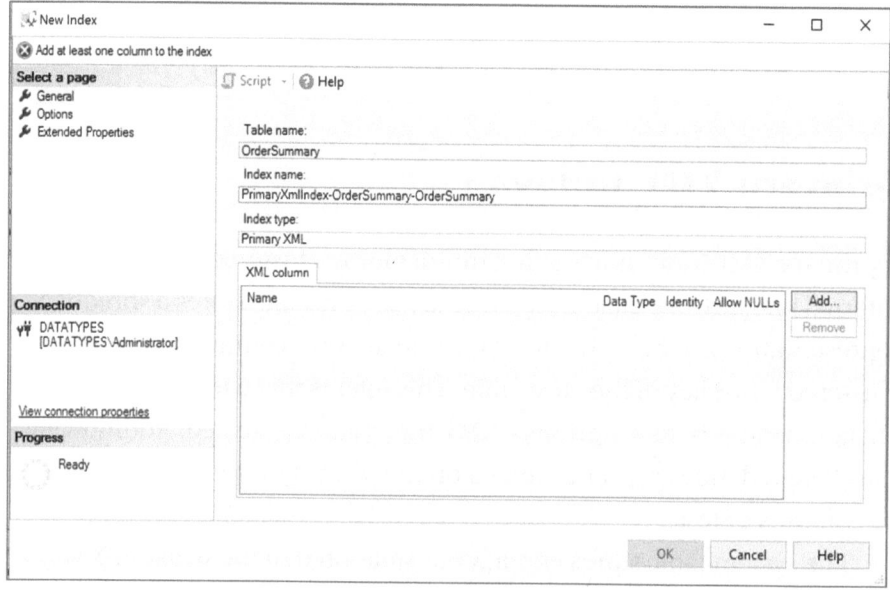

Figure 5-5. *New Index dialog box (Primary XML)*

Here, we will give the index a descriptive name and then use the Add button, to add the required XML column, as shown in Figure 5-6.

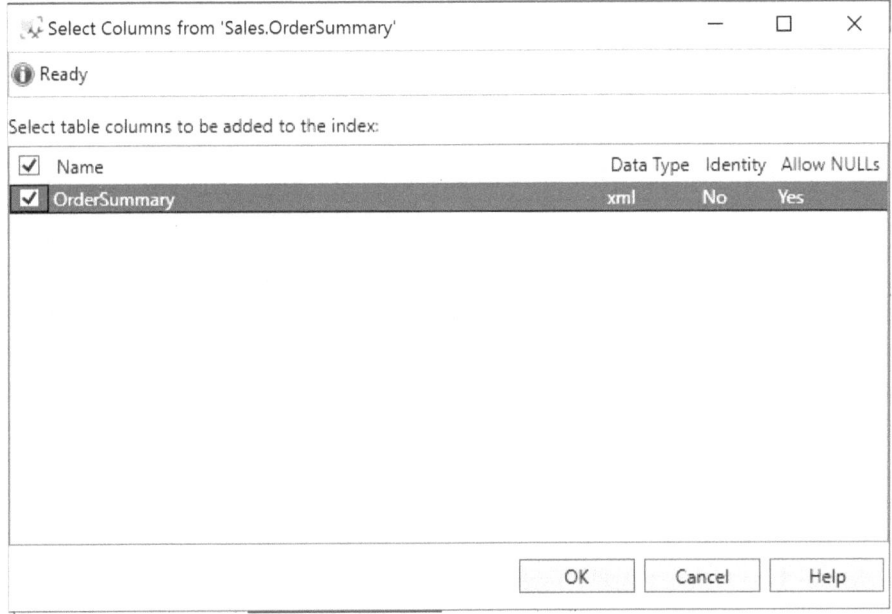

Figure 5-6. *Add column dialog box (Primary XML)*

From the Options tab of the New Index dialog box (Figure 5-7), we can set the options detailed in Table 5-1.

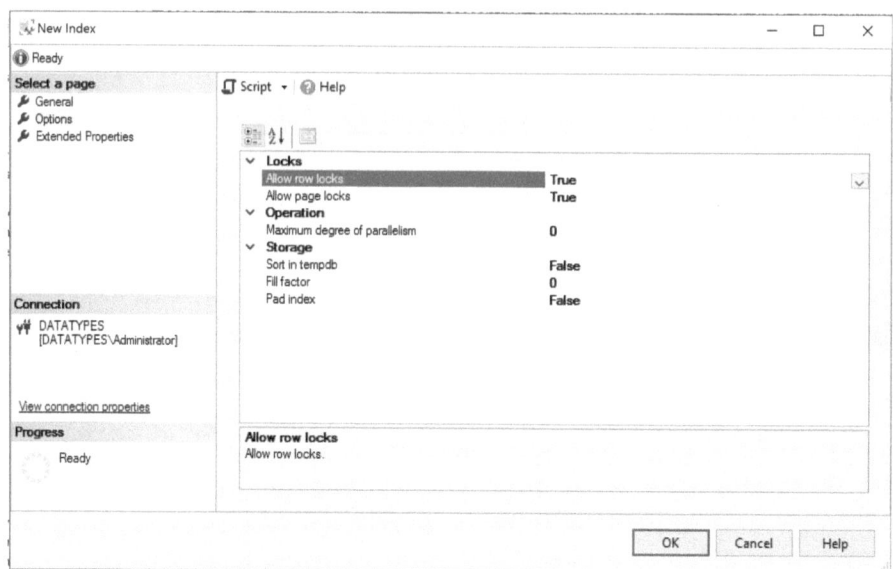

Figure 5-7. *New Index dialog box—Options page (Primary XML)*

Table 5-1. *Primary XML Index Options*

Option	Description
Allow Row Locks	Specifies if row locks can be acquired when accessing the index
Allow Page Locks	Specifies if page locks can be acquired when accessing the index
MaxDoP	Has no effect for building primary XML indexes, as this operation is always single threaded
Sort in TempDB	If specified, sort in TempDB will cause the intermediate result set to be stored in TempDB, as opposed to the user database. This could mean that the index is built faster.

(*continued*)

Table 5-1. (*continued*)

Option	Description
Fill Factor	Specifies a percentage of free space that will be left on each index page at the lowest level of the index. The default is 0 (100% full), meaning that only enough space for a single row will be left. Specifying a percentage lower than 100, for example, specifying 70, will leave 30% free space and can reduce page splits, if there are likely to be frequent row inserts.
Pad Index	Applies a fill factor (see preceding) to the intermediate levels of a B-Tree

Alternatively, to create the index via T-SQL, you could use the script in Listing 5-4.

Listing 5-4. Creating a Primary XML Index

```
USE WideWorldImporters
GO

CREATE PRIMARY XML INDEX [PrimaryXmlIndex-OrderSummary-
OrderSummary]
        ON Sales.OrderSummary ([OrderSummary]) ;
GO
```

Secondary XML Indexes

Secondary XML indexes can only be created on XML columns that already have a primary XML index. Behind the scenes, secondary XML indexes are actually nonclustered indexes on the internal Node table. Secondary XML indexes can improve query performance for queries that use specific types of XQuery processing.

171

A PATH secondary XML index is built on the Node ID and VALUE columns of the Node table. This type of index offers performance improvements to queries that use path expressions, such as the exists() XQuery method. A VALUE secondary XML index is the reverse of this and is built on the VALUE and Node ID columns. This type of index will offer performance improvements to queries that search for values, without knowing the name of the XML element or attribute that contains the value being searched for.

Finally, a PROPERTY secondary XML index is built on the clustered index key of the base table, the Node ID, and the VALUE columns of the Node table. This type of index performs very well if the query is trying to retrieve nodes from multiple tuples of the column.

Creating Secondary XML Indexes

To create a secondary XML index in SSMS, drill through Databases ➤ WideWorldImporters ➤ Tables ➤ OrderSummary in Object Explorer. Next, select New Index ➤ Secondary XML Index from the context menu of the Indexes node. This will cause the New Index dialog box to be displayed, as illustrated in Figure 5-8.

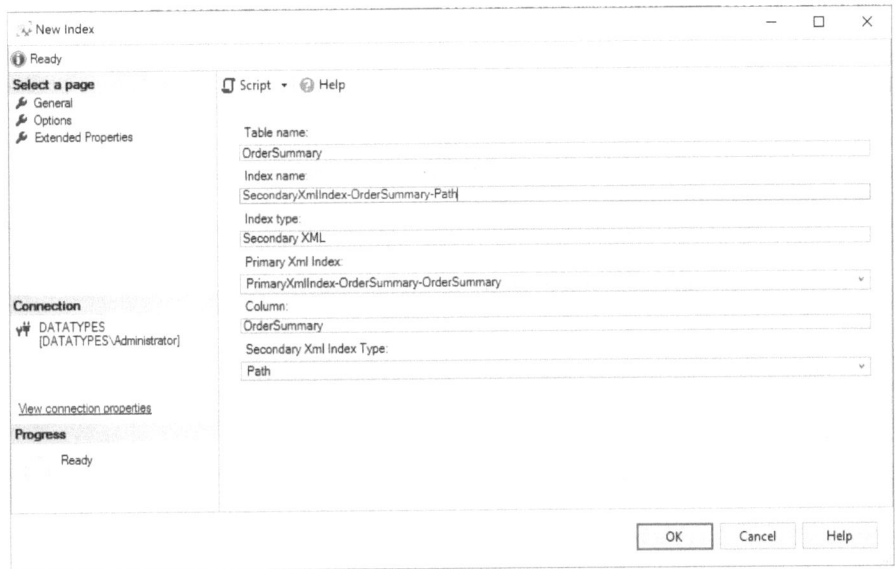

Figure 5-8. *New Index dialog box (Secondary XML)*

On the General tab of the New Index dialog box, we have first given the index a descriptive name. Next, we select the appropriate primary XML index from the Primary XML Index drop-down list. Finally, we select the type of secondary XML index that we wish to create, from the Secondary XML Index Type drop-down box. In this case, we have chosen to create a PATH index.

Figure 5-9 illustrates the Options tab of the New Index dialog box. For details of each option, please refer to Table 5-1.

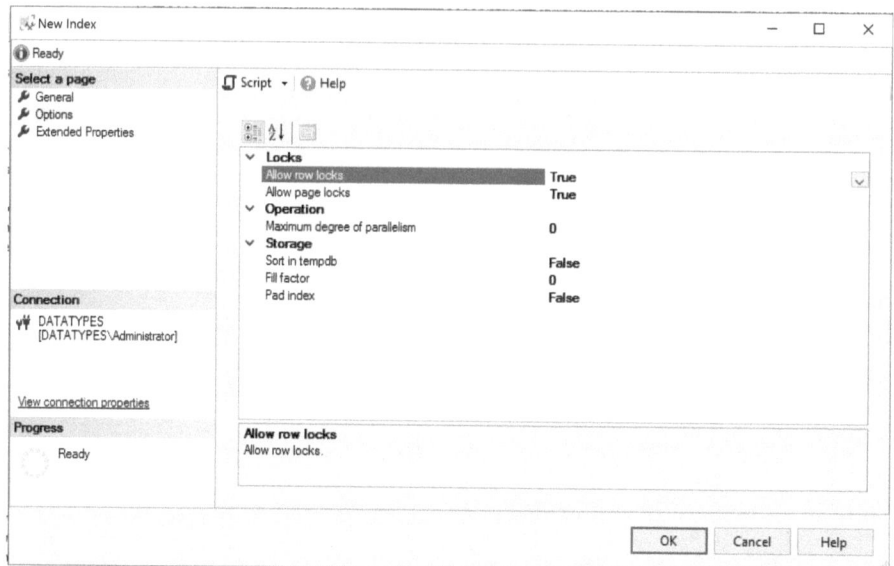

Figure 5-9. *New Index dialog box—Options tab (Secondary XML Index)*

Alternatively, to create this index with T-SQL, you could use the script in Listing 5-5.

Listing 5-5. Creating a Secondary XML Index

```
USE WideWorldImporters
GO

CREATE XML INDEX [SecondaryXmlIndex-OrderSummary-Path]
        ON Sales.OrderSummary (OrderSummary)
USING XML INDEX [PrimaryXmlIndex-OrderSummary-OrderSummary] FOR
PATH ;
GO
```

Performance Considerations for XML Indexes

In order to discuss the performance of XML indexes, let's write a query that is well-suited to the PATH secondary XML index that we have created on the OrderSummary table. The query in Listing 5-6 runs a query against the OrderSummary table and returns all rows indicating customers who have ordered the Chocolate echidnas 250g product, which has a StockItemID of 223. The first part of the script removes unchanged pages from the buffer cache and drops the plan cache, making it a fair test. The middle part of the script turns on time statistics, so we can accurately tell how long the query took to run.

Tip   Performance will vary, based on the specification of your server and how many resources are being consumed by concurrent processes. You should always check performance within your own environment.

Listing 5-6. Return Rows Where Customers Have Ordered StockItemID 23

```
--Clear buffer cache and plan cache
DBCC DROPCLEANBUFFERS
DBCC FREEPROCCACHE
GO

--Turn on IO statistics to appear with results
SET STATISTICS TIME ON
GO

--Run query
SELECT *
```

```
FROM Sales.OrderSummary
WHERE OrderSummary.exist('/SalesOrders/Order/OrderDetails/
Product/.[@ProductID = 223]') = 1 ;
```

The statistics shown in Figure 5-10 show that the query took 1.95 seconds to complete.

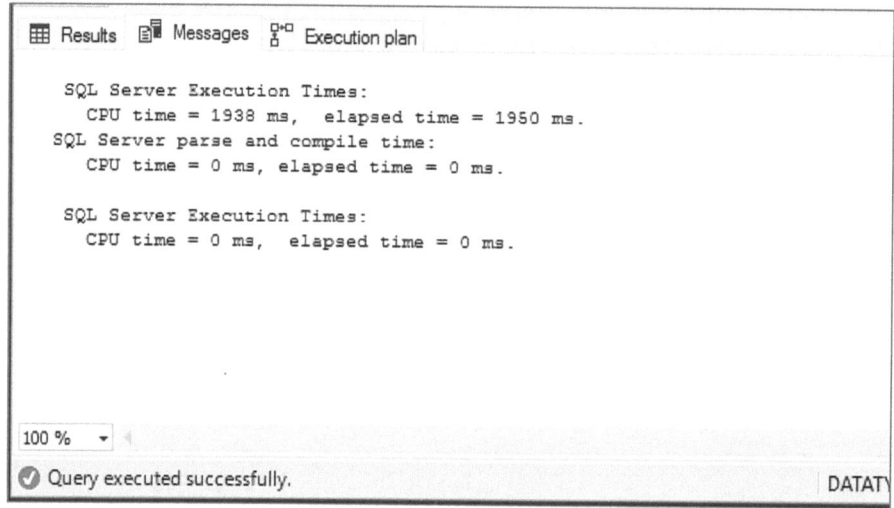

Figure 5-10. *Query results with PATH index*

Now let's use the script in Listing 5-7 to drop the PATH index and run the query again. This time, only the primary XML index is available for use.

Listing 5-7. Run Query Without PATH Index

```
DROP INDEX [SecondaryXmlIndex-OrderSummary-Path] ON Sales.
OrderSummary ;
GO

DBCC DROPCLEANBUFFERS
DBCC FREEPROCCACHE
GO
```

```
SET STATISTICS TIME ON
GO

SELECT *
FROM Sales.OrderSummary
WHERE OrderSummary.exist('/SalesOrders/Order/OrderDetails/
Product/.[@ProductID = 223]') = 1 ;
```

This time, as we can see from the statistics in Figure 5-11, the query
took more than 2.7 seconds to complete.

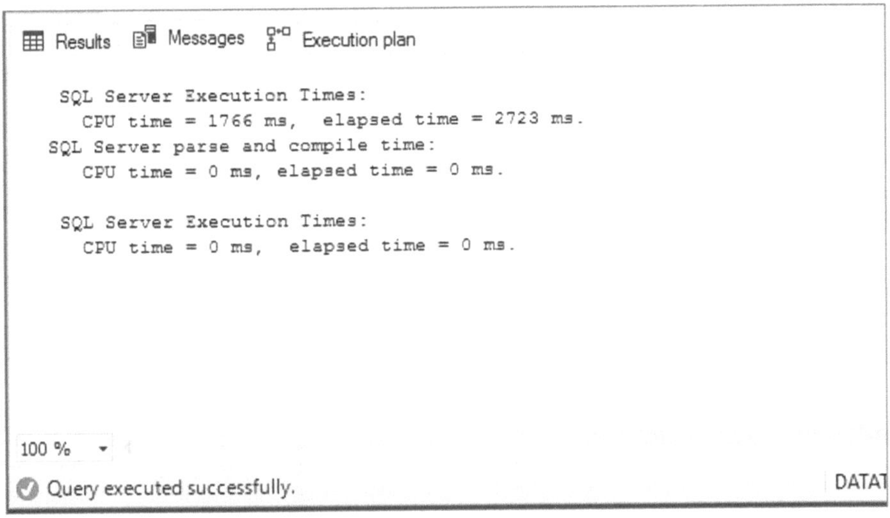

Figure 5-11. *Query results without PATH index*

Finally, let's use the script in Listing 5-8 to drop the primary XML
Index, and run the query again, with no XML index support.

Listing 5-8. Drop Primary XML Index and Rerun Query

```
DROP INDEX [PrimaryXmlIndex-OrderSummary-OrderSummary] ON
Sales.OrderSummary ;
GO

DBCC DROPCLEANBUFFERS
DBCC FREEPROCCACHE
GO

SET STATISTICS TIME ON
GO

SELECT *
FROM Sales.OrderSummary
WHERE OrderSummary.exist('/SalesOrders/Order/OrderDetails/
Product/.[@ProductID = 223]') = 1 ;
```

You will notice from the statistics in Figure 5-12 that the query execution time has now risen to more than 4 seconds. While our table only has fewer than 700 rows and results you see will vary, depending on the performance of your machine, this example shows why creating XML indexes is so important.

⊞ Results   📄 Messages   ⌗ Execution plan

```
 SQL Server Execution Times:
   CPU time = 2125 ms,  elapsed time = 4083 ms.
 SQL Server parse and compile time:
   CPU time = 0 ms, elapsed time = 0 ms.

 SQL Server Execution Times:
   CPU time = 0 ms,  elapsed time = 0 ms.
```

100 % ▾

✅ Query executed successfully.   DATA

Figure 5-12. *Results of query with no XML indexes*

Summary

Specialized XML indexes can be created on XML columns, to improve the performance of queries that rely on interrogating XML data. There are four types of XML Index: Primary, Secondary PATH, Secondary VALUE, and Secondary PROPERTY.

A primary XML index cannot be created on an XML column, unless the table has a clustered primary key (a clustered index built on a primary key column). A secondary XML cannot be created unless a primary XML index already exists on the XML column. XML indexes can be created before a table is populated with data, however.

Queries that interrogate XML columns can be quite inefficient and perform poorly, unless the correct XML indexes are created to support them. XML indexes will always be more efficient on XML columns than full-text indexes will be. As demonstrated in this chapter, XML query performance is significantly impaired if XML indexes are not created appropriately.

CHAPTER 6

Understanding JSON

As SQL Server evolves, more and more nonrelational features are being added to the product, blurring the lines between relational and NoSQL technologies. JSON is an example of this. JSON (JavaScript object notation) is a document format, designed as a method of lightweight data interchange. It is similar to XML, in the respect that it is a self-describing, hierarchical data-interchange format. Unlike XML, however, JSON tags are minimal, making JSON documents shorter and both easier to read and quicker to parse.

In this chapter, I will introduce the JSON format. I will discuss the structure of a JSON document and compare it to an XML document. Finally, I will discuss usage scenarios for JSON data within SQL Server.

Understanding the JSON Format

The basic JSON syntax uses name/value pairs, separated by a colon. The JSON object is then enclosed by braces. The name must be a string, enclosed with double quotes, and the value must be

- A string (enclosed by double quotes)
- A number
- A nested JSON object
- A Boolean value
- An array (enclosed by square brackets)
- NULL

© Peter A. Carter 2018
P. A. Carter, *SQL Server Advanced Data Types*,
https://doi.org/10.1007/978-1-4842-3901-8_6

For instance, consider the simple example in Listing 6-1.

Listing 6-1. Simple JSON Document

```
{ "FirstName" : "Pete" }
```

If multiple name/value pairs occur within a JSON document, they are separated by a comma. For example, consider the JSON document in Listing 6-2. You will notice that the value for age is not enclosed in double quotes, because it is a number, as opposed to a string.

Listing 6-2. Simple JSON Document with Multiple Name/Value Pairs

```
{ "FirstName" : "Pete" , "LastName" : "Carter" , "Age" : 38 }
```

If you were to represent as a JSON flat document a row set in a table, the result would be an array of JSON objects. For example, consider the query in Listing 6-3.

Listing 6-3. Top Vehicle Temperatures

```
USE WideWorldImporters
GO

SELECT TOP 3
        VehicleRegistration
      , ChillerSensorNumber
      , Temperature
FROM Warehouse.VehicleTemperatures
ORDER BY Temperature DESC ;
```

This query will produce the results displayed in Figure 6-1.

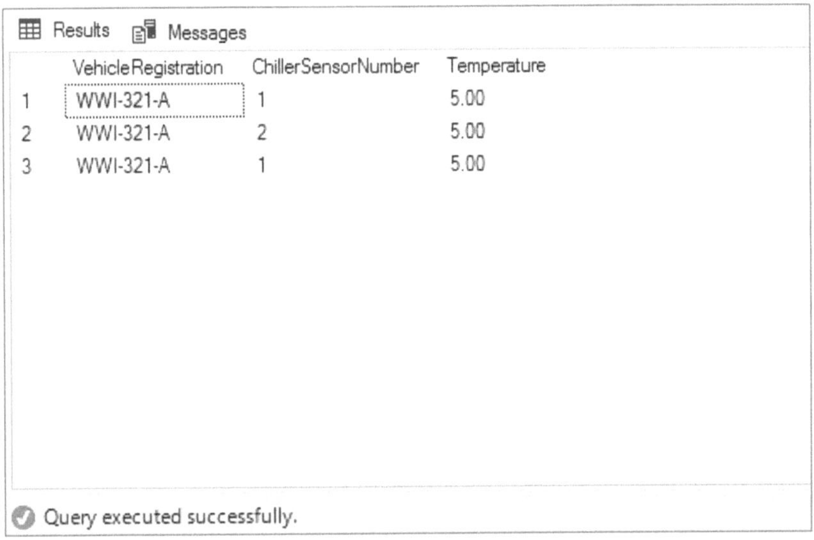

	VehicleRegistration	ChillerSensorNumber	Temperature
1	WWI-321-A	1	5.00
2	WWI-321-A	2	5.00
3	WWI-321-A	1	5.00

Figure 6-1. *Top vehicle temperatures*

If this result set were to be expressed as a JSON document, it would look like the document in Listing 6-4.

Listing 6-4. Top Vehicle Temperatures Expressed As JSON

```
[
   {
      "VehicleRegistration": "WWI-321-A",
      "ChillerSensorNumber": 1,
      "Temperature": 5
   },
   {
      "VehicleRegistration": "WWI-321-A",
      "ChillerSensorNumber": 2,
      "Temperature": 5
   },
   {
```

```
    "VehicleRegistration": "WWI-321-A",
    "ChillerSensorNumber": 1,
    "Temperature": 5
  }
]
```

You can see that the results are an array of JSON objects; therefore, the document is enclosed in square brackets. Each JSON object (representing a single row in the table) is enclosed in braces and separated by commas. Within each JSON object, comma separated name/value pairs represent each column in the tabular representation of the results.

The Warehouse.VehicleTemperatures table, in the WideWorldImporters database also includes a column with the JSON data type, which records the full sensor data. Consider the query in Listing 6-5.

Listing 6-5. Vehicle Temperatures with Full Sensor Data

```
USE WideWorldImporters
GO

SELECT TOP 3
          VehicleRegistration
        , ChillerSensorNumber
        , Temperature
        , FullSensorData
FROM Warehouse.VehicleTemperatures
ORDER BY Temperature DESC ;
```

This query returns the results displayed in Figure 6-2.

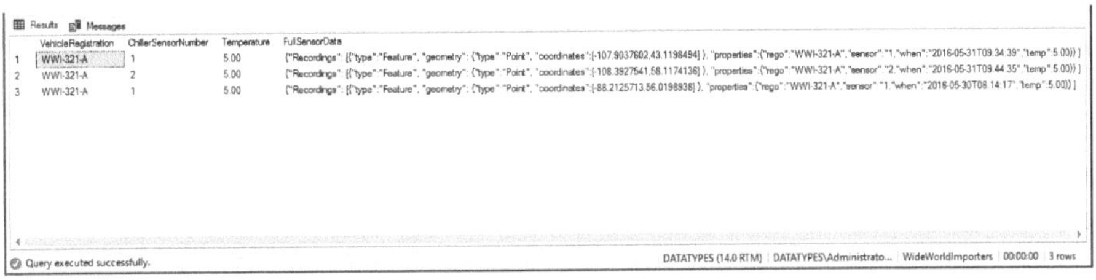

Figure 6-2. *Results of temperatures with full sensor data*

If we were to represent this result set as a JSON document, we would have an array of JSON objects in which one of the objects is a nested JSON object, as shown in Listing 6-6.

Listing 6-6. Vehicle Temperatures with Full Sensor Data Expressed As JSON

```
[
    {
        "VehicleRegistration": "WWI-321-A",
        "ChillerSensorNumber": 1,
        "Temperature": 5,
        "FullSensorData": "{\"Recordings\": [{\"type\":\"Feature\",
        \"geometry\": {\"type\":\"Point\",
        \"coordinates\":[-107.9037602,43.1198494] },
        \"properties\":{\"rego\":\"WWI-321-A\",
        \"sensor\":\"1,\"when\":\"2016-05-31T09:34:39\",
        \"temp\":5.00}} ]"
    },
    {
        "VehicleRegistration": "WWI-321-A",
        "ChillerSensorNumber": 2,
        "Temperature": 5,
```

```
      "FullSensorData": "{\"Recordings\": [{\"type\":\"Feature\",
      \"geometry\": {\"type\":\"Point\",
      \"coordinates\":[-108.3927541,58.1174136] },
      \"properties\":{\"rego\":\"WWI-321-A\",
      \"sensor\":\"2,\"when\":\"2016-05-31T09:44:35\",
      \"temp\":5.00}} ]"
  },
  {
      "VehicleRegistration": "WWI-321-A",
      "ChillerSensorNumber": 1,
      "Temperature": 5,
      "FullSensorData": "{\"Recordings\": [{\"type\":\"Feature\",
      \"geometry\": {\"type\":\"Point\",
      \"coordinates\":[-88.2125713,56.0198938] },
      \"properties\":{\"rego\":\"WWI-321-A\",
      \"sensor\":\"1,\"when\":\"2016-05-30T08:14:17\",
      \"temp\":5.00}} ]"
  }
]
```

Tip   The nested JSON objects contain a backslash before each double quote, as an escape character.

You will notice, in this example, that the value for each FullSensorData node is a JSON object nested inside the JSON object, which represents a row within the tabular result set.

A root node can also be added to a JSON document, sometimes used to represent the name of the object's type or abstraction. This can help give the document context. Listing 6-7 shows the same document as Listing 6-6, but with a root node added.

Listing 6-7. Adding a Root Node

```
{
    "VehicleTemperatures": [
        {
            "VehicleRegistration": "WWI-321-A",
            "ChillerSensorNumber": 1,
            "Temperature": 5,
            "FullSensorData": "{\"Recordings\": [{\"type\":\"Feature\",
            \"geometry\": {\"type\":\"Point\",
            \"coordinates\":[-107.9037602,43.1198494] },
            \"properties\":{\"rego\":\"WWI-321-A\",
            \"sensor\":\"1,\"when\":\"2016-05-31T09:34:39\",
            \"temp\":5.00}} ]"
        },
        {
            "VehicleRegistration": "WWI-321-A",
            "ChillerSensorNumber": 2,
            "Temperature": 5,
            "FullSensorData": "{\"Recordings\": [{\"type\":\"Feature\",
            \"geometry\": {\"type\":\"Point\",
            \"coordinates\":[-108.3927541,58.1174136] },
            \"properties\":{\"rego\":\"WWI-321-A\",
            \"sensor\":\"2,\"when\":\"2016-05-31T09:44:35\",
            \"temp\":5.00}} ]"
        },
        {
            "VehicleRegistration": "WWI-321-A",
            "ChillerSensorNumber": 1,
            "Temperature": 5,
```

```
        "FullSensorData": "{\"Recordings\": [{\"type\":\"Feature\",
        \"geometry\": {\"type\":\"Point\",
        \"coordinates\":[-88.2125713,56.0198938] },
        \"properties\":{\"rego\":\"WWI-321-A\",
        \"sensor\":\"1,\"when\":\"2016-05-30T08:14:17\",
        \"temp\":5.00}} ]"
    }
  ]
}
```

JSON vs. XML

Let's compare a simple JSON document against an XML equivalent and examine the differences. Consider the XML document in Listing 6-8, which represents the salespeople within the WideWorldImporters database.

Listing 6-8. Sales People—XML

```
<SalesPeople>
  <SalesPerson>
    <PersonID>2</PersonID>
    <FullName>Kayla Woodcock</FullName>
    <PreferredName>Kayla</PreferredName>
    <LogonName>kaylaw@wideworldimporters.com</LogonName>
    <PhoneNumber>(415) 555-0102</PhoneNumber>
    <EmailAddress>kaylaw@wideworldimporters.com</EmailAddress>
  </SalesPerson>
  <SalesPerson>
    <PersonID>3</PersonID>
    <FullName>Hudson Onslow</FullName>
    <PreferredName>Hudson</PreferredName>
```

```
  <LogonName>hudsono@wideworldimporters.com</LogonName>
  <PhoneNumber>(415) 555-0102</PhoneNumber>
  <EmailAddress>hudsono@wideworldimporters.com</EmailAddress>
</SalesPerson>
<SalesPerson>
  <PersonID>6</PersonID>
  <FullName>Sophia Hinton</FullName>
  <PreferredName>Sophia</PreferredName>
  <LogonName>sophiah@wideworldimporters.com</LogonName>
  <PhoneNumber>(415) 555-0102</PhoneNumber>
  <EmailAddress>sophiah@wideworldimporters.com</EmailAddress>
</SalesPerson>
<SalesPerson>
  <PersonID>7</PersonID>
  <FullName>Amy Trefl</FullName>
  <PreferredName>Amy</PreferredName>
  <LogonName>amyt@wideworldimporters.com</LogonName>
  <PhoneNumber>(415) 555-0102</PhoneNumber>
  <EmailAddress>amyt@wideworldimporters.com</EmailAddress>
</SalesPerson>
<SalesPerson>
  <PersonID>8</PersonID>
  <FullName>Anthony Grosse</FullName>
  <PreferredName>Anthony</PreferredName>
  <LogonName>anthonyg@wideworldimporters.com</LogonName>
  <PhoneNumber>(415) 555-0102</PhoneNumber>
  <EmailAddress>anthonyg@wideworldimporters.com</EmailAddress>
</SalesPerson>
<SalesPerson>
  <PersonID>13</PersonID>
  <FullName>Hudson Hollinworth</FullName>
```

```xml
    <PreferredName>Hudson</PreferredName>
    <LogonName>hudsonh@wideworldimporters.com</LogonName>
    <PhoneNumber>(415) 555-0102</PhoneNumber>
    <EmailAddress>hudsonh@wideworldimporters.com</EmailAddress>
  </SalesPerson>
  <SalesPerson>
    <PersonID>14</PersonID>
    <FullName>Lily Code</FullName>
    <PreferredName>Lily</PreferredName>
    <LogonName>lilyc@wideworldimporters.com</LogonName>
    <PhoneNumber>(415) 555-0102</PhoneNumber>
    <EmailAddress>lilyc@wideworldimporters.com</EmailAddress>
  </SalesPerson>
  <SalesPerson>
    <PersonID>15</PersonID>
    <FullName>Taj Shand</FullName>
    <PreferredName>Taj</PreferredName>
    <LogonName>tajs@wideworldimporters.com</LogonName>
    <PhoneNumber>(415) 555-0102</PhoneNumber>
    <EmailAddress>tajs@wideworldimporters.com</EmailAddress>
  </SalesPerson>
  <SalesPerson>
    <PersonID>16</PersonID>
    <FullName>Archer Lamble</FullName>
    <PreferredName>Archer</PreferredName>
    <LogonName>archerl@wideworldimporters.com</LogonName>
    <PhoneNumber>(415) 555-0102</PhoneNumber>
    <EmailAddress>archerl@wideworldimporters.com</EmailAddress>
  </SalesPerson>
  <SalesPerson>
```

```
    <PersonID>20</PersonID>
    <FullName>Jack Potter</FullName>
    <PreferredName>Jack</PreferredName>
    <LogonName>jackp@wideworldimporters.com</LogonName>
    <PhoneNumber>(415) 555-0102</PhoneNumber>
    <EmailAddress>jackp@wideworldimporters.com</EmailAddress>
  </SalesPerson>
</SalesPeople>
```

Each salesperson has an opening and closing tag element, containing an opening and closing tag element, for each property related to a salesperson. A root node, called SalesPeople, has also been added.

Note   This XML document is element-centric. We could, of course, also represent the salespeoples' properties as attributes. Please see Chapter 3, for further details.

Let's compare this XML to the JSON document in Listing 6-9.

Listing 6-9. Sales People—JSON

```
{
    "SalesPeople": [
      {
          "PersonID": 2,
          "FullName": "Kayla Woodcock",
          "PreferredName": "Kayla",
          "LogonName": "kaylaw@wideworldimporters.com",
          "PhoneNumber": "(415) 555-0102",
          "EmailAddress": "kaylaw@wideworldimporters.com"
      },
      {
```

```json
      "PersonID": 3,
      "FullName": "Hudson Onslow",
      "PreferredName": "Hudson",
      "LogonName": "hudsono@wideworldimporters.com",
      "PhoneNumber": "(415) 555-0102",
      "EmailAddress": "hudsono@wideworldimporters.com"
   },
   {

      "PersonID": 6,
      "FullName": "Sophia Hinton",
      "PreferredName": "Sophia",
      "LogonName": "sophiah@wideworldimporters.com",
      "PhoneNumber": "(415) 555-0102",
      "EmailAddress": "sophiah@wideworldimporters.com"
   },
   {

      "PersonID": 7,
      "FullName": "Amy Trefl",
      "PreferredName": "Amy",
      "LogonName": "amyt@wideworldimporters.com",
      "PhoneNumber": "(415) 555-0102",
      "EmailAddress": "amyt@wideworldimporters.com"
   },
   {

      "PersonID": 8,
      "FullName": "Anthony Grosse",
      "PreferredName": "Anthony",
      "LogonName": "anthonyg@wideworldimporters.com",
      "PhoneNumber": "(415) 555-0102",
      "EmailAddress": "anthonyg@wideworldimporters.com"
   },
   {
```

```
      "PersonID": 13,
      "FullName": "Hudson Hollinworth",
      "PreferredName": "Hudson",
      "LogonName": "hudsonh@wideworldimporters.com",
      "PhoneNumber": "(415) 555-0102",
      "EmailAddress": "hudsonh@wideworldimporters.com"
   },
   {
      "PersonID": 14,
      "FullName": "Lily Code",
      "PreferredName": "Lily",
      "LogonName": "lilyc@wideworldimporters.com",
      "PhoneNumber": "(415) 555-0102",
      "EmailAddress": "lilyc@wideworldimporters.com"
   },
   {
      "PersonID": 15,
      "FullName": "Taj Shand",
      "PreferredName": "Taj",
      "LogonName": "tajs@wideworldimporters.com",
      "PhoneNumber": "(415) 555-0102",
      "EmailAddress": "tajs@wideworldimporters.com"
   },
   {
      "PersonID": 16,
      "FullName": "Archer Lamble",
      "PreferredName": "Archer",
      "LogonName": "archerl@wideworldimporters.com",
      "PhoneNumber": "(415) 555-0102",
      "EmailAddress": "archerl@wideworldimporters.com"
   },
```

```
        {
            "PersonID": 20,
            "FullName": "Jack Potter",
            "PreferredName": "Jack",
            "LogonName": "jackp@wideworldimporters.com",
            "PhoneNumber": "(415) 555-0102",
            "EmailAddress": "jackp@wideworldimporters.com"
        }
    ]
}
```

Instead of using elements, as in the XML document, the JSON document consists simply of name/value pairs in an array of JSON objects. A root node, called SalesPeople, has also been added.

The most obvious observation about the JSON document is that the character count is much shorter, largely due to the lack of closing tags. The main consequence of this is that the document is easier to parse, and there is less information to be transferred between application tiers. Arguably, the document is also more human-readable. These advantages have made JSON a very popular choice with application developers.

The main disadvantage of the JSON document is that it cannot be bound to a schema in the way that XML can. The impact of this is that although the document can be parsed, to ensure that it has valid syntax, it isn't possible (without custom code) to ensure that it meets the contract expected by the recipient before sending.

Other than the differences mentioned, despite their different appearance, the documents are actually quite similar. They are both self-describing, extensible documents that can be used for data-interchange. Both formats are widely used and work with many REST APIs and web service end points.

> **Tip**   REST is short for representational state transfer. It is an
> architectural style of providing a uniform interface, often between
> layers of an application. It provides a stateless approach, with client/
> server separation.

JSON Usage Scenarios

There are many use cases for JSON data within SQL Server. The following
sections will introduce some of these potential uses.

n-Tier Applications with Rest APIs

Modern apps often have a lot of logic at the client side. The application
tier of the application often has to have complex code, or even multiple
sublayers, to broker a conversation between the client and the back-end
RDBMS. This is because you will have to use an object relational mapper
to execute the query against the database, write these results into data
transfer object, and then serialize the results in JSON format before they
can be sent to the client.

With JSON support in SQL Server, however, you can simply expose the
data from SQL Server to a REST API and return the data in JSON format,
meaning that the application tier can simply send the data as is to the
client. While there may be resistance to this approach from middle-tier
purists, it certainly allows architects to simplify the application design.

De-Normalizing Data

Using a normalized data model is perfect when high-frequency updates
are made to data. In a normalized model, data is separated into multiple
tables, which are joined together using primary and foreign key

constraints, with the intention of storing data only once. For example, if customers have multiple addresses, then core details about a customer, such as name and phone number, may be stored in a table called Customers. Their addresses may then be stored in a separate table called CustomerAddresses, which contains a foreign key (CustomerID), which joins to the primary key of the Customers table. This means that the core details about the customer are only stored once, as opposed to having to repeat the details for every address.

Tip   While a detailed discussion of normalization is beyond the scope of this book, a full discussion can be found in *Expert Scripting and Automation for SQL Server DBAs* (Apress, 2016).

A traditional normalized model can cause issues in some instances, however. For example, performance can decrease when data is split across multiple tables and joined together in a SELECT statement, owing to the matching of primary and foreign key values that is required. Also, when data is updated across multiple tables, a transaction must be used, to ensure a consistent update. This can lead to locking issues, in which pessimistic isolation levels are in use, or IO performance issues, in which optimistic isolation levels are used.

Tip   A full discussion of transaction isolation levels can be found in *Pro SQL Server Administration* (Apress, 2015).

To work around this issue, data architects will sometimes use NoSQL structures to store details of entities such as customers, so that logical entities can be stored as a single record. Coincidently, JSON is often the format used for these records. This approach creates its own issues, however, when the NoSQL data must be combined with data that is still stored in a relational format.

JSON can help resolve these kinds of modeling challenges, by allowing the JSON record to be stored in a table in SQL Server, meaning that updates can be made to a single table, while the table can still easily be joined back to relational data.

Config As Code

In DevOps environments, there is a requirement to have infrastructure as code, platforms as code, and config as code. Essentially, an entire virtual estate will be written in code, so that it is highly portable between data centers or, more commonly, between data centers and the cloud. It is also highly recoverable, in the event of a disaster, such as the loss of a data center.

SQL Server management has been slow to be incorporated into the DevOps space, because there is a lack of crossover skills between SQL Server and desired state configuration tooling, such as Chef and Puppet. The DBA world is slowly starting to get on board, however, and as part of an SQL-Server-platform-as-code approach, a configuration management database (CMDB) will often be used on a central management server, to store the details of member servers (SQL Server VMs) within the estate. A central management server (in this context) refers to an instance of SQL Server that is used to help DBAs manage the rest of the SQL Server estate. It will often be the master server in SQL Server Agent master/target job configurations and may have other management features installed, such as Management Data Warehouse, which is used as a central hub for SQL Server monitoring.

When a platform-as-code approach is being used, however, a config-as-code approach should be applied alongside. In the SQL Server world, this involves being able to rebuild the CMDB from code, which is stored in a source control provider, such as GitHub of TFS.

Config as code for the SQL Server CMBD can easily be managed with a circular process. The first step in this process is a Server Agent job, which will periodically run and export the data from the tables into JSON files in the operating system. These files will then be pushed to a source-control repository and checked in.

When a desired state configuration management tool such as Chef or Puppet builds a new central management server, it will look, in the source control repository, to find the JSON files containing the configuration data. It will create the config database and then repopulate the tables with the data from the repo. This provides an easily configurable RPO (recover point objective) for the config database, without the challenges that are often associated with enterprise backup management tools and the lead times often associated with recovering data from tape robots. It also means that the core management utility for SQL Server can be easily moved to the cloud or other data centers, helping to make the SQL Server estate extremely portable.

Tip   The principle of desired state management tools, such as Puppet and Chef, is that they run periodically on a server, with a manifest that describes the desired state of the server. At the Windows level, this may include code to disable the guest account or ensure that user rights assignments are configured correctly. At the SQL Server level, it may check that a specific login exists or that xp_cmdshell is disabled. First, the tool will check to see if a resource is already configured as expected. If not, it will correct the configuration. This means that if an unauthorized change is made to a server, it will be corrected the next time the manifest is applied. The result is that Windows engineers and DBAs can also be sure of the state of their servers.

Analyzing the Log Data

Devices such as sensors or RFID (radio frequency identification) can generate very large amounts of data. This means that data architects will often choose to store this data in NoSQL solutions. Often, JSON is used as the file format for such logging.

When large logs are stored in JSON format, the SQL Server's native JSON support means that these logs can easily be read into SQL Server and analyzed using T-SQL, without any complex parsing requirements. This can reduce the time to market for reports against log data.

Summary

JSON is a lightweight data-interchange format that is supported by many REST APIs and web service end points. It is similar to XML, in that it is an extensible, self-describing, hierarchical document format, but it differs in the following ways:

- It cannot be validated against a schema.

- It does not have closing tags.

- It is shorter.

- It is easier to parse.

- It supports arrays.

JSON's basic format is a series of name/value pairs, which are separated by commas. JSON objects are always enclosed in braces, and arrays are always enclosed in brackets. JSON objects can be nested inside other JSON objects. When this is the case, a backslash should be used to escape characters, such as double quotes and braces.

JSON has many use cases in SQL Server, including the simplification of REST APIs interacting with back-end databases. JSON is also a good choice when NoSQL solutions must be integrated with SQL Server, such as when device logs must be analyzed or NoSQL semi-structured data must be stored alongside structured data. JSON is also very useful when DBAs or platform engineers implement config as code solutions.

CHAPTER 7

Constructing JSON from T-SQL

Just as the FOR XML clause (see Chapter 3) can be used to construct XML documents from relational results sets, the FOR JSON clause can be used to construct JSON data from relational results sets. This is useful for exchanging data between SQL Server and traditional programming languages. Unlike FOR XML, however, FOR JSON only offers two modes: AUTO and PATH. This chapter discusses the use of the FOR JSON clause in both AUTO mode and PATH mode.

FOR JSON AUTO

FOR JSON AUTO is the simplest of the two FOR JSON modes. It can automatically nest JSON data, based on table joins, or provide flat JSON documents from a single table. To explain FOR JSON at the most basic level, consider the query in Listing 7-1, which returns the order dates, alongside customer, order, and salesperson keys, for customer 1060.

Listing 7-1. Return Keys and Dates for Sales Orders

```
USE WideWorldImporters
GO
```

© Peter A. Carter 2018
P. A. Carter, *SQL Server Advanced Data Types*,
https://doi.org/10.1007/978-1-4842-3901-8_7

```
SELECT
        OrderID
        , CustomerID
        , SalespersonPersonID
        , OrderDate
FROM Sales.Orders
WHERE CustomerID = 1060 ;
```

This query returns the results illustrated in Figure 7-1.

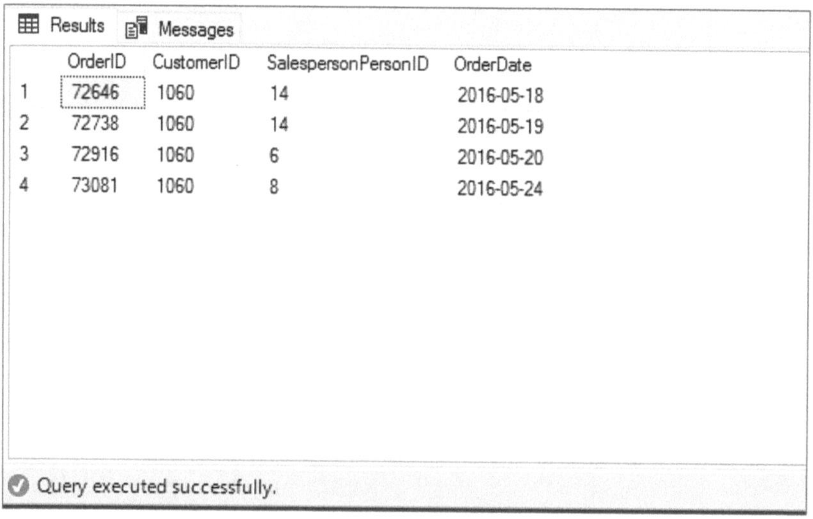
Results
Messages
OrderID CustomerID SalespersonPersonID OrderDate
1 72646 1060 14 2016-05-18
2 72738 1060 14 2016-05-19
3 72916 1060 6 2016-05-20
4 73081 1060 8 2016-05-24
Query executed successfully.

Figure 7-1. *Results of keys and dates for sales orders*

If we wanted to return these results in JSON format, we could append the `FOR JSON` clause, as demonstrated in Listing 7-2.

Listing 7-2. Return Results As JSON

```
USE WideWorldImporters
GO

SELECT
        OrderID
        , CustomerID
        , SalespersonPersonID
        , OrderDate
FROM Sales.Orders
WHERE CustomerID = 1060
FOR JSON AUTO ;
```

This query will produce the results shown in Listing 7-3.

Listing 7-3. Results of Returning Data As JSON

```
[
   {
      "OrderID": 72646,
      "CustomerID": 1060,
      "SalespersonPersonID": 14,
      "OrderDate": "2016-05-18"
   },
   {
      "OrderID": 72738,
      "CustomerID": 1060,
      "SalespersonPersonID": 14,
      "OrderDate": "2016-05-19"
   },
   {
      "OrderID": 72916,
      "CustomerID": 1060,
```

```
      "SalespersonPersonID": 6,
      "OrderDate": "2016-05-20"
   },
   {
      "OrderID": 73081,
      "CustomerID": 1060,
      "SalespersonPersonID": 8,
      "OrderDate": "2016-05-24"
   }
]
```

Working with Root Nodes

Because our results have no root node, an array wrapper (in the form of square brackets) must be placed around the document. If we did not want our results to be enclosed in square brackets, we could remove them by amending our query, as shown in Listing 7-4.

Listing 7-4. Removing an Array Wrapper

```
USE WideWorldImporters
GO

SELECT
        OrderID
        , CustomerID
        , SalespersonPersonID
        , OrderDate
FROM Sales.Orders
WHERE CustomerID = 1060
FOR JSON AUTO, WITHOUT_ARRAY_WRAPPER ;
```

This amended query will return the results shown in Listing 7-5.

Listing 7-5. Results Without an Array Wrapper

```
{
    "OrderID": 72646,
    "CustomerID": 1060,
    "SalespersonPersonID": 14,
    "OrderDate": "2016-05-18"
},
{
    "OrderID": 72738,
    "CustomerID": 1060,
    "SalespersonPersonID": 14,
    "OrderDate": "2016-05-19"
},
{
    "OrderID": 72916,
    "CustomerID": 1060,
    "SalespersonPersonID": 6,
    "OrderDate": "2016-05-20"
},
{
    "OrderID": 73081,
    "CustomerID": 1060,
    "SalespersonPersonID": 8,
    "OrderDate": "2016-05-24"
}
```

Alternatively, we could resolve the issue by adding a root node to our document. This can be achieved by using the amended query shown in Listing 7-6, which will cause a root node, SalesOrders, to be added to the resultant document.

Caution   ROOT and WITHOUT_ARRAY_WRAPPER are not compatible with each other. Attempting to use both will cause the query to generate an error.

Listing 7-6. Adding a Root Node

```
USE WideWorldImporters
GO

SELECT
        OrderID
        , CustomerID
        , SalespersonPersonID
        , OrderDate
FROM Sales.Orders
WHERE CustomerID = 1060
FOR JSON AUTO, ROOT('SalesOrders') ;
```

This query produced the results illustrated in Listing 7-7.

Listing 7-7. Results of Adding a Root Node

```
{
    "SalesOrders": [
      {
          "OrderID": 72646,
          "CustomerID": 1060,
          "SalespersonPersonID": 14,
          "OrderDate": "2016-05-18"
      },
      {
          "OrderID": 72738,
```

```
         "CustomerID": 1060,
         "SalespersonPersonID": 14,
         "OrderDate": "2016-05-19"
      },
      {
         "OrderID": 72916,
         "CustomerID": 1060,
         "SalespersonPersonID": 6,
         "OrderDate": "2016-05-20"
      },
      {
         "OrderID": 73081,
         "CustomerID": 1060,
         "SalespersonPersonID": 8,
         "OrderDate": "2016-05-24"
      }
   ]
}
```

Working with NULL Values

What if NULL values were returned by our dataset? Consider the example in
Listing 7-8, where the Comments column has been added to the
SELECT list.

Listing 7-8. Adding Comments to the SELECT List

```
USE WideWorldImporters
GO

SELECT
        OrderID
        , CustomerID
```

```
        , SalespersonPersonID
        , OrderDate
        , Comments
FROM Sales.Orders
WHERE CustomerID = 1060 ;
```

The results of this query are displayed in Figure 7-2.

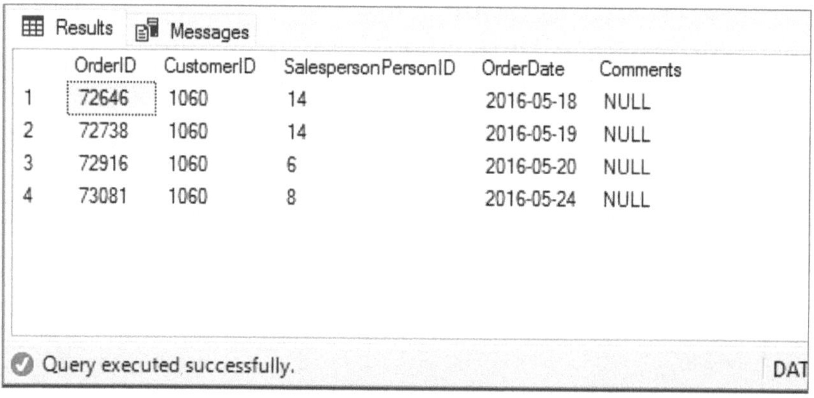
Results
Messages
OrderID CustomerID SalespersonPersonID OrderDate Comments
1 72646 1060 14 2016-05-18 NULL
2 72738 1060 14 2016-05-19 NULL
3 72916 1060 6 2016-05-20 NULL
4 73081 1060 8 2016-05-24 NULL
Query executed successfully.
DAT

Figure 7-2. *Results of adding comments*

You will notice that there are no comments associated with any of the orders returned. Let's see how this affects the JSON, using the query in Listing 7-9.

Listing 7-9. JSON with `NULL` Comments Added

```
USE WideWorldImporters
GO

SELECT
        OrderID
        , CustomerID
        , SalespersonPersonID
        , OrderDate
```

```
        , Comments
FROM Sales.Orders
WHERE CustomerID = 1060
FOR JSON AUTO, ROOT('SalesOrders') ;
```

The results of this query can be found in Listing 7-10.

Listing 7-10. Results of JSON with NULL Comments

```
{
    "SalesOrders": [
        {
            "OrderID": 72646,
            "CustomerID": 1060,
            "SalespersonPersonID": 14,
            "OrderDate": "2016-05-18"
        },
        {
            "OrderID": 72738,
            "CustomerID": 1060,
            "SalespersonPersonID": 14,
            "OrderDate": "2016-05-19"
        },
        {
            "OrderID": 72916,
            "CustomerID": 1060,
            "SalespersonPersonID": 6,
            "OrderDate": "2016-05-20"
        },
        {
            "OrderID": 73081,
            "CustomerID": 1060,
            "SalespersonPersonID": 8,
```

```
      "OrderDate": "2016-05-24"
    }
  ]
}
```

You can see that the default behavior is to omit any name/value pairs with NULL values from the results set. We can change this behavior, however, by using the INCLUDE_NULL_VALUES option, as demonstrated in Listing 7-11.

Listing 7-11. Including NULL Values in Results

```
USE WideWorldImporters
GO

SELECT
        OrderID
      , CustomerID
      , SalespersonPersonID
      , OrderDate
      , Comments
FROM Sales.Orders
WHERE CustomerID = 1060
FOR JSON AUTO, ROOT('SalesOrders'), INCLUDE_NULL_VALUES ;
```

The results of this query can be found in Listing 7-12. You will notice that, this time, the name/value pairs with NULL values have been included in the results.

Listing 7-12. Results of Including NULL Values in Results

```
{
   "SalesOrders": [
      {
```

```
      "OrderID": 72646,
      "CustomerID": 1060,
      "SalespersonPersonID": 14,
      "OrderDate": "2016-05-18",
      "Comments": null
   },
   {
      "OrderID": 72738,
      "CustomerID": 1060,
      "SalespersonPersonID": 14,
      "OrderDate": "2016-05-19",
      "Comments": null
   },
   {
      "OrderID": 72916,
      "CustomerID": 1060,
      "SalespersonPersonID": 6,
      "OrderDate": "2016-05-20",
      "Comments": null
   },
   {
      "OrderID": 73081,
      "CustomerID": 1060,
      "SalespersonPersonID": 8,
      "OrderDate": "2016-05-24",
      "Comments": null
   }
 ]
}
```

Using Column Aliases

When considering the format of the JSON output, it is also possible to use column aliases, such as in Listing 7-13.

Listing 7-13. Using Column Aliases

```
USE WideWorldImporters
GO

SELECT
        OrderID
        , CustomerID
        , SalespersonPersonID
        , OrderDate
        , Comments AS 'Orders Comments'
FROM Sales.Orders
WHERE CustomerID = 1060
FOR JSON AUTO, ROOT('SalesOrders'), INCLUDE_NULL_VALUES ;
```

This query returns the results shown in Listing 7-14.

Listing 7-14. Results of Using Column Aliases

```
{
   "SalesOrders": [
      {
         "OrderID": 72646,
         "CustomerID": 1060,
         "SalespersonPersonID": 14,
         "OrderDate": "2016-05-18",
         "Orders Comments": null
      },
      {
```

```
      "OrderID": 72738,
      "CustomerID": 1060,
      "SalespersonPersonID": 14,
      "OrderDate": "2016-05-19",
      "Orders Comments": null
   },
   {
      "OrderID": 72916,
      "CustomerID": 1060,
      "SalespersonPersonID": 6,
      "OrderDate": "2016-05-20",
      "Orders Comments": null
   },
   {
      "OrderID": 73081,
      "CustomerID": 1060,
      "SalespersonPersonID": 8,
      "OrderDate": "2016-05-24",
      "Orders Comments": null
   }
 ]
}
```

You will notice that the comments key now has the name Orders
Comments, instead of Comments. This behavior is also true if you use dot-
separated aliases, such as the example in Listing 7-15.

Listing 7-15. Using Dot-Separated Aliases

```
USE WideWorldImporters
GO

SELECT
        OrderID
        , CustomerID
        , SalespersonPersonID
        , OrderDate
        , Comments AS 'Orders.Comments'
FROM Sales.Orders
WHERE CustomerID = 1060
FOR JSON AUTO, ROOT('SalesOrders'), INCLUDE_NULL_VALUES ;
```

This query returns the results illustrated in Listing 7-16.

Listing 7-16. Results of Using Dot-Separated Aliases

```
{
   "SalesOrders": [
      {
         "OrderID": 72646,
         "CustomerID": 1060,
         "SalespersonPersonID": 14,
         "OrderDate": "2016-05-18",
         "Orders.Comments": null
      },
      {
         "OrderID": 72738,
         "CustomerID": 1060,
         "SalespersonPersonID": 14,
         "OrderDate": "2016-05-19",
         "Orders.Comments": null
      },
```

```
{
    "OrderID": 72916,
    "CustomerID": 1060,
    "SalespersonPersonID": 6,
    "OrderDate": "2016-05-20",
    "Orders.Comments": null
},
{
    "OrderID": 73081,
    "CustomerID": 1060,
    "SalespersonPersonID": 8,
    "OrderDate": "2016-05-24",
    "Orders.Comments": null
}
]
}
```

You will notice that the key is simply given a dot-separated name. This is important behavior to note, as when using FOR JSON PATH, dot-separated aliases result in nested JSON objects. You will learn more about this as you progress through the chapter.

Automatic Nesting

So far, all our examples have focused on the behavior of FOR JSON AUTO, when used against a single table. So now, let's turn our attention to how FOR JSON AUTO automatically nests data, based on table joins and subqueries.

Consider the query in Listing 7-17. This query inspects order 72646 in more detail, by enhancing it to retrieve the details of the stock items ordered on each of the three orders placed.

Listing 7-17. Added Order Line Details

```
USE WideWorldImporters
GO

SELECT
          Orders.OrderID
        , Orders.CustomerID
        , Orders.SalespersonPersonID
        , Orders.OrderDate
        , Orders.Comments
        , OrderLines.StockItemID
        , OrderLines.UnitPrice
        , OrderLines.Quantity
FROM Sales.Orders Orders
INNER JOIN Sales.OrderLines OrderLines
        ON OrderLines.OrderID = Orders.OrderID
WHERE CustomerID = 1060
        AND Orders.OrderID = 72646
FOR JSON AUTO, ROOT('SalesOrders'), INCLUDE_NULL_VALUES ;
```

The results of this query are illustrated in Listing 7-18.

Listing 7-18. Results of Adding Order Line Details

```
{
   "SalesOrders": [
      {
         "OrderID": 72646,
         "CustomerID": 1060,
         "SalespersonPersonID": 14,
         "OrderDate": "2016-05-18",
         "Comments": null,
         "OrderLines": [
```

```
        {
            "StockItemID": 45,
            "UnitPrice": 13,
            "Quantity": 6
        },
        {
            "StockItemID": 146,
            "UnitPrice": 18,
            "Quantity": 108
        },
        {
            "StockItemID": 8,
            "UnitPrice": 240,
            "Quantity": 2
        },
        {
            "StockItemID": 212,
            "UnitPrice": 4.3,
            "Quantity": 20
        }
      ]
    }
  ]
}
```

You will notice that a new key, the name of which matches the alias of the second table, has been added to the representation of each order. The value is a nested array of JSON objects containing the name/value pairs, which represent the columns returned from the second (based on the order of columns within the SELECT list) table.

So, what if we added a nested join, so that we can retrieve the product name from the Warehouse.StockItems table, as demonstrated in Listing 7-19?

Listing 7-19. Using Nested Joins

```
USE WideWorldImporters
GO

SELECT
          Orders.OrderID
        , Orders.CustomerID
        , Orders.SalespersonPersonID
        , Orders.OrderDate
        , Orders.Comments
        , OrderLines.StockItemID
        , OrderLines.UnitPrice
        , OrderLines.Quantity
        , Products.StockItemName
FROM Sales.Orders Orders
INNER JOIN Sales.OrderLines OrderLines
        ON OrderLines.OrderID = Orders.OrderID
INNER JOIN Warehouse.StockItems Products
        ON Products.StockItemID = OrderLines.StockItemID
WHERE CustomerID = 1060
        AND Orders.OrderID = 72646
FOR JSON AUTO, ROOT('SalesOrders'), INCLUDE_NULL_VALUES ;
```

The results of this query can be found in Listing 7-20.

Listing 7-20. Results of Using Nested Joins

```
{
   "SalesOrders": [
      {
         "OrderID": 72646,
         "CustomerID": 1060,
         "SalespersonPersonID": 14,
         "OrderDate": "2016-05-18",
         "Comments": null,
         "OrderLines": [
            {
               "StockItemID": 45,
               "UnitPrice": 13,
               "Quantity": 6,
               "Products": [
                  {
                     "StockItemName": "Developer joke mug - there
                     are 10 types of people in the world (Black)"
                  }
               ]
            },
            {
               "StockItemID": 146,
               "UnitPrice": 18,
               "Quantity": 108,
               "Products": [
                  {
                     "StockItemName": "Halloween skull mask
                     (Gray) S"
                  }
               ]
```

```
            },
            {
                "StockItemID": 212,
                "UnitPrice": 4.3,
                "Quantity": 20,
                "Products": [
                    {
                        "StockItemName": "Large   replacement
                        blades 18mm"
                    }
                ]
            },
            {
                "StockItemID": 8,
                "UnitPrice": 240,
                "Quantity": 2,
                "Products": [
                    {
                        "StockItemName": "USB food flash drive -
                        dim sum 10 drive variety pack"
                    }
                ]
            }
        ]
    }
]
}
```

You will notice that an additional layer of nesting has been added to the document, with an array, Products, containing the StockItemName being added to each OrderLines array.

Just as nesting is automatic, based on table joins, the same applies to subqueries. Consider the query in Listing 7-21, which includes two correlated subqueries in the SELECT list that return the name of the customer who placed the order and the name of the salesperson who sold it.

Tip   Nested structures can be processed more easily by programming languages.

Listing 7-21. Using Subqueries to Nest Data

```
USE WideWorldImporters
GO
SELECT
        Orders.OrderID
      , (SELECT FullName FROM Application.People WHERE
        PersonID = Orders.CustomerID FOR JSON AUTO) AS 'Customer'
      , (SELECT FullName FROM Application.People WHERE
        PersonID = Orders.SalespersonPersonID FOR JSON AUTO) AS
        'SalesPerson'
      , Orders.OrderDate
      , Orders.Comments
      , OrderLines.UnitPrice
      , OrderLines.Quantity
      , Products.StockItemName
FROM Sales.Orders Orders
INNER JOIN Sales.OrderLines OrderLines
        ON OrderLines.OrderID = Orders.OrderID
INNER JOIN Warehouse.StockItems Products
        ON Products.StockItemID = OrderLines.StockItemID
WHERE CustomerID = 1060
        AND Orders.OrderID = 72646
FOR JSON AUTO, ROOT('SalesOrders'), INCLUDE_NULL_VALUES ;
```

The results of this query are detailed in Listing 7-22.

Listing 7-22. Results of Nesting Data Using Subqueries

```
{
    "SalesOrders": [
        {
            "OrderID": 72646,
            "Customer": [
                {
                    "FullName": "Konrads Sprogis"
                }
            ],
            "SalesPerson": [
                {
                    "FullName": "Lily Code"
                }
            ],
            "OrderDate": "2016-05-18",
            "Comments": null,
            "OrderLines": [
                {
                    "UnitPrice": 13,
                    "Quantity": 6,
                    "Products": [
                        {
                            "StockItemName": "Developer joke mug - there
                            are 10 types of people in the world (Black)"
                        }
                    ]
                },
                {
```

```
        "UnitPrice": 18,
        "Quantity": 108,
        "Products": [
           {
              "StockItemName": "Halloween skull mask
              (Gray) S"
           }
        ]
    },
    {
        "UnitPrice": 4.3,
        "Quantity": 20,
        "Products": [
           {
              "StockItemName": "Large   replacement
              blades 18mm"
           }
        ]
    },
    {
        "UnitPrice": 240,
        "Quantity": 2,
        "Products": [
           {
              "StockItemName": "USB food flash drive -
              dim sum 10 drive variety pack"
           }
        ]
    }
  ]
 }
 ]
}
```

FOR JSON PATH

While the final example in the FOR JSON AUTO section of this chapter returns all the required data for the sales order summary, the format of the document leaves something to be desired. The document is a lot longer than necessary, because of unrequired nesting. For example, there can only be one product name per line item, so the Products array should ideally be a simple name/value pair in the OrderLines array. The same principle applies to the customer and salesperson names.

Therefore, let's imagine that we wanted to produce a JSON document with the format illustrated in Listing 7-23, which has a more concise, easier-to-read layout.

Listing 7-23. Desired JSON Format

```
{
   "SalesOrders": [
      {
         "OrderDetails": {
            "OrderID": 72646,
            "Customer": "Konrads Sprogis",
            "SalesPerson": "Lily Code",
            "OrderDate": "2016-05-18",
            "Comments": null,
            "LineItems": {
               "UnitPrice": 13,
               "Quantity": 6,
               "ProductName": "Developer joke mug - there are
               10 types of people in the world (Black)"
            }
         }
      },
```

```json
{
   "OrderDetails": {
      "OrderID": 72646,
      "Customer": "Konrads Sprogis",
      "SalesPerson": "Lily Code",
      "OrderDate": "2016-05-18",
      "Comments": null,
      "LineItems": {
         "UnitPrice": 18,
         "Quantity": 108,
         "ProductName": "Halloween skull mask (Gray) S"
      }
   }
},
{
   "OrderDetails": {
      "OrderID": 72646,
      "Customer": "Konrads Sprogis",
      "SalesPerson": "Lily Code",
      "OrderDate": "2016-05-18",
      "Comments": null,
      "LineItems": {
         "UnitPrice": 4.3,
         "Quantity": 20,
         "ProductName": "Large  replacement blades 18mm"
      }
   }
},
{
   "OrderDetails": {
      "OrderID": 72646,
```

```
        "Customer": "Konrads Sprogis",
        "SalesPerson": "Lily Code",
        "OrderDate": "2016-05-18",
        "Comments": null,
        "LineItems": {
           "UnitPrice": 240,
           "Quantity": 2,
           "ProductName": "USB food flash drive - dim sum
           10 drive variety pack"
        }
      }
    }
  ]
}
```

We could easily achieve these results by using FOR JSON PATH, which provides granular control over how the resultant document is formatted. This control is provided through the use of column aliases, which allow you to specify desired nesting, through dot separation. Consider the query in Listing 7-24. The query is similar to that in Listing 7-21, but there are two key differences to note. The first is that FOR XML AUTO has changed to FOR XML PATH. The second is that each column has been given column aliases, which designate not just the name of the node but its position within the document. The customer's full name, for example, will be placed into a node called Customer, which is nested directly under OrderDetails. The ProductName node, in contrast, will be nested alongside the unit price and quantity, under a node called LineItems. This causes a LineItems key to be created with a value that consists of an array of JSON objects, including all nodes that are specified in the preceding text. The result is the document found in Listing 7-23.

Listing 7-24. Using FOR JSON PATH

```
USE WideWorldImporters
GO

SELECT
        Orders.OrderID AS 'OrderDetails.OrderID'
        , Customers.FullName AS 'OrderDetails.Customer'
        , SalesPeople.FullName AS 'OrderDetails.SalesPerson'
        , Orders.OrderDate AS 'OrderDetails.OrderDate'
        , Orders.Comments AS 'OrderDetails.Comments'
        , OrderLines.UnitPrice AS 'OrderDetails.LineItems.
        UnitPrice'
        , OrderLines.Quantity AS 'OrderDetails.LineItems.
        Quantity'
        , Products.StockItemName AS 'OrderDetails.LineItems.
        ProductName'
FROM Sales.Orders Orders
INNER JOIN Sales.OrderLines OrderLines
        ON OrderLines.OrderID = Orders.OrderID
INNER JOIN Warehouse.StockItems Products
        ON Products.StockItemID = OrderLines.StockItemID
INNER JOIN Application.People Customers
        ON Customers.PersonID = Orders.CustomerID
INNER JOIN Application.People SalesPeople
        ON SalesPeople.PersonID = Orders.SalespersonPersonID
WHERE CustomerID = 1060
        AND orders.OrderID = 72646
FOR JSON PATH, ROOT('SalesOrders'), INCLUDE_NULL_VALUES ;
```

Summary

The FOR JSON clause of a SELECT statement can be used to convert a result set into JSON format. It can be used in two modes: either AUTO or PATH. When used in AUTO mode, FOR JSON will automatically nest data, based on the joins within your query.

When used in PATH mode, FOR JSON gives the developer more control, by allowing the location of each relational column to be defined within the JSON result set, by using dot-separated column aliases, which control nesting.

The FOR JSON clause has multiple options for controlling the document format. For example, a root node can be added to the document, by using the ROOT option, or if no root node is present, the outer array wrapper can be removed by using the WITHOUT_ARRAY_WRAPPER option. You can also specify if NULL values should be included in the resultant document, by using the INCLUDE_NULL_VALUES option.

CHAPTER 8

Shredding JSON Data

In Chapter 7, I discussed how we can convert relational data into JSON documents, but what if we had to shred a JSON document (just as you learned to shred XML documents in Chapter 4) into a relational dataset? We could achieve this by using the OPENJSON() function. The OPENJSON() function accepts a single JSON document as an input parameter and outputs a tabular result set. The OPENJSON() function can be called either with or without specifying an explicit schema for the result set. OPENJSON() also supports the use of JSON path expressions. This chapter will examine each of these options.

OPENJSON() with Default Schema

In order to understand how the OPENJSON() function works with the default schema, let's examine the CustomFields column of the Application. People table in the WideWorldImporters database. The query in Listing 8-1, returns the PersonID (the primary key of the table), the FullName column, and the CustomFields column, which contains a JSON document.

Tip Unlike the other data types discussed in this book, a JSON data type has not actually been created in SQL Server 2017. Instead, JSON documents are stored in NVARCHAR columns, and JSON-aware functions are called against the data, to parse and interact with the JSON.

© Peter A. Carter 2018
P. A. Carter, *SQL Server Advanced Data Types*,
https://doi.org/10.1007/978-1-4842-3901-8_8

Listing 8-1. Inspecting the Application.Person Table

```
USE WideWorldImporters
GO

SELECT
      PersonID
      , FullName
      , CustomFields
FROM Application.People ;
```

You will notice, from the partial result set shown in Figure 8-1, that the CustomFields column contains a JSON document specifying each person's properties, such as their hire data (for staff), languages spoken, and their title.

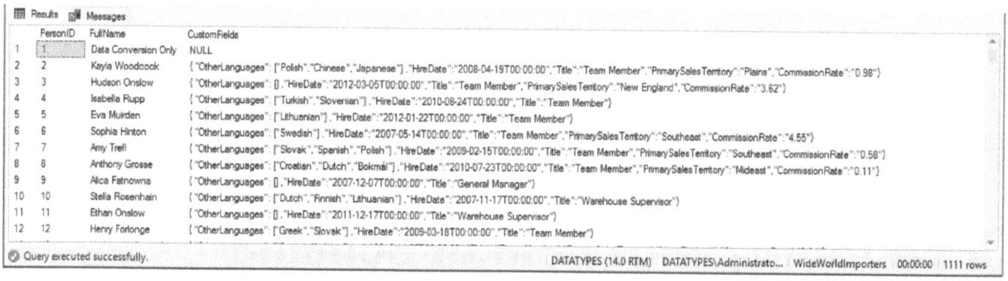

Figure 8-1. *Results of inspecting the Application.Person table*

If we wanted to use OPENJSON() to shred the details of a specific user, we would first have to pass the JSON document into a variable, before passing the variable into the OPENJSON() function. This technique is demonstrated in Listing 8-2, which returns the custom fields for Anthony Grosse.

Listing 8-2. Shredding a Single JSON Document

```
USE WideWorldImporters
GO

DECLARE @CustomFields NVARCHAR(MAX) ;
```

```
SET @CustomFields = (
        SELECT CustomFields
        FROM Application.People
        WHERE FullName = 'Anthony Grosse'
) ;

SELECT *
FROM OPENJSON(@CustomFields) ;
```

The results of this script are illustrated in Figure 8-2.

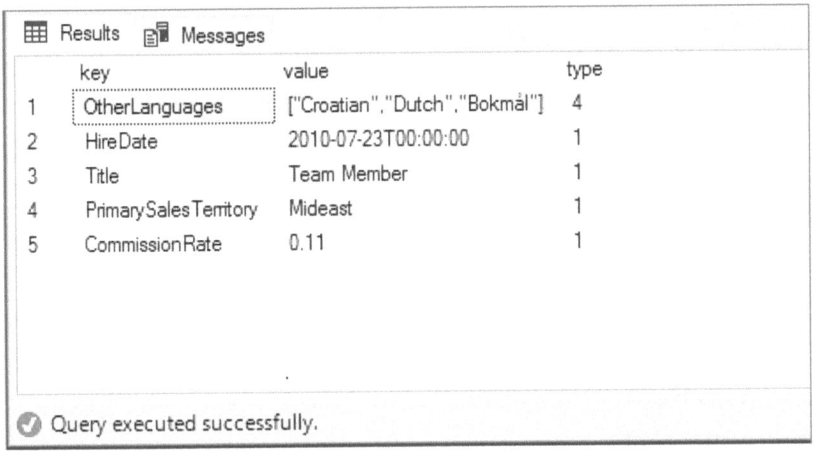
Results Messages

	key	value	type
1	OtherLanguages	["Croatian","Dutch","Bokmål"]	4
2	HireDate	2010-07-23T00:00:00	1
3	Title	Team Member	1
4	PrimarySalesTerritory	Mideast	1
5	CommissionRate	0.11	1

Query executed successfully.

***Figure 8-2.** Results of shredding a single JSON document*

The key column contains the name of the name/value pair; the value column contains the value of the name/value pair; and the type column indicates the data type. Table 8-1 details the data types that can be returned.

Table 8-1. *Data Types*

Data Type ID	Data Type
1	String
2	Number
3	Boolean
4	Array
5	Object

Shredding a Column

But what if we wanted to shred an entire column? The OPENJSON()
function only accepts a single JSON object, so we could not pass in values
from multiple rows. Instead, we would have to use the OUTER APPLY
operator against the table.

The OUTER APPLY operator applies a function to every row in a result
set. If the function returns a NULL value, the row will be included in the
result set. This contrasts with the CROSS APPLY operator, which also applies
a function to every row in a result set but omits the row, if the applied
function returns NULL.

The query in Listing 8-3 demonstrates how to use the OUTER APPLY
operator against the Application.People table, to shred the CustomFields
document.

Listing 8-3. Using OUTER APPLY with OPENJSON()

```
USE WideWorldImporters
GO

SELECT PersonID, FullName, CustomFields, JSON.*
FROM Application.People
OUTER APPLY OPENJSON(CustomFields) JSON ;
```

Partial results from this query are shown in Figure 8-3.

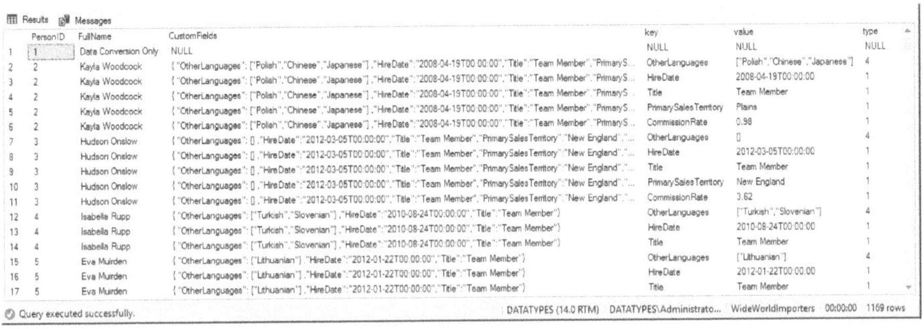

	PersonID	FullName	CustomFields	key	value	type
1	1	Data Conversion Only	NULL	NULL	NULL	NULL
2	2	Kayla Woodcock	{ "OtherLanguages": ["Polish","Chinese","Japanese"] ,"HireDate":"2008-04-19T00:00:00","Title":"Team Member","PrimaryS...	OtherLanguages	["Polish","Chinese","Japanese"]	4
3	2	Kayla Woodcock	{ "OtherLanguages": ["Polish","Chinese","Japanese"] ,"HireDate":"2008-04-19T00:00:00","Title":"Team Member","PrimaryS...	HireDate	2008-04-19T00:00:00	1
4	2	Kayla Woodcock	{ "OtherLanguages": ["Polish","Chinese","Japanese"] ,"HireDate":"2008-04-19T00:00:00","Title":"Team Member","PrimaryS...	Title	Team Member	1
5	2	Kayla Woodcock	{ "OtherLanguages": ["Polish","Chinese","Japanese"] ,"HireDate":"2008-04-19T00:00:00","Title":"Team Member","PrimaryS...	PrimarySalesTerritory	Plains	1
6	2	Kayla Woodcock	{ "OtherLanguages": ["Polish","Chinese","Japanese"] ,"HireDate":"2008-04-19T00:00:00","Title":"Team Member","PrimaryS...	CommissionRate	0.98	1
7	3	Hudson Onslow	{ "OtherLanguages": [] ,"HireDate":"2012-03-05T00:00:00","Title":"Team Member","PrimarySalesTerritory":"New England","...	OtherLanguages	[]	4
8	3	Hudson Onslow	{ "OtherLanguages": [] ,"HireDate":"2012-03-05T00:00:00","Title":"Team Member","PrimarySalesTerritory":"New England","...	HireDate	2012-03-05T00:00:00	1
9	3	Hudson Onslow	{ "OtherLanguages": [] ,"HireDate":"2012-03-05T00:00:00","Title":"Team Member","PrimarySalesTerritory":"New England","...	Title	Team Member	1
10	3	Hudson Onslow	{ "OtherLanguages": [] ,"HireDate":"2012-03-05T00:00:00","Title":"Team Member","PrimarySalesTerritory":"New England","...	PrimarySalesTerritory	New England	1
11	3	Hudson Onslow	{ "OtherLanguages": [] ,"HireDate":"2012-03-05T00:00:00","Title":"Team Member","PrimarySalesTerritory":"New England","...	CommissionRate	3.62	1
12	4	Isabella Rupp	{ "OtherLanguages": ["Turkish","Slovenian"] ,"HireDate":"2010-08-24T00:00:00","Title":"Team Member"}	OtherLanguages	["Turkish","Slovenian"]	4
13	4	Isabella Rupp	{ "OtherLanguages": ["Turkish","Slovenian"] ,"HireDate":"2010-08-24T00:00:00","Title":"Team Member"}	HireDate	2010-08-24T00:00:00	1
14	4	Isabella Rupp	{ "OtherLanguages": ["Turkish","Slovenian"] ,"HireDate":"2010-08-24T00:00:00","Title":"Team Member"}	Title	Team Member	1
15	5	Eva Muirden	{ "OtherLanguages": ["Lithuanian"] ,"HireDate":"2012-01-22T00:00:00","Title":"Team Member"}	OtherLanguages	["Lithuanian"]	4
16	5	Eva Muirden	{ "OtherLanguages": ["Lithuanian"] ,"HireDate":"2012-01-22T00:00:00","Title":"Team Member"}	HireDate	2012-01-22T00:00:00	1
17	5	Eva Muirden	{ "OtherLanguages": ["Lithuanian"] ,"HireDate":"2012-01-22T00:00:00","Title":"Team Member"}	Title	Team Member	1

Figure 8-3. *Results of using* `OUTER APPLY` *with* `OPENJSON()`

You will notice that the results from the Application.Person table are duplicated for each row returned from the `OPENJSON()` function. This is known as a Cartesian product.

Tip If we had used `CROSS APPLY` instead of `OUTER APPLY`, the results for `PersonID 1` would have been omitted.

To turn this data into columns, to avoid rows being duplicated, you could use the `PIVOT` operator. The `PIVOT` operator works by rotating unique values from a column into separate columns. This could also be described as changing rows to columns. It will then perform aggregations on remaining columns, as required. The same could be achieved by using multiple `CASE` statements, but the `PIVOT` operator is far more efficient.

The syntax of the `PIVOT` operator has an outer query, followed by two subqueries. The first subquery contains the base query, while the second contains the pivot specification. Because our values are often textual, and aggregation isn't appropriate, we will use the `MAX()` aggregate function. This is demonstrated with the query in Listing 8-4.

Listing 8-4. Using PIVOT with OPENJSON()

```
USE WideWorldImporters
GO
SELECT
        PersonID
      , FullName
      , [OtherLanguages]
      , [HireDate]
      , [Title]
      , [PrimarySalesTerritory]
      , [CommissionRate]
FROM (
SELECT
        PersonID
      , FullName
      , JSON.[Key] AS JSONName
      , JSON.value AS JSONValue
FROM Application.People
OUTER APPLY OPENJSON(CustomFields) JSON
) Src
PIVOT
(
MAX(JSONValue)
FOR JSONName IN ([OtherLanguages], [HireDate], [Title],
[PrimarySalesTerritory], [CommissionRate])
) pvt ;
```

The partial results of this query can be seen in Figure 8-4.

	PersonID	FullName	OtherLanguages	HireDate	Title	PrimarySalesTerritory	CommissionRate
1	1	Data Conversion Only	NULL	NULL	NULL	NULL	NULL
2	2	Kayla Woodcock	["Polish","Chinese","Japanese"]	2008-04-19T00:00:00	Team Member	Plains	0.98
3	3	Hudson Onslow	[]	2012-03-05T00:00:00	Team Member	New England	3.62
4	4	Isabella Rupp	["Turkish","Slovenian"]	2010-08-24T00:00:00	Team Member	NULL	NULL
5	5	Eva Muirden	["Lithuanian"]	2012-01-22T00:00:00	Team Member	NULL	NULL
6	6	Sophia Hinton	["Swedish"]	2007-05-14T00:00:00	Team Member	Southeast	4.55
7	7	Amy Trefl	["Slovak","Spanish","Polish"]	2009-02-15T00:00:00	Team Member	Southeast	0.58
8	8	Anthony Grosse	["Croatian","Dutch","Bokmål"]	2010-07-23T00:00:00	Team Member	Mideast	0.11
9	9	Alica Fatnowna	[]	2007-12-07T00:00:00	General Manager	NULL	NULL
10	10	Stella Rosenhain	["Dutch","Finnish","Lithuanian"]	2007-11-17T00:00:00	Warehouse Supervisor	NULL	NULL
11	11	Ethan Onslow	[]	2011-12-17T00:00:00	Warehouse Supervisor	NULL	NULL
12	12	Henry Forlonge	["Greek","Slovak"]	2009-03-18T00:00:00	Team Member	NULL	NULL
13	13	Hudson Hollinworth	["Croatian"]	2010-11-27T00:00:00	Team Member	New England	0.24
14	14	Lily Code	["Finnish","Bulgarian"]	2010-06-06T00:00:00	Team Member	Southeast	3.98
15	15	Taj Shand	["Arabic","Greek"]	2009-03-14T00:00:00	Manager	Far West	2.29
16	16	Archer Lamble	["Greek"]	2009-05-13T00:00:00	Team Member	Plains	1.88
17	17	Piper Koch	["Romanian","Portuguese"]	2011-10-15T00:00:00	Manager	NULL	NULL
18	18	Katie Darwin	["Estonian","Romanian"]	2008-07-12T00:00:00	Team Member	NULL	NULL
19	19	Jai Shand	["Finnish","Dutch"]	2011-11-13T00:00:00	Team Member	NULL	NULL
20	20	Jack Potter	["Arabic"]	2009-05-29T00:00:00	General Manager	Southeast	3.97

Figure 8-4. Results of using PIVOT *with* OPENJSON()

The limitation of using this approach is that you must know the name of each key in the JSON document before writing the query. If any key names are missed, or added later, the data will not appear in the result set. This can be particularly challenging, as JSON documents cannot be bound to a schema.

Dynamic Shredding Based on Document Content

The way to resolve the issue of not knowing the document contents at development time is to use a dynamic PIVOT. This involves using dynamic SQL to define the current list of JSON keys to pivot before the query is run. This technique is demonstrated in Listing 8-5.

Tip QUOTENAME() is a system function that delimits a value by wrapping it in square brackets.

Listing 8-5. Using Dynamic PIVOT with OPENJSON()

```
DECLARE @Columns NVARCHAR(MAX) ;
DECLARE @SQL NVARCHAR(MAX) ;

SET @Columns = ";

SELECT @Columns += ', p.' + QUOTENAME(JSONName)
FROM (
SELECT DISTINCT
        JSON.[Key] AS JSONName
FROM Application.People p
CROSS APPLY OPENJSON(CustomFields) JSON
) AS cols ;

SET @SQL =
'SELECT
        PersonID
      , FullName
      , ' + STUFF(@Columns, 1, 2, ") + '
FROM
(
  SELECT
        PersonID
      , FullName
      , JSON.[Key] AS JSONName
      , JSON.value AS JSONValue
FROM Application.People
OUTER APPLY OPENJSON(CustomFields) JSON
) AS src
PIVOT
```

```
(
  MAX(JSONValue) FOR JSONName IN ('
  + STUFF(REPLACE(@Columns, ', p.[', ',['), 1, 1, ")
  + ')
) AS p ;' ;

EXEC (@SQL) ;
```

OPENJSON( ) with Explicit Schema

When using OPENJSON( ) with an explicit schema, you are able to provide
control over the format of the result set that is returned. Instead of a three-
column result set, a column will be returned for every column that you
have specified in the WITH clause. You can also specify the data type of each
column. These data types are T-SQL data types, not JSON data types, so
types such as DATE or DECIMAL can be specified. For example, consider the
script in Listing 8-6.

Listing 8-6. Using OPENJSON( ) with an Explicit Schema

```
DECLARE @CustomFields NVARCHAR(MAX) ;

SET @CustomFields =
(
SELECT
        CustomFields
FROM Application.People
WHERE PersonID = 2
) ;

SELECT *
FROM OPENJSON(@CustomFields)
WITH (
```

237

```
      HireDate DATETIME2
    , Title NVARCHAR(50)
    , PrimarySalesTerritory NVARCHAR(50)
    , CommissionRate DECIMAL(5,2)
) ;
```

This query returns the results shown in Figure 8-5.

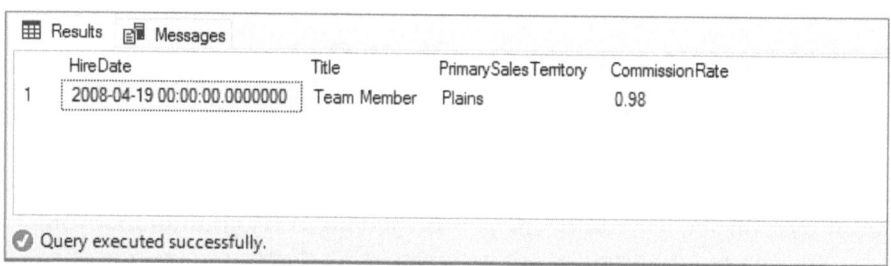

Figure 8-5. *Results of using OPENJSON( ) with an explicit schema*

A slight complexity arises when one of the columns returned is a JSON object. For example, consider the query in Listing 8-7, which adds the OtherLanguages column to the query. As there is no specific JSON data type, we will use NVARCHAR(MAX), as it can be stored as NVARCHAR(MAX) in a table.

Listing 8-7. Adding a JSON Column

```
DECLARE @CustomFields NVARCHAR(MAX) ;

SET @CustomFields =
(
SELECT
        CustomFields
FROM Application.People
WHERE PersonID = 2
) ;
```

```
SELECT *
FROM OPENJSON(@CustomFields)
WITH (
        OtherLanguages NVARCHAR(MAX)
      , HireDate DATETIME2
      , Title NVARCHAR(50)
      , PrimarySalesTerritory NVARCHAR(50)
      , CommissionRate DECIMAL(5,2)
) ;
```

This query returns the results shown in Figure 8-6.

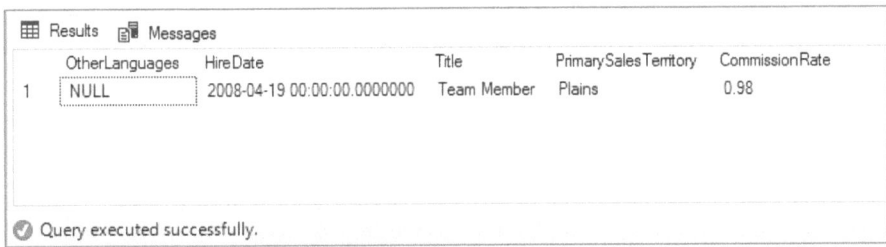

Figure 8-6. *Results of adding a JSON column*

So why has the OtherLanguages column returned NULL? We know that the column exists, and that it contains data for PersonID 2, owing to the previous examples in this chapter. When returning a JSON object from OPENJSON(), we must use additional syntax in the WITH clause, to specify that the NVARCHAR actually represents a JSON object, as demonstrated in Listing 8-8.

Listing 8-8. Correctly Returning a JSON Array or Object

```
DECLARE @CustomFields NVARCHAR(MAX) ;

SET @CustomFields =
(
```

```
SELECT
        CustomFields
FROM Application.People
WHERE PersonID = 2
) ;

SELECT *
FROM OPENJSON(@CustomFields)
WITH (
        OtherLanguages NVARCHAR(MAX) AS JSON
        , HireDate DATETIME2
        , Title NVARCHAR(50)
        , PrimarySalesTerritory NVARCHAR(50)
        , CommissionRate DECIMAL(5,2)
) ;
```

The script will now return the results that we expect, as shown in Figure 8-7.

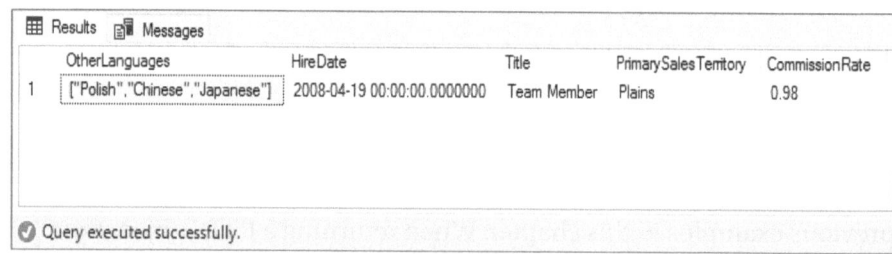

Figure 8-7. *Correctly returning JSON data*

When you must shred multiple rows, an explicit schema can also be specified, when using the OUTER APPLY operator. Remember that the OUTER APPLY operator will not remove rows that return NULL values, in the way that CROSS APPLY does. This is demonstrated in Listing 8-9.

Listing 8-9. Using an Explicit Schema with OUTER APPLY

```
SELECT
          PersonID
        , FullName
        , JSON.*
FROM Application.People
OUTER APPLY OPENJSON(CustomFields)
                              WITH (
                                      OtherLanguages
                                      NVARCHAR(MAX) AS JSON
                                    , HireDate DATETIME2
                                    , Title NVARCHAR(50)
                                    , PrimarySalesTerritory
                                      NVARCHAR(50)
                                    , CommissionRate
                                      DECIMAL(5,2)
                              ) JSON ;
```

As you can see from the partial results in Figure 8-8, some of the need-to-pivot data has been eliminated. The issue remains, however, that you must know every possible key in the JSON document before the query is written. Therefore, if there is not a discrete set of possible values, you may still be required to use dynamic SQL.

	PersonID	FullName	OtherLanguages	HireDate	Title	Primary Sales Territory	CommissionRate
1	1	Data Conversion Only	NULL	NULL	NULL	NULL	NULL
2	2	Kayla Woodcock	["Polish","Chinese","Japanese"]	2008-04-19 00:00:00.0000000	Team Member	Plains	0.98
3	3	Hudson Onslow	[]	2012-03-05 00:00:00.0000000	Team Member	New England	3.62
4	4	Isabella Rupp	["Turkish","Slovenian"]	2010-08-24 00:00:00.0000000	Team Member	NULL	NULL
5	5	Eva Muirden	["Lithuanian"]	2012-01-22 00:00:00.0000000	Team Member	NULL	NULL
6	6	Sophia Hinton	["Swedish"]	2007-05-14 00:00:00.0000000	Team Member	Southeast	4.55
7	7	Amy Trefl	["Slovak","Spanish","Polish"]	2009-02-15 00:00:00.0000000	Team Member	Southeast	0.58
8	8	Anthony Grosse	["Croatian","Dutch","Bokmål"]	2010-07-23 00:00:00.0000000	Team Member	Mideast	0.11
9	9	Alica Fatnowna	[]	2007-12-07 00:00:00.0000000	General Manager	NULL	NULL
10	10	Stella Rosenhain	["Dutch","Finnish","Lithuanian"]	2007-11-17 00:00:00.0000000	Warehouse Supervisor	NULL	NULL
11	11	Ethan Onslow	[]	2011-12-17 00:00:00.0000000	Warehouse Supervisor	NULL	NULL
12	12	Henry Forlonge	["Greek","Slovak"]	2009-03-18 00:00:00.0000000	Team Member	NULL	NULL

Query executed successfully.   DATATYPES (14.0 RTM)   DATATYPES\Administ

Figure 8-8. *Results of using an explicit schema with OUTER APPLY*

OPENJSON( ) with Path Expressions

As well as the use of explicit schema, OPENJSON( ) also supports JSON path expressions. A path expression allows you to reference specific properties within a JSON document. For example, consider the JSON document in Listing 8-10.

Tip   You may recognize this document, as we created it in Chapter 7.

Listing 8-10. Sales Orders with Root Node

```
{
   "SalesOrders": [
      {
         "OrderID": 72646,
         "CustomerID": 1060,
         "SalespersonPersonID": 14,
         "OrderDate": "2016-05-18"
      },
```

```
{
   "OrderID": 72738,
   "CustomerID": 1060,
   "SalespersonPersonID": 14,
   "OrderDate": "2016-05-19"
},
{
   "OrderID": 72916,
   "CustomerID": 1060,
   "SalespersonPersonID": 6,
   "OrderDate": "2016-05-20"
},
{
   "OrderID": 73081,
   "CustomerID": 1060,
   "SalespersonPersonID": 8,
   "OrderDate": "2016-05-24"
}
   ]
}
```

If we used a basic OPENJSON() statement against this document, it would
return the entire SalesOrders array, as partially shown in Figure 8-9.

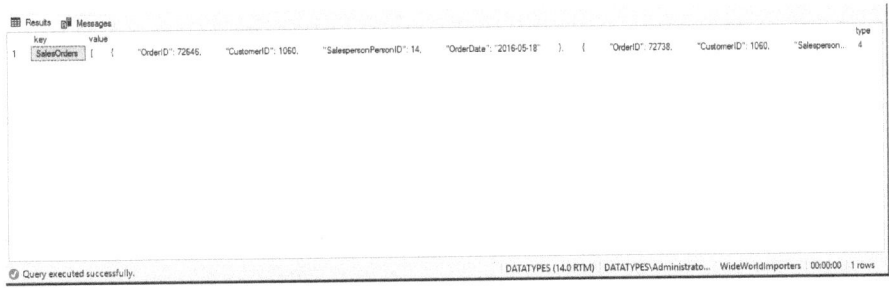

Figure 8-9. *Results of basic OPENJSON()*

If we were to use a PATH statement, however, we could choose to only return the *n*th item in this array. This would drastically alter the results set, as OPENJSON() would be able to map each item within the array element to a relational column, meaning that a row for each key within the element would be returned, instead of a single row containing a JSON document, as shown in Figure 8-10, which contains the results of shredding the first array element (OrderID 72646).

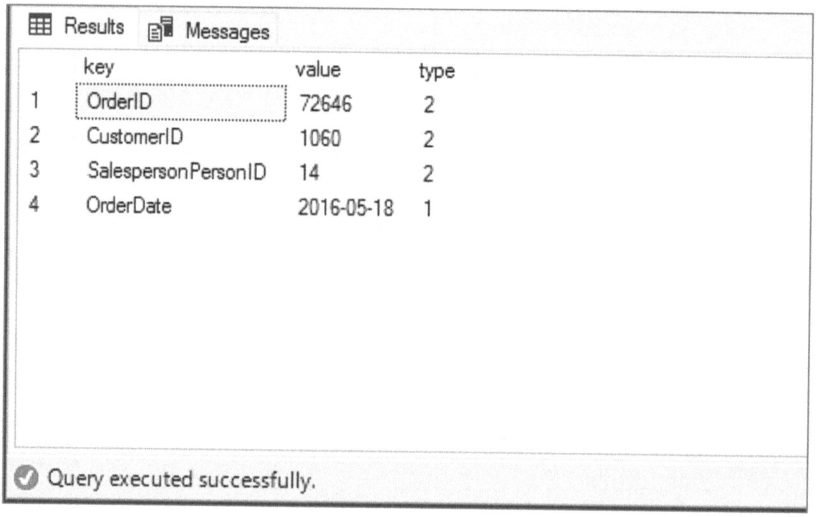

	key	value	type
1	OrderID	72646	2
2	CustomerID	1060	2
3	SalespersonPersonID	14	2
4	OrderDate	2016-05-18	1

Query executed successfully.

Figure 8-10. *Results of shredding a single array element*

So, let's look at how we can get to this result. First, we must understand that path expressions can be run in one of two modes: strict or lax. If you run a path expression in lax mode, and the path expression contains an error, OPENJSON() will "eat the error" and return an empty result set. If you use strict mode, however, if the path expression contains an error, OPENJSON() will throw an error message.

We now must understand the elements of the path itself. First, we use a $ to specify the context, followed by dot-separated, nested key names. Finally, we specify the array element number in square brackets. So, to produce the results in Figure 8-10, we would use the query in Listing 8-11.

Listing 8-11. Using Path Expressions to Return a Single Array Element

```
DECLARE @JSON NVARCHAR(MAX) ;

SET @JSON = '{
   "SalesOrders": [
      {
         "OrderID": 72646,
         "CustomerID": 1060,
         "SalespersonPersonID": 14,
         "OrderDate": "2016-05-18"
      },
      {
         "OrderID": 72738,
         "CustomerID": 1060,
         "SalespersonPersonID": 14,
         "OrderDate": "2016-05-19"
      },
      {
         "OrderID": 72916,
         "CustomerID": 1060,
         "SalespersonPersonID": 6,
         "OrderDate": "2016-05-20"
      },
      {
         "OrderID": 73081,
         "CustomerID": 1060,
         "SalespersonPersonID": 8,
         "OrderDate": "2016-05-24"
      }
   ]
}
' ;
```

```
SELECT *
FROM OPENJSON(@JSON, 'lax $.SalesOrders[0]') ;
```

You will notice, in this script, that after passing in the JSON document, we use the lax (or, alternatively, strict) keyword to specify the mode we will use. After a space comes the path expression itself. Here, we start with $, to set the context, and then point to the SalesOrders key. We then use square brackets to specify the array element that we wish to use.

Tip   JSON path expressions always use zero-base arrays.

Shredding Data into Tables

You can now imagine how simple looping techniques could be used to shred each element within an array. For example, consider the script in Listing 8-12. This script will shred each of the array elements into a temporary table called Orders.

Listing 8-12. Shredding Each Element into a Temporary Table

```
DECLARE @JSON NVARCHAR(MAX) ;

SET @JSON = '{
   "SalesOrders": [
      {
         "OrderID": 72646,
         "CustomerID": 1060,
         "SalespersonPersonID": 14,
         "OrderDate": "2016-05-18"
      },
```

```
    {
        "OrderID": 72738,
        "CustomerID": 1060,
        "SalespersonPersonID": 14,
        "OrderDate": "2016-05-19"
    },
    {
        "OrderID": 72916,
        "CustomerID": 1060,
        "SalespersonPersonID": 6,
        "OrderDate": "2016-05-20"
    },
    {
        "OrderID": 73081,
        "CustomerID": 1060,
        "SalespersonPersonID": 8,
        "OrderDate": "2016-05-24"
    }
    ]
}
' ;

CREATE TABLE #Orders
(
        OrderID                 INT,
        CustomerID              INT,
        SalespersonPersonID     INT,
        OrderDate               DATE
) ;
```

```
DECLARE @ArrayElement INT = 0 ;

DECLARE @path NVARCHAR(MAX) = 'lax $.SalesOrders[' + CAST(
@ArrayElement AS NVARCHAR) + ']' ;

WHILE @ArrayElement <=3
BEGIN
        INSERT INTO #Orders (OrderID, CustomerID,
        SalespersonPersonID, OrderDate)
        SELECT
                OrderID
              , CustomerID
              , SalespersonPersonID
              , OrderDate
        FROM OPENJSON(@JSON, @Path)
        WITH( OrderID INT, CustomerID INT, SalespersonPersonID
        INT, OrderDate DATE) ;

        SET @ArrayElement = @ArrayElement + 1 ;

        SET @path = 'lax $.SalesOrders[' + CAST(@ArrayElement
        AS NVARCHAR) + ']' ;
END

SELECT * FROM #Orders ;

DROP TABLE #Orders ;
```

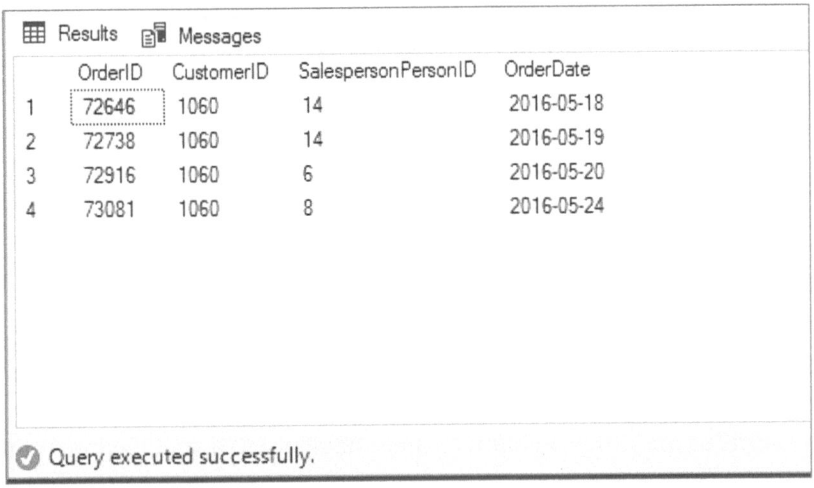

	OrderID	CustomerID	SalespersonPersonID	OrderDate
1	72646	1060	14	2016-05-18
2	72738	1060	14	2016-05-19
3	72916	1060	6	2016-05-20
4	73081	1060	8	2016-05-24

⊞ Results ▤ Messages

✓ Query executed successfully.

Figure 8-11. *Results of shredding multiple array elements*

The final SELECT statement in this script produces the results illustrated in Figure 8-11.

Caution   While I have used a WHILE loop in this example, I have done so only because it provides a clear and easy example of how path expressions can be used. I would never use a WHILE loop or CURSOR in production code. There is always a way to achieve the same results, using a set-based approach.

Summary

JSON data can be shredded into tabular results sets by using the OPENJSON() function. OPENJSON() can be used either with or without an explicit schema. When a schema is not explicitly defined, OPENJSON(), using a WITH clause, returns a standard row set, detailing the key (name), value, and JSON data type ID of each node in the document.

When an explicit schema is supplied, OPENJSON() will return a formatted result set, which contains a column for each specified in the WITH clause. Using an explicit schema avoids the need to pivot the data when you know every node in the document at development time. If the list of columns is not discrete, however, dynamic SQL will be required, to build a list of possible results before processing.

OPENJSON() also supports JSON path expressions. Passing path expressions to the function allows you to navigate to a specific item within an array, meaning that you can shred data to a more granular level. For example, instead of shredding an array of JSON objects into a table, you can use looping methodologies to shred the contents of each array element into relational data.

CHAPTER 9

Working with the JSON Data Type

In this chapter, I will discuss the T-SQL functions that allow developers to query JSON data. I will then discuss how JSON data can be indexed.

Querying JSON Data

SQL Server has introduced the JSON_VALUE(), JSON_QUERY(), JSON_MODIFY(), and ISJSON() functions to help developers interrogate and interact with JSON data. The following sections will discuss each of these functions.

Using ISJSON( )

Because JSON data is stored in NVARCHAR(MAX) columns, as opposed to using its own data type, it is very useful to ensure that a tuple contains a valid JSON document, before calling a JSON function against it. The ISJSON() function will evaluate a string to check if it is a valid JSON document. The function will return a value of 1 if the string is valid JSON and 0 if it is not. Therefore, a common usage of the function is within an IF statement. For example, consider the query in Listing 9-1.

© Peter A. Carter 2018
P. A. Carter, *SQL Server Advanced Data Types*,
https://doi.org/10.1007/978-1-4842-3901-8_9

Listing 9-1. Incorrectly Formatted JSON

```
DECLARE @JSON NVARCHAR(MAX) ;

SET @JSON = '{"I am not:"Correctly formatted"}' ;

SELECT *
FROM OPENJSON(@JSON) ;
```

Because the name of the key is missing a closing double quotation mark, the query will fail, with the error shown in Figure 9-1.

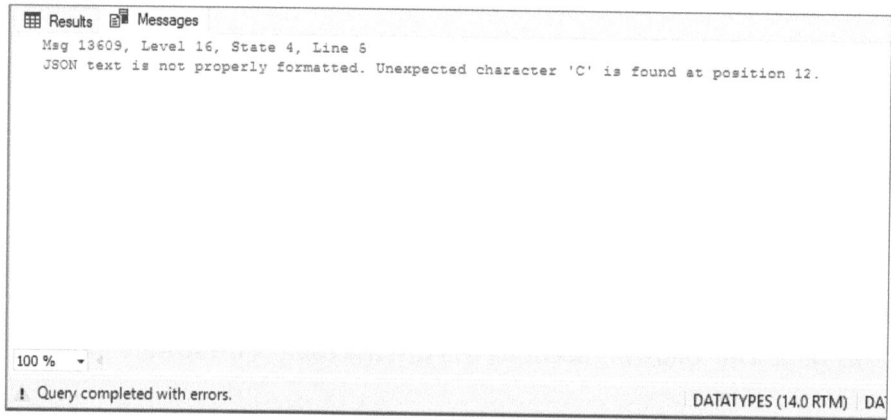

Figure 9-1. *Error thrown by invalid JSON*

Instead of our script failing, we could instead use the ISJSON() function in an IF statement, as demonstrated in Listing 9-2.

Listing 9-2. Use ISJSON() in an IF Statement

```
DECLARE @JSON NVARCHAR(MAX) ;

SET @JSON = '{"I am not:"Correctly formatted"}' ;

IF ISJSON(@JSON) = 1
```

```
BEGIN
        SELECT *
        FROM OPENJSON(@JSON) ;
END
```

This time, the script will complete without errors, as the query against the OPENJSON() function will never run.

Tip   A full description of the usage of OPENJSON() can be found in Chapter 8.

The ISJSON() function could also be used in the WHERE clause of a SELECT statement. For example, consider the script in Listing 9-3. The script creates a simple temporary table and inserts two values into an NVARCHAR(MAX) column. One of the values is valid JSON data, and the other is not. The script then calls the OPENJSON() function against the column.

Listing 9-3. Filter Results That Are Not JSON

```
--Create a temp table

CREATE TABLE #JsonTemp
(
        JSONData        NVARCHAR(MAX)
) ;

--Populate temp table with one JSON value and one non-JSON value

INSERT INTO #JsonTemp
VALUES ('{"I am JSON":"True"}'),
        ('I am JSON - False') ;

--Call OPENJSON() against only rows where data is JSON
```

```
SELECT JSON.*
FROM #JsonTemp Base
OUTER APPLY OPENJSON(Base.JSONData) JSON
WHERE ISJSON(Base.JSONData) = 1 ;

--Drop temp table

DROP TABLE #JsonTemp ;
```

Because the WHERE clause removes any rows that do not contain valid JSON data, before the OPENJSON() function is applied, the script completes successfully and returns the results shown in Figure 9-2.

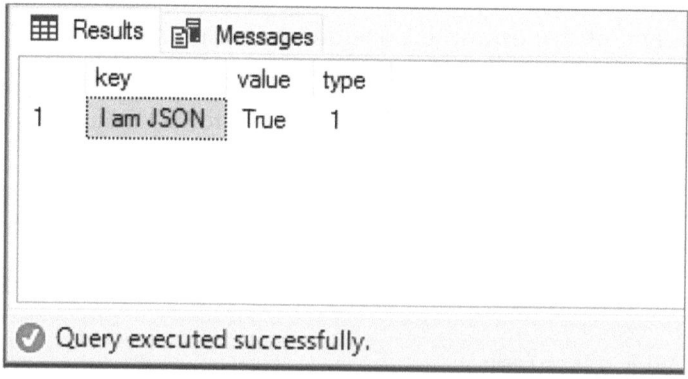

Figure 9-2. *Results of filtering non-JSON data*

Using JSON_VALUE( )

The JSON_VALUE() function can be used to return a single scalar value from a JSON document. The function accepts two parameters. The first parameter is the JSON document, from which to retrieve the data. The second is a path expression to the value you wish to return. As described in Chapter 8, when using path expressions with OPENJSON(), path expressions can be used in either lax mode or strict mode. When lax mode is used, if there is an error in the path expression, NULL results will be returned, and no error will be raised. When used in strict mode, if there is an error in the path expression, an error will be thrown.

The value returned is always of data type NVARCHAR(4000). This means that if the value exceeds 4000 characters, JSON_VALUE() will either return NULL or throw an error, depending on whether lax mode or strict mode has been used.

To look more closely at the JSON_VALUE() function, let's consider the Warehouse.StockItems table in the WideWorldImporters database. The CustomFields column of this table contains a JSON document that includes a key called Tags, which has a value of an array, containing product tags.

The script in Listing 9-4 will first populate a variable with the content of CustomFields for a single product. Subsequently, it will check that the variable contains a valid JSON document, by using the ISJSON() function, before passing the document into the JSON_VALUE() function.

The path expression of the JSON_VALUE() function starts by specifying that we wish to use the path expression in lax mode. It then uses a $ to represent the context, before using a dot-separated path to the node we wish to extract. Because the Tags node is an array, and the JSON_VALUE() function can only return a scalar value, we will use square brackets to denote the element within the array that we would like to extract. This is mandatory syntax, even if there is only a single element in the array.

Tip   The array is always zero-based.

Listing 9-4. UsingJSON_VALUE() Against a JSON Document

```
DECLARE @JSON NVARCHAR(MAX) ;

--The CustomFields column for StockItem ID 61 contains the
following JSON document:
--'{ "CountryOfManufacture": "China", "Tags": ["Radio
Control","Realistic Sound"], "MinimumAge": "10" }'

SET @JSON = (SELECT CustomFields FROM Warehouse.StockItems
WHERE StockItemID = 61) ;

IF ISJSON(@JSON) = 1
BEGIN
        SELECT JSON_VALUE(@Json,'lax $.Tags[0]') ;
END
```

This script produces the results illustrated in Figure 9-3.

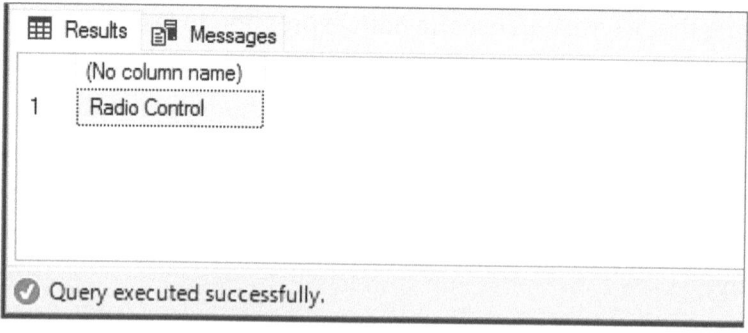

Figure 9-3. *Results of using JSON_VALUE() against a JSON document*

So, what if we want to use the JSON_VALUE() function against a column in a table? Where it is a scalar function, we cannot use OUTER APPLY or CROSS APPLY. Instead, we must include it in the SELECT list of our query. This is demonstrated in Listing 9-5.

Listing 9-5. Using `JSON_VALUE()` in a `SELECT` List

```
USE WideWorldImporters
GO

SELECT
          StockItemName
        , JSON_VALUE(customfields,'lax $.Tags[0]')
FROM Warehouse.StockItems ;
```

You will notice that instead of passing in a variable, we simply pass in the name of the column that contains the JSON document. Partial results of this query can be found in Figure 9-4.

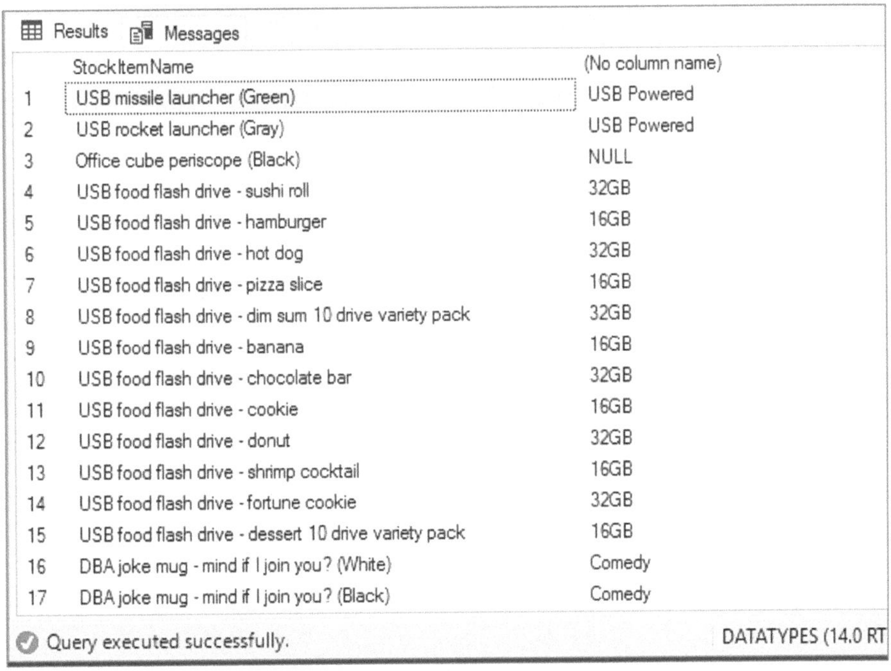
Results Messages

	StockItemName	(No column name)
1	USB missile launcher (Green)	USB Powered
2	USB rocket launcher (Gray)	USB Powered
3	Office cube periscope (Black)	NULL
4	USB food flash drive - sushi roll	32GB
5	USB food flash drive - hamburger	16GB
6	USB food flash drive - hot dog	32GB
7	USB food flash drive - pizza slice	16GB
8	USB food flash drive - dim sum 10 drive variety pack	32GB
9	USB food flash drive - banana	16GB
10	USB food flash drive - chocolate bar	32GB
11	USB food flash drive - cookie	16GB
12	USB food flash drive - donut	32GB
13	USB food flash drive - shrimp cocktail	16GB
14	USB food flash drive - fortune cookie	32GB
15	USB food flash drive - dessert 10 drive variety pack	16GB
16	DBA joke mug - mind if I join you? (White)	Comedy
17	DBA joke mug - mind if I join you? (Black)	Comedy

Query executed successfully. DATATYPES (14.0 RT

Figure 9-4. *Results of using `JSON_VALUE()` against a table*

Our original JSON document referred to Stock Item ID 61, which is a remote-controlled car. We could also use JSON_VALUE in the WHERE clause of our query, to filter the result set, so that only rows in which the first tag contains the value Radio Control are returned. This is demonstrated in Listing 9-6, in which we have also enhanced the query, to ensure that only valid JSON documents are returned, by using the ISJSON() function.

Listing 9-6. Using JSON_VALUE() in a WHERE Clause

```
USE WideWorldImporters
GO

SELECT
        StockItemName
      , JSON_VALUE(CustomFields,'lax $.Tags[0]') AS Tag0
FROM Warehouse.StockItems
WHERE JSON_VALUE(CustomFields,'lax $.Tags[0]') = 'Radio Control'
        AND       ISJSON(CustomFields) = 1 ;
```

The results of this query are illustrated in Figure 9-5.

	StockItemName	Tag0
1	RC toy sedan car with remote control (Black) 1/50 scale	Radio Control
2	RC toy sedan car with remote control (Red) 1/50 scale	Radio Control
3	RC toy sedan car with remote control (Blue) 1/50 scale	Radio Control
4	RC toy sedan car with remote control (Green) 1/50 scale	Radio Control
5	RC toy sedan car with remote control (Yellow) 1/50 scale	Radio Control
6	RC toy sedan car with remote control (Pink) 1/50 scale	Radio Control
7	RC vintage American toy coupe with remote control (Red) 1/50 scale	Radio Control
8	RC vintage American toy coupe with remote control (Black) 1/50 scale	Radio Control
9	RC big wheel monster truck with remote control (Black) 1/50 scale	Radio Control

Query executed successfully.   DATATYPES (14.0

Figure 9-5. *Results of using JSON_VALUE() in a WHERE clause*

The third tag of remote-controlled car products denotes if the item is vintage. There are two vintage cars in the product table. Therefore, in Listing 9-7, we will further filter the result set to include only products for which the third tag has a value of Vintage. We will also enhance the SELECT list, to contain the first three tags in the array. Finally, we will change the JSON_VALUE() functions in the WHERE clause, to use strict path expressions, so that an error will result in the query failing.

Listing 9-7. Enhancing the Query

```
USE WideWorldImporters
GO

SELECT
        StockItemName
      , JSON_VALUE(CustomFields,'lax $.Tags[0]') AS Tag0
      , JSON_VALUE(CustomFields,'lax $.Tags[1]') AS Tag1
      , JSON_VALUE(CustomFields,'lax $.Tags[2]') AS Tag2
FROM Warehouse.StockItems
WHERE JSON_VALUE(CustomFields,'strict $.Tags[0]') = 'Radio Control'
        AND JSON_VALUE(CustomFields,'strict $.Tags[2]') = 'Vintage'
        AND     ISJSON(CustomFields) = 1 ;
```

Unfortunately, this time, even though the ISJSON() function is ensuring that any non-valid JSON documents are not in the result set, the query returns the error shown in Figure 9-6. This is because not all JSON documents in the CustomFields column have a Tags key. From those that do, not all documents have three tags. Therefore, the path expressions for two JSON_VALUE() calls in the WHERE clause are not valid. Because we have changed from lax mode to strict mode, the query fails.

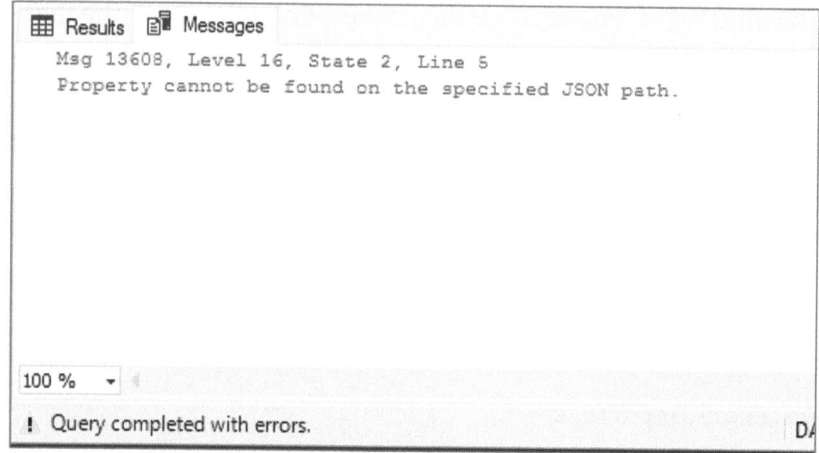

Figure 9-6. *Error thrown by the query*

If we were to change back to lax mode path expressions, the query would return the results displayed in Figure 9-7.

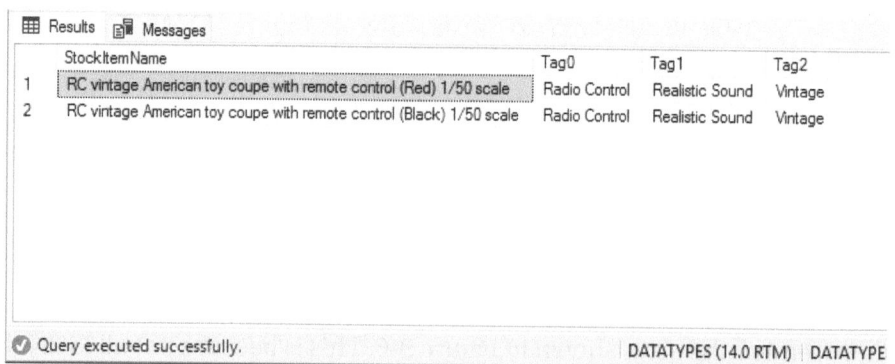

Figure 9-7. *Query results with lax mode path expressions*

With SQL Server 2017 and later versions, it is also possible to pass in a path expression as a variable. Therefore, the query in Listing 9-8 will return the same results as shown in Figure 9-7.

> **Tip**   You must use SQL Server 2017 or later versions, to run the
> query in Listing 9-8.

Listing 9-8. Using a Variable As a Path

```
USE WideWorldImporters
GO
DECLARE @Path NVARCHAR(MAX) = 'lax $.Tags[2]' ;

SELECT
        StockItemName
      , JSON_VALUE(CustomFields,'lax $.Tags[0]') AS Tag0
      , JSON_VALUE(CustomFields,'lax $.Tags[1]') AS Tag1
      , JSON_VALUE(CustomFields,@Path) AS Tag2
FROM Warehouse.StockItems
WHERE JSON_VALUE(CustomFields,'lax $.Tags[0]') = 'Radio Control'
        AND JSON_VALUE(CustomFields,'lax $.Tags[2]') = 'Vintage'
        AND     ISJSON(CustomFields) = 1 ;
```

Using JSON_QUERY( )

Unlike JSON_VALUE(), which returns a scalar value, JSON_QUERY() can
be used to extract a JSON object, or an array, from a JSON document.
For example, consider the script in Listing 9-9. The script uses the same
JSON document that we used in Listing 9-4, which extracted a single array
element from the Tags array for Stock Item ID 61. This time, however,
instead of extracting a single array element, we will extract the entire Tags
array. Because we are extracting the entire array, there is no need to specify
the array element number in square brackets, as we did when using JSON_
VALUE() against the document.

Listing 9-9. Using JSON_QUERY() Against a JSON Document

```
DECLARE @JSON NVARCHAR(MAX) ;

--The CustomFields column for StockItem ID 61 contains the
following JSON document:
--'{ "CountryOfManufacture": "China", "Tags": ["Radio
Control","Realistic Sound"], "MinimumAge": "10" }'

SET @JSON = (SELECT CustomFields FROM Warehouse.StockItems
WHERE StockItemID = 61) ;

IF ISJSON(@JSON) = 1
BEGIN
        SELECT JSON_QUERY(@Json,'lax $.Tags') ;
END
```

The results of this script are illustrated in Figure 9-8.

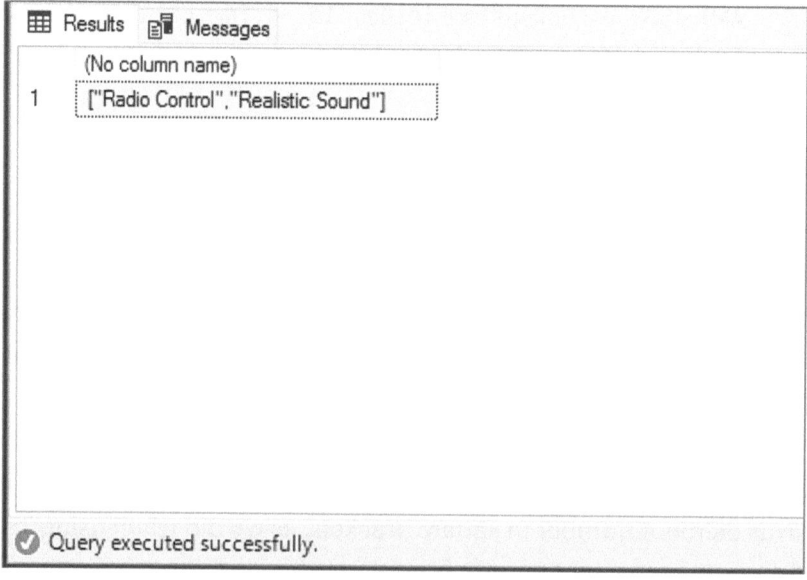

Figure 9-8. *Results of using JSON_QUERY() against a JSON document*

As with JSON_VALUE(), if we want to use JSON_QUERY() against a column in a table, we will use it in the SELECT list, as opposed to using a CROSS APPLY or OUTER APPLY operator. The difference between JSON_VALUE() and JSON_QUERY() is demonstrated in Listing 9-10. Here, we use the same query as in Listing 9-7 but enhance it to include a column in the result set that includes the whole Tags array, using JSON_QUERY().

Listing 9-10. Using JSON_QUERY() in a SELECT List

```
USE WideWorldImporters
GO

SELECT
         StockItemName
      , JSON_VALUE(CustomFields,'lax $.Tags[0]') AS Tag0
      , JSON_VALUE(CustomFields,'lax $.Tags[1]') AS Tag1
      , JSON_VALUE(CustomFields,'lax $.Tags[2]') AS Tag2
      , JSON_QUERY(CustomFields,'lax $.Tags') AS TagsArray
FROM Warehouse.StockItems
WHERE JSON_VALUE(CustomFields,'lax $.Tags[0]') = 'Radio Control'
       AND JSON_VALUE(CustomFields,'lax $.Tags[2]') = 'Vintage'
       AND       ISJSON(CustomFields) = 1 ;
```

This query returns the results shown in Figure 9-9.

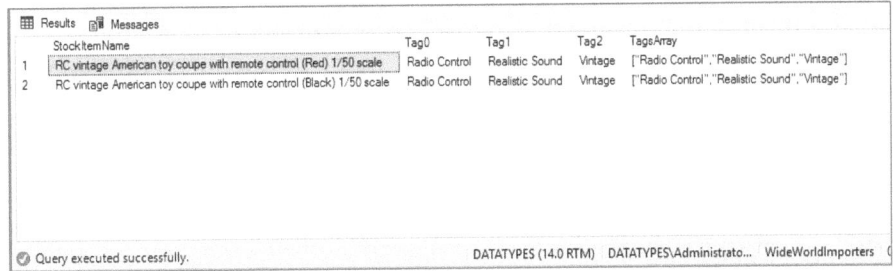

Figure 9-9. *Results of using JSON_QUERY() in a SELECT list*

The JSON_QUERY() function can also be used in a WHERE clause. Consider the query in Listing 9-11, which has been rewritten, so that the JSON_QUERY() function is used to filter out any rows in which the JSON document does contain an empty Tags array. You will notice that the query uses a mix of lax mode and strict mode.

Listing 9-11. Using JSON_QUERY() in a WHERE Clause

```
USE WideWorldImporters
GO

SELECT
          StockItemName
        , JSON_VALUE(CustomFields,'lax $.Tags[0]') AS Tag0
        , JSON_VALUE(CustomFields,'lax $.Tags[1]') AS Tag1
        , JSON_VALUE(CustomFields,'lax $.Tags[2]') AS Tag2
        , JSON_QUERY(CustomFields,'lax $.Tags') AS TagsArray
FROM Warehouse.StockItems
WHERE JSON_QUERY(CustomFields,'strict $.Tags') <> '[]'
        AND        ISJSON(CustomFields) = 1 ;
```

If only the document context ($) is passed to the path expression, the entire JSON document will be returned. It is also worth noting that a variable can be used to pass the path, from SQL Server 2017 onward, just as it can for OPENJSON() and JSON_VALUE(). Both these concepts are demonstrated in Listing 9-12, which uses a variable to pass only the document context, as the path expression, to an additional column in the result set.

Tip   You must be running SQL Server 2017 or later versions to run the query in Listing 9-12.

Listing 9-12. Using Path Variables and Document Context

```
USE WideWorldImporters
GO

DECLARE @Path NVARCHAR(MAX) = '$' ;

SELECT
          StockItemName
        , JSON_VALUE(CustomFields,'lax $.Tags[0]') AS Tag0
        , JSON_VALUE(CustomFields,'lax $.Tags[1]') AS Tag1
        , JSON_VALUE(CustomFields,'lax $.Tags[2]') AS Tag2
        , JSON_QUERY(CustomFields,'lax $.Tags') AS TagsArray
        , JSON_QUERY(CustomFields, @Path) AS EntireDocument
FROM Warehouse.StockItems
WHERE JSON_QUERY(CustomFields,'strict $.Tags') <> '[]'
        AND      ISJSON(CustomFields) = 1 ;
```

The partial results of this query can be seen in Figure 9-10.

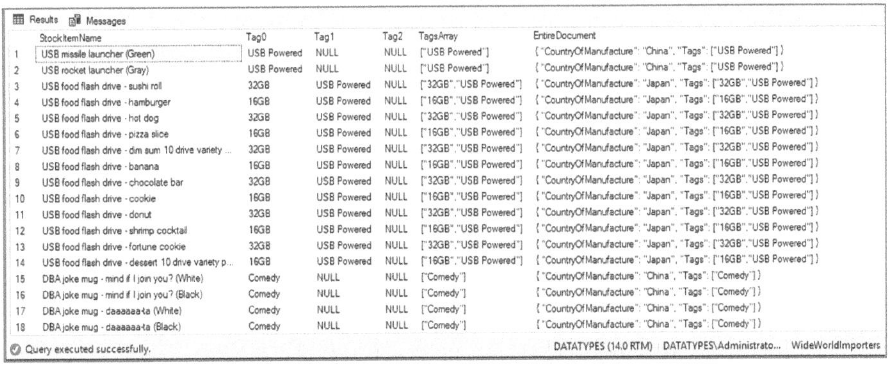

	StockItemName	Tag0	Tag1	Tag2	TagsArray	EntireDocument
1	USB missile launcher (Green)	USB Powered	NULL	NULL	["USB Powered"]	{ "CountryOfManufacture": "China", "Tags": ["USB Powered"] }
2	USB rocket launcher (Gray)	USB Powered	NULL	NULL	["USB Powered"]	{ "CountryOfManufacture": "China", "Tags": ["USB Powered"] }
3	USB food flash drive - sushi roll	32GB	USB Powered	NULL	["32GB","USB Powered"]	{ "CountryOfManufacture": "Japan", "Tags": ["32GB","USB Powered"] }
4	USB food flash drive - hamburger	16GB	USB Powered	NULL	["16GB","USB Powered"]	{ "CountryOfManufacture": "Japan", "Tags": ["16GB","USB Powered"] }
5	USB food flash drive - hot dog	32GB	USB Powered	NULL	["32GB","USB Powered"]	{ "CountryOfManufacture": "Japan", "Tags": ["32GB","USB Powered"] }
6	USB food flash drive - pizza slice	16GB	USB Powered	NULL	["16GB","USB Powered"]	{ "CountryOfManufacture": "Japan", "Tags": ["16GB","USB Powered"] }
7	USB food flash drive - dim sum 10 drive variety ...	32GB	USB Powered	NULL	["32GB","USB Powered"]	{ "CountryOfManufacture": "Japan", "Tags": ["32GB","USB Powered"] }
8	USB food flash drive - banana	16GB	USB Powered	NULL	["16GB","USB Powered"]	{ "CountryOfManufacture": "Japan", "Tags": ["16GB","USB Powered"] }
9	USB food flash drive - chocolate bar	32GB	USB Powered	NULL	["32GB","USB Powered"]	{ "CountryOfManufacture": "Japan", "Tags": ["32GB","USB Powered"] }
10	USB food flash drive - cookie	16GB	USB Powered	NULL	["16GB","USB Powered"]	{ "CountryOfManufacture": "Japan", "Tags": ["16GB","USB Powered"] }
11	USB food flash drive - donut	32GB	USB Powered	NULL	["32GB","USB Powered"]	{ "CountryOfManufacture": "Japan", "Tags": ["32GB","USB Powered"] }
12	USB food flash drive - shrimp cocktail	16GB	USB Powered	NULL	["16GB","USB Powered"]	{ "CountryOfManufacture": "Japan", "Tags": ["16GB","USB Powered"] }
13	USB food flash drive - fortune cookie	32GB	USB Powered	NULL	["32GB","USB Powered"]	{ "CountryOfManufacture": "Japan", "Tags": ["32GB","USB Powered"] }
14	USB food flash drive - dessert 10 drive variety p...	16GB	USB Powered	NULL	["16GB","USB Powered"]	{ "CountryOfManufacture": "Japan", "Tags": ["16GB","USB Powered"] }
15	DBA joke mug - mind if I join you? (White)	Comedy	NULL	NULL	["Comedy"]	{ "CountryOfManufacture": "China", "Tags": ["Comedy"] }
16	DBA joke mug - mind if I join you? (Black)	Comedy	NULL	NULL	["Comedy"]	{ "CountryOfManufacture": "China", "Tags": ["Comedy"] }
17	DBA joke mug - daaaaaa-ta (White)	Comedy	NULL	NULL	["Comedy"]	{ "CountryOfManufacture": "China", "Tags": ["Comedy"] }
18	DBA joke mug - daaaaaa-ta (Black)	Comedy	NULL	NULL	["Comedy"]	{ "CountryOfManufacture": "China", "Tags": ["Comedy"] }

Figure 9-10. *Results of using path variables and document context*

Using JSON_MODIFY()

So far, all the JSON functions that we have examined have allowed us to interrogate JSON documents. The JSON_MODIFY() function, however, as its name suggests, allows us to modify the contents of the JSON document. To explain this further, let's once again use the CustomFields JSON document for Stock Item ID 61, as used in Listing 9-4 and Listing 9-9.

The script in Listing 9-13 will modify the second element of the Tags array, so that the second element is updated to read 'Very Realistic Sound'. The output of the function is the complete, modified document.

Listing 9-13. Updating a Value

```
DECLARE @JSON NVARCHAR(MAX) ;

--The CustomFields column for StockItem ID 61 contains the
following JSON document:
--'{ "CountryOfManufacture": "China", "Tags": ["Radio
Control","Realistic Sound"], "MinimumAge": "10" }'

SET @JSON = (SELECT CustomFields FROM Warehouse.StockItems
WHERE StockItemID = 61) ;

IF ISJSON(@JSON) = 1
BEGIN
        SELECT JSON_MODIFY(@Json,'lax $.Tags[1]', 'Very
        Realistic Sound') ;
END
```

This script returns the results in Figure 9-11.

```
Results    Messages
     (No column name)
1    { "CountryOfManufacture": "China", "Tags": ["Radio Control","Very Realistic Sound"], "MinimumAge": "10" }




    ⊘ Query executed successfully.
```

Figure 9-11. *Results of updating a value*

You can see how the output from this function could be used subsequently to update a row in a table containing a JSON document, as demonstrated in Listing 9-14. Here, instead of passing in a variable as the JSON document, we pass in the CustomFields column from the table.

Listing 9-14. Using `MODIFY_JSON()` to Update a Row in a Table

```
USE WideWorldImporters
GO

UPDATE StockItems
        SET CustomFields = JSON_MODIFY(CustomFields,'lax
        $.Tags[1]', 'Very Realistic Sound')
FROM Warehouse.StockItems
WHERE StockItemID = 61 ;
```

The `MODIFY_JSON()` function can also be used to add an element to an array. Consider the query in Listing 9-15, which marks Stock Item ID 61 as being vintage, by adding an additional element to the `Tags` array. You will notice that because we are adding an additional value to an array, as opposed to updating an existing value, we have used the append keyword at the beginning of the path expression. Note, too, that because we are updating the array, rather than a single element, the array element in square brackets is not included.

Listing 9-15. Adding an Additional Array Element

```
USE WideWorldImporters
GO

UPDATE StockItems
        SET CustomFields = JSON_MODIFY(CustomFields,'append lax
        $.Tags', 'Vintage')
FROM Warehouse.StockItems
WHERE StockItemID = 61 ;
```

Let's now use the query in Listing 9-16, to examine the updated record.

Listing 9-16. Examining the Updated Record

```
USE WideWorldImporters
GO

SELECT
        StockItemName
    , JSON_VALUE(CustomFields,'lax $.Tags[0]') AS Tag0
    , JSON_VALUE(CustomFields,'lax $.Tags[1]') AS Tag1
    , JSON_VALUE(CustomFields,'lax $.Tags[2]') AS Tag2
    , JSON_QUERY(CustomFields,'lax $.Tags') AS TagsArray
FROM Warehouse.StockItems
WHERE StockItemID = 61 ;
```

This query returns the results in Figure 9-12. You will notice that the second array element now reads "Very Realistic Sound", and the array now contains a third element, marking the product as vintage.

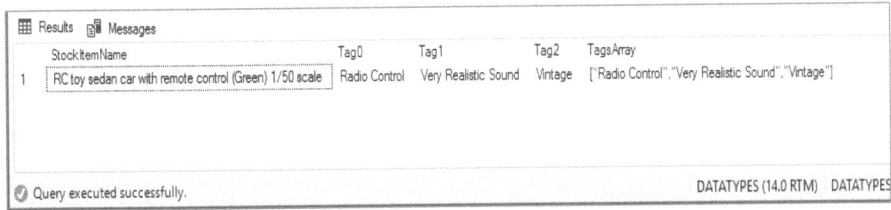

Figure 9-12. *Results of examining the modified row*

As you might expect, the MODIFY_JSON() function can also be used to delete data. This is achieved by updating a value with a NULL. For example, imagine that marking Stock Item ID 61 as vintage was a mistake. We could correct that mistake by using the query in Listing 9-17.

Listing 9-17. Deleting Data with MODIFY_JSON()

```
USE WideWorldImporters
GO

UPDATE StockItems
        SET CustomFields = JSON_MODIFY(CustomFields,
        'lax $.Tags[2]', NULL)
FROM Warehouse.StockItems
WHERE StockItemID = 61 ;
```

Rerunning the query in Listing 9-16 now returns the results shown in Figure 9-13.

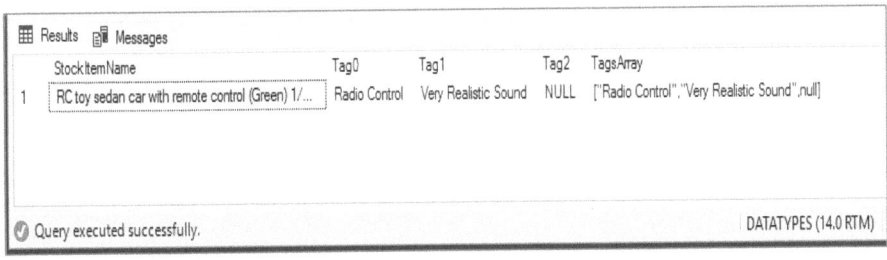

Figure 9-13. *Results of reexamining the modified row*

Alternatively, we could delete the entire Tags array, by using the query in Listing 9-18.

Listing 9-18. Deleting the Tags Array

```
USE WideWorldImporters
GO

UPDATE StockItems
        SET CustomFields = JSON_MODIFY(CustomFields,'lax
        $.Tags',NULL)
FROM Warehouse.StockItems
WHERE StockItemID = 61 ;
```

The query in Listing 9-19 allows us to examine the modified JSON document. You will notice that the Tags array no longer exists.

Listing 9-19. Examining the Modified Document

```
USE WideWorldImporters
GO

SELECT
        StockItemName
        , JSON_QUERY(CustomFields,'lax $') AS EntireDocument
FROM Warehouse.StockItems
WHERE StockItemID = 61 ;
```

The results of this query are shown in Figure 9-14.

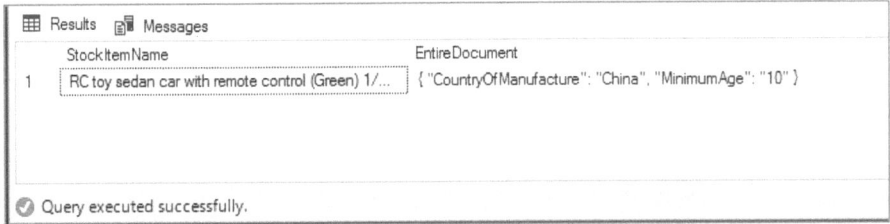

Figure 9-14. *Examining the modified JSON document*

Indexing JSON Data

When querying a table and filtering, grouping, or ordering by properties within a JSON document, you can improve the performance of your queries by indexing the data. Because JSON doesn't have its own data type, as XML does, there are no JSON indexes, as there are XML indexes. Instead, to index JSON properties, you must create a computed column that includes a JSON_VALUE() call, which mirrors the logic in the query you are optimizing. You can then create an index on the computed column, and SQL Server will use this index when optimizing the query.

Note Actual query performance depends on many factors, including system hardware, and other resource constraints, such as other queries that may be running simultaneously. The performance analysis in this section is meant to illustrate potential impacts, but performance should always be tested on your own servers, under realistic workloads.

Before demonstrating this technique, let's first take a baseline of query performance against the Warehouse.StockItems table. We will do this by turning on TIME STATISTICS in our session, before running the query that we are trying to optimize. Prior to this, however, we will first copy the data from the StockItems table to a new table. The reason for this is twofold. First, the StockItems table already has a number of indexes, which could potentially influence our results. The second reason is because the StockItems table is system-versioned with indexes. This means that when we alter the table, to add computed columns, instead of a simple ALTER TABLE script, we would be required to script out the data to a temp table, drop and re-create both the table and the archive table, and then script the data back in. This amount of code would distract from how to add a computed column, which is the point of this exercise. This is demonstrated in Listing 9-20.

Tip   We use DBCC FREEPROCCACHE to drop any existing plans from the plan cache. We then use DBCC DROPCLEANBUFFERS to remove pages from the buffer cache that have not been modified. This helps make it a fair test.

Listing 9-20. Creating a Performance Baseline

```
USE WideWorldImporters
GO

--Copy data to a new table

SELECT *
INTO Warehouse.NewStockItems
FROM Warehouse.StockItems

--Clear plan cache

DBCC FREEPROCCACHE

--Clear buffer cache
```

```
DBCC DROPCLEANBUFFERS

--Turn on statistics

SET STATISTICS TIME ON

SELECT
        StockItemName
      , JSON_VALUE(CustomFields,'lax $.Tags[0]') AS Tag0
      , JSON_VALUE(CustomFields,'lax $.Tags[1]') AS Tag1
      , JSON_VALUE(CustomFields,'lax $.Tags[2]') AS Tag2
      , JSON_QUERY(CustomFields,'lax $.Tags') AS TagsArray
FROM Warehouse.NewStockItems
WHERE JSON_VALUE(CustomFields,'lax $.Tags[0]') = 'Radio Control' ;
```

The results in Figure 9-15 show that the query took 6ms to execute.

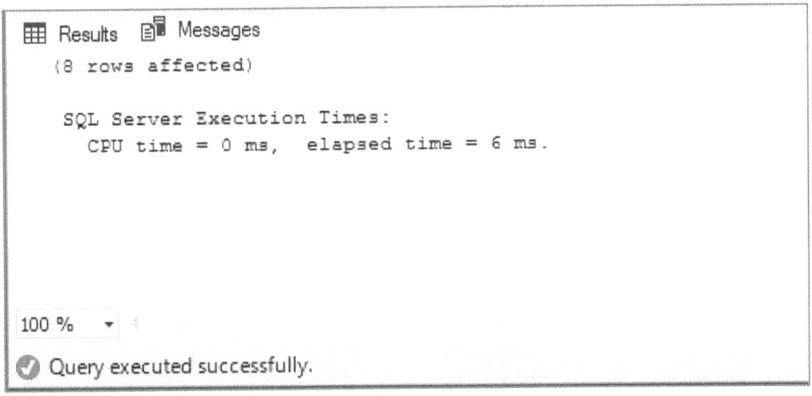

Figure 9-15. *Time statistics*

Let's now create a computer column on the Warehouse.StockItems table, using the same logic as in our WHERE clause. This can be achieved by using the script in Listing 9-21.

Listing 9-21. Creating a Computer Column

```
USE WideWorldImporters
GO

ALTER TABLE Warehouse.NewStockItems
        ADD CustomFieldsTag0 AS JSON_VALUE(CustomFields,
        'lax $.Tags[0]') ;
```

We can now index the computed column (which will also cause the column to be persisted, as opposed to calculated on the fly, when queried), by using the script in Listing 9-22.

Listing 9-22. Indexing the Computed Column

```
USE WideWorldImporters
GO

CREATE NONCLUSTERED INDEX NCI_CustomFieldsTag0
        ON Warehouse.NewStockItems(CustomFieldsTag0) ;
```

Let's now check the performance of our query, once again, by using the simplified script in Listing 9-23.

Listing 9-23. Checking Index Performance

```
USE WideWorldImporters
GO
--Clear plan chahe

DBCC FREEPROCCACHE

--Clear buffer cache

DBCC DROPCLEANBUFFERS
```

```
--Turn on statistics

SET STATISTICS TIME ON

SELECT
        StockItemName
      , JSON_VALUE(CustomFields,'lax $.Tags[0]') AS Tag0
      , JSON_VALUE(CustomFields,'lax $.Tags[1]') AS Tag1
      , JSON_VALUE(CustomFields,'lax $.Tags[2]') AS Tag2
      , JSON_QUERY(CustomFields,'lax $.Tags') AS TagsArray
FROM Warehouse.NewStockItems
WHERE JSON_VALUE(CustomFields,'lax $.Tags[0]') = 'Radio Control' ;
```

You can see from the time statistics shown in Figure 9-16 that the query executed in 3ms. That's a 50% performance improvement!

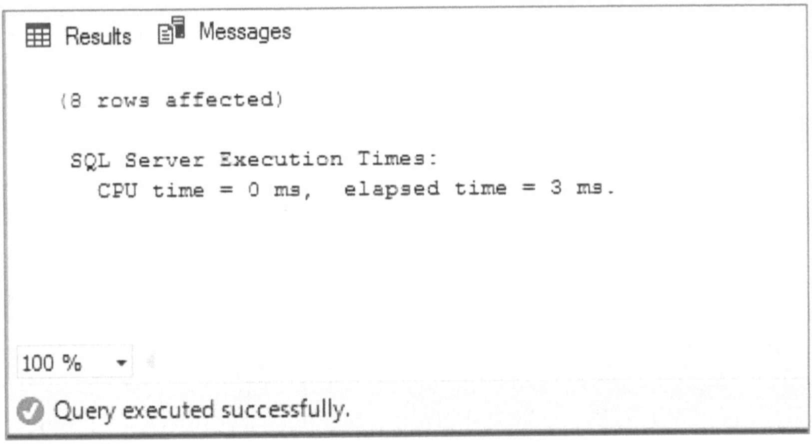

Figure 9-16. *Results of checking index performance*

> **Tip**   Because the NewStockItems table is so small, there is a
> chance that the query optimizer will choose not to use your index.
> If this happens, you can force it to use the index, by adding the
> WITH (INDEX(NCI_CustomFieldsTag0)) query hint. It is very
> important to note, however, that on a general basis, the optimizer is
> smart and rarely should be given hints. If you do need to use hints,
> then you should always work with the optimizer, rather than against it.
> For example, if the optimizer is incorrectly choosing a LOOP JOIN
> physical operator, force it to use either MERGE JOIN or HASH JOIN.
> Do not choose for it which is better!

Summary

SQL Server provides the ability to interrogate and modify JSON data with
the ISJSON(), JSON_VALUE(), JSON_QUERY(), and JSON_MODIFY() functions.
The ISJSON() function provides a simple validation that the document has
a valid JSON format. It returns 1 if the document is JSON and 0 if not.

The JSON_VALUE() function can be included in the SELECT list, WHERE
clause, ORDER BY clause, or GROUP BY clause of your query. It returns a
single scalar value from a JSON document that is passed to it, based on a
path expression.

The JSON_QUERY() function can also be included in the SELECT list,
WHERE clause, ORDER BY, or GROUP BY, but instead of returning a single
scalar value, it returns a JSON object or array. As with JSON_VALUE(),
the object returned is based on a path expression that is passed to the
function.

The MODIFY_JSON() function can be used to update, insert, or delete key values. A JSON document and a path expression are passed to the function, and the complete modified document is returned, making it easy to use in a standard UPDATE statement. The optional append keyword in the path expression is used to denote that the intention is to add an additional value to an array, as opposed to modifying an existing value. Updating a key value with NULL deletes the key.

Query performance can be improved by indexing the properties of a JSON document. This is achieved by creating a computed column, based on the path expression that you wish to optimize. You can then create an index on the computed column. This allows the query optimizer to use the index when the column containing the JSON data is queried.

CHAPTER 10

Understanding Spatial Data

Spatial data is data that describes a location. It is said that 80% of the world's data has a spatial element to it, so you can see how, for many data-tier applications, the ability to construct or interrogate spatial data may be critical. In this chapter, I will give an overview of spatial data and its implementation in SQL Server, before looking at the spatial standards that are used in the SQL Server implementation.

Note This chapter is intended to provide a theoretical overview of spatial data. Practical examples of usage can be found in Chapter 11.

Understanding Spatial Data

SQL Server provides two data types that are able to store spatial data: GEOMETRY and GEOGRAPHY. These data types are implemented through CLR (Common Language Runtime) and, behind the scenes, are .NET classes, which provide a series of methods and properties that allow you to interact with the data.

© Peter A. Carter 2018
P. A. Carter, *SQL Server Advanced Data Types*,
https://doi.org/10.1007/978-1-4842-3901-8_10

Caution   A geospatial object can be referred to as a geometry, with simple objects referred to as primitive geometries and collections of objects referred to as geometry collections. Because geometry is also the name of the data type that implements spatial data as a flat-earth model, this can cause confusion. Therefore, please note that when this chapter refers to a geospatial object, the word *geometry* will be used in lowercase. When referring to the data type, the word will be in uppercase letters (GEOMETRY).

The GEOMETRY data type uses the Euclidean coordinates system, which provides a flat-earth model. GEOMETRY is the correct data type to use when you are dealing with 2D objects or small objects that are not required to consider the curvature of the earth.

When using the GEOMETRY data type, objects are plotted using x and y axes. For example, the point in Figure 10-1 is located (or plotted) at 5, 3.

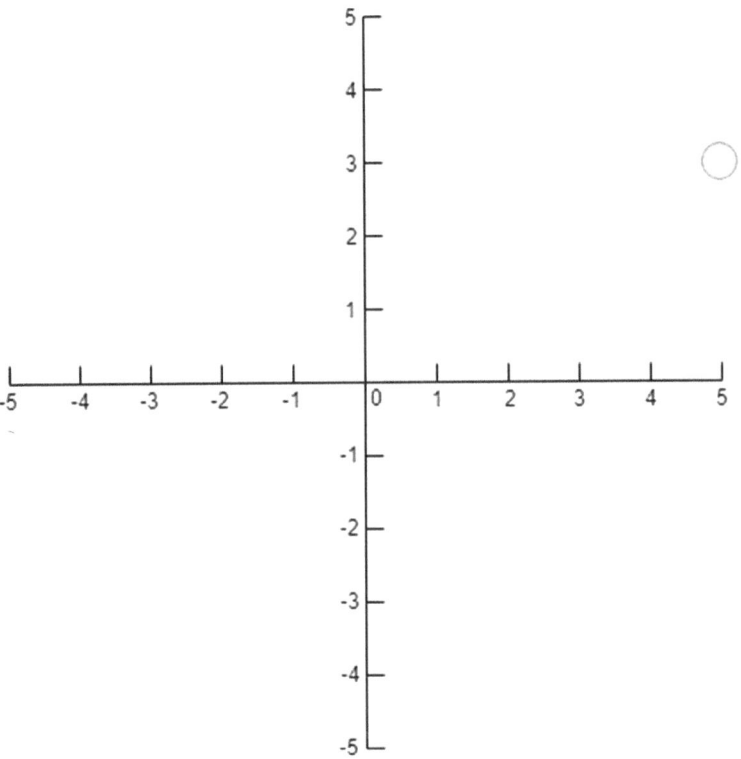

Figure 10-1. *Plotting a point in a Euclidean system*

Tip   A shape is referred to as a surface.

Similarly, the polygon (closed surface) in Figure 10-2 is drawn using the coordinates (-1 -1, -1 2, 2 2, 2 -1, -1 -1).

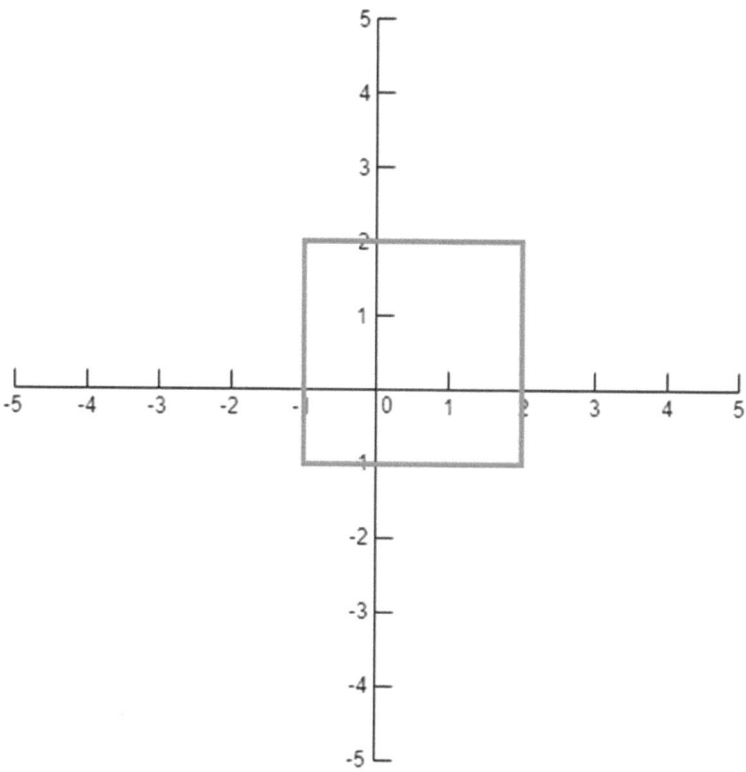

Figure 10-2. *Plotting a polygon in a Euclidean system*

The GEOGRAPHY data type, on the other hand, uses a round-earth model (or, actually, multiple round-earth models) and is ideal for representing 3D objects or large areas that must consider the curvature of the earth.

When working with data for a round-earth model, instead of x and y coordinates, a point can be identified by providing longitude and latitude. Lines of longitude, also called meridians, indicate the number of degrees east or west of a baseline of longitude, known as the prime meridian. The prime meridian runs through the borough of Greenwich in London and is regarded as the point where Eastern and Western Hemispheres meet. Sometimes, longitude coordinates are referenced as positive and negative values, with meridians east of the prime meridian being positive and meridians west of the prime meridian being negative. Other times, meridians will always be referred to as positive numbers, with either E (East) or W (West) being used to denote direction from the prime meridian. This is illustrated in Figure 10-3.

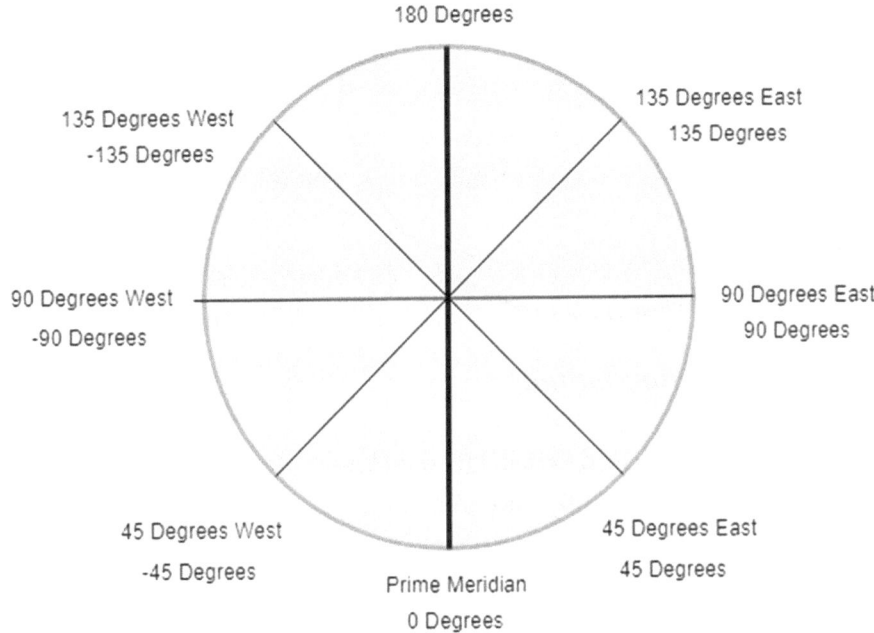

Figure 10-3. *Plotting longitude*

The equator is the central point between the North and South Poles. Latitude indicates the number of degrees north or south of the equator. Therefore, the equator has a latitude of 0 degrees. A line of latitude represents all points on Earth that have the same degree of latitude. As indicated in Figure 10-4, sometimes degrees of latitude are referred to as positive and negative values, with the Northern Hemisphere being positive values and the Southern Hemisphere being negative values. Other times, latitude is always referenced with positive values, differentiated by a suffix of either north latitude or south latitude.

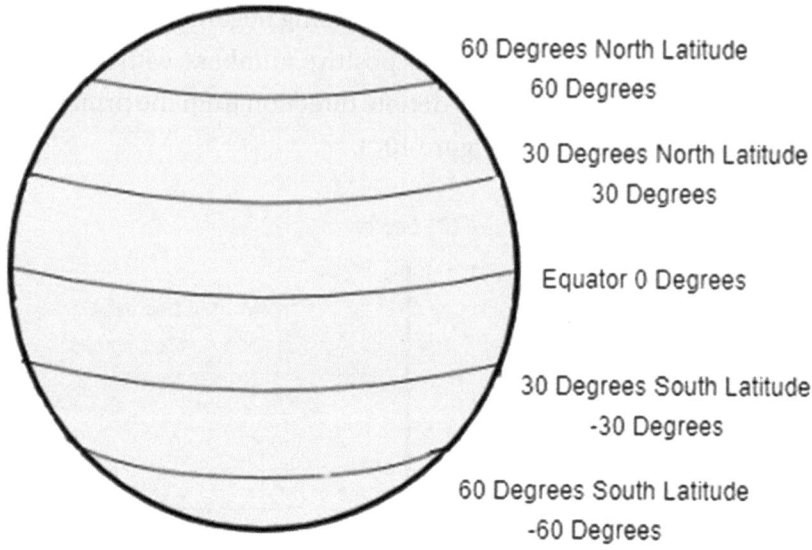

60 Degrees North Latitude
60 Degrees

30 Degrees North Latitude
30 Degrees

Equator 0 Degrees

30 Degrees South Latitude
-30 Degrees

60 Degrees South Latitude
-60 Degrees

Figure 10-4. *Plotting latitude*

Both the GEOMETRY and GEOGRAPHY data types allow you to instantiate a number of objects. These objects can be broken down into two categories. The first category is single geometry instances, also known as primitive geometries. The second category is geometry collections, also known as multipart geometries. Table 10-1 details the primitive geometries that are supported by SQL Server.

Table 10-1. *Primitive Geometries*

Geometry	Description
Point	A single point specified with a single set of coordinates
LineString	A path that joins multiple points, defined with multiple sets of coordinates. A line string can either be enclosed or unenclosed.*
CircularString	A path, in the form of an arc, between multiple points. There must be an odd number of points defined, with a minimum of three. The points cannot all be on the same axis (or it will be treated as a LineString).
CompoundCurve	A path that joins multiple sets of points. It can be defined by using multiple LineStrings and/or CircularStrings, to create surfaces such as circles or semicircles.
Polygon	An enclosed surface defined by specifying the points that map each corner of the polygon. Each side of the polygon is essentially a LineString.
CurvePolygon	An enclosed surface. This is similar to Polygon, except that it may be defined using LineStrings, CircularString, or CompoundCurves, instead of just LineStrings, as is the case of Polygon.

An enclosed surface is one in which the points used to define it join. Therefore, the first coordinates defined will also be the last coordinates defined.

Table 10-2 defines the multipart geometries that are supported by SQL Server.

Table 10-2. *Multipart Geometries*

Geometry	Description
MultiPoint	A collection of 0 or more points
MultiLineString	A collection of 0 or more LineStrings
MultiPolygon	A collection of 0 or more Polygons
GeometryCollection	A collection of 0 or more geometries. Can include any primitive or multipart geometries

In SQL Server 2017, a new surface type has been added, which is applicable only to the GEOGRAPHY data type. FullGlobe represents the entire surface of the planet. Therefore, it has an area, but no borders.

Tip   Practical examples of creating and working with primitive geometries and geometry collections can be found in Chapter 11.

Spatial Data Standards

Spatial data in SQL Server has been implemented around the standards set out by the Open Geospatial Consortium (OGC). These standards can be found at www.opengeospatial.org/standards/gml.

The following sections will provide an overview of the spatial surfaces available within SQL Server and how they can be represented, using well-known text and well-known binary. I will also discuss spatial reference systems.

Well-Known Text

The OGC lays out two methods of referencing spatial data: well-known text (WKT) and well-known binary (WKB). I'll first discuss WKT, and how each geometry can be specified using this approach. Table 10-3 details the WKT for each primitive geometry.

Table 10-3. *Primitive Geometry WKT*

Geometry	WKT	Description
Point	POINT(x y z m)	x indicates the x axis or longitude; y indicates the y axis or latitude; z is optional and indicates the elevation; m is optional and indicates the measure.
LineString	LINESTRING(POINT 1, POINT 2, POINT n)	
CircularString	CIRCULARSTRING(Start POINT, Anchor POINT 1, Anchor POINT n, End POINT)	
CompoundCurve	COMPOUNDCURVE((POINT 1, POINT n), CIRCULARSTRING(Start POINT, Anchor POINT, End POINT))	When an arc segment is a CircularString, the set of points must be prefixed with the geometry type. When the arc segment is a LineString, there is no need to specify the geometry type.

(continued)

Table 10-3. (*continued*)

Geometry	WKT	Description
Polygon	POLYGON((POINT 1, POINT 2, POINT n))	Polygon can also contain an inner Polygon, by defining a second set of points within parentheses, separated by a comma.
CurvePolygon	CURVEPOLYGON((CIRCULARSTRING(POINT 1, POINT 2, POINT n))	A CurvePolygon can also contain an inner CurvePolygon, by defining a second set of points within parentheses, separated by a comma.

Table 10-4 details the WKT for multipart geometries.

Table 10-4. *Multipart Geometry WKT*

Geometry	WKT
MultiPoint	MULTIPOINT((POINT 1),(POINT n))
MultiLineString	MULTILINESTRING((POINT 1, POINT n), (POINT 1, POINT n))
MultiPolygon	MULTIPOLYGON((POINT 1, POINT 2, POINT n),(POINT 1, POINT 2, POINT n))
GeometryCollection	GEOMETRYCOLLECTION(GEOMETRYTYPENAME(POINT n),GEOMETRYTYPENAME(POINT n))

Well-Known Binary

WKB can also be used to represent a geometry. This binary data is usually represented as a hexadecimal value. When working with WKB, you can control the order of bytes before specifying the surface type and, finally, the points specification. This section will discuss how each of the bytes in WKB are used.

The first byte indicates the byte order, in which 00 is big endian and 01 is little endian.

Tip Big endian means that the least significant byte in the sequence is stored last, and little endian means that the least significant byte is stored first.

The following four bytes represent the type of surface being defined. Table 10-5 describes the integer codes for each of these bytes.

Table 10-5. *WKB Surface Type Integer Codes*

Type	2D	Z	M	ZM
Point	0001	1001	2001	3001
LineString	0002	1002	2002	3002
CircularString	0008	1008	2008	3008
CompoundCurve	0009	1009	2009	3009
Polygon	0003	1003	2003	3003
CurvePolygon	0010	1010	2010	3010
MultiPoint	0004	1004	2004	3004
MultiLineString	0005	1005	2005	3005
MultiPolygon	0006	1006	2006	3006
GeometryCollection	0007	1007	2007	3007

The remaining bytes consist of eight-byte floats, which describe the points. For example, imagine a POINT, with coordinates 4, 2. Using big endian, the hexadecimal representation would be 0x0101000000000000000000 00010400000000000000040. If we break this down into its constituent parts

01—Indicates the byte direction

01000000—Indicates the surface type

0000000000001040—Indicates the x axis

0000000000000040—Indicates the y axis

Tip   Each byte is represented by a two-character hexadecimal reference.

Table 10-6 provides some examples of this.

Table 10-6. *WKB Examples*

WKT	WKB (Hexadecimal Representation—Big Endian)
POINT(1 1)	0x0101000000000000000000F03F000000000000 0F03F
POINT(1 1 1)	0x00000000010F0000000000000F03F0000000000 00F03F000000000000F03F000000000000F03F
LINESTRING(1 1, 2 2)	0x0000000000114000000000000F03F0000000000 00F03F00000000000000004000000000000000040
POLYGON((1 1, 2 2, 2 1, 1 1))	0x00000000010404000000000000000000000F03F00 0000000000F03F0000000000000004000000000000 000040000000000000000040000000000000F03F00 0000000000F03F000000000000F03F0100000002 0000000001000000FFFFFFFF0000000003
GEOMETRYCOLLECTION (POINT(1 1),POINT(2 2))	0x00000000010402000000000000000000F03 F000000000000F03F000000000000000400000 0000000040020000000100000000101000 00003000000FFFFFFFF0000000007000000000- 0000000010000000000100000001

Spatial Reference Systems

When working with the GEOGRAPHY data type, we must be aware that there is not one single unified view of how to represent the earth. Instead, there are multiple reference systems, known as spatial reference systems. Each system provides its own map projections. Each system is identified by an SRID (spatial reference identifier). The SRIDs supported by SQL Server can be found by interrogating the sys.spatial_reference_systems system table, as demonstrated in Listing 10-1.

Tip The earth cannot be modeled on a plane without being distorted. A map projection defines the distortions that are acceptable and unacceptable. Each projection allows for different distortions.

Listing 10-1. Discovering Spatial References

```
SELECT *
FROM sys.spatial_reference_systems ;
```

Partial results of this query can be found in Figure 10-5.

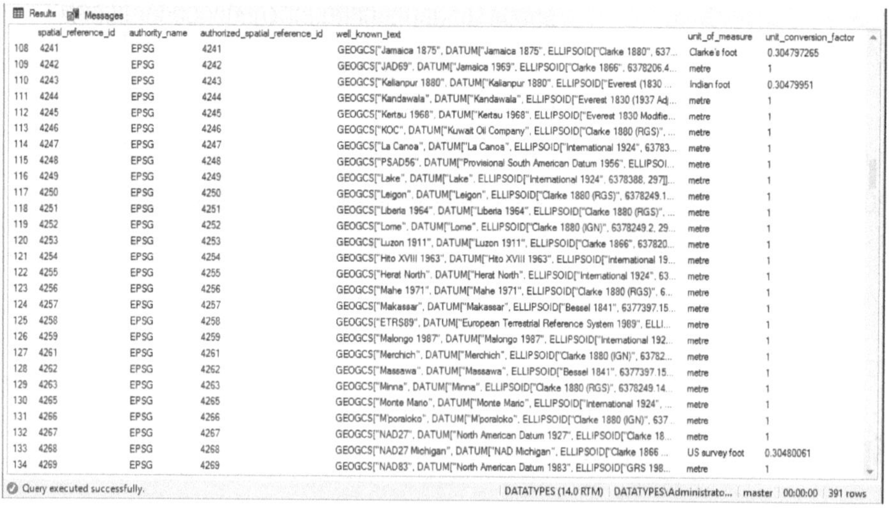

	spatial_reference_id	authority_name	authorized_spatial_reference_id	well_known_text	unit_of_measure	unit_conversion_factor
108	4241	EPSG	4241	GEOGCS["Jamaica 1875", DATUM["Jamaica 1875", ELLIPSOID["Clarke 1880", 637...	Clarke's foot	0.304797265
109	4242	EPSG	4242	GEOGCS["JAD69", DATUM["Jamaica 1969", ELLIPSOID["Clarke 1866", 6378206.4...	metre	1
110	4243	EPSG	4243	GEOGCS["Kalianpur 1880", DATUM["Kalianpur 1880", ELLIPSOID["Everest (1830 ...	Indian foot	0.30479951
111	4244	EPSG	4244	GEOGCS["Kandawala", DATUM["Kandawala", ELLIPSOID["Everest 1830 (1937 Adj...	metre	1
112	4245	EPSG	4245	GEOGCS["Kertau 1968", DATUM["Kertau 1968", ELLIPSOID["Everest 1830 Modifie...	metre	1
113	4246	EPSG	4246	GEOGCS["KOC", DATUM["Kuwait Oil Company", ELLIPSOID["Clarke 1880 (RGS)", ...	metre	1
114	4247	EPSG	4247	GEOGCS["La Canoa", DATUM["La Canoa", ELLIPSOID["International 1924", 63783...	metre	1
115	4248	EPSG	4248	GEOGCS["PSAD56", DATUM["Provisional South American Datum 1956", ELLIPSOI...	metre	1
116	4249	EPSG	4249	GEOGCS["Lake", DATUM["Lake", ELLIPSOID["International 1924", 6378388, 297]]...	metre	1
117	4250	EPSG	4250	GEOGCS["Leigon", DATUM["Leigon", ELLIPSOID["Clarke 1880 (RGS)", 6378249.1...	metre	1
118	4251	EPSG	4251	GEOGCS["Liberia 1964", DATUM["Liberia 1964", ELLIPSOID["Clarke 1880 (RGS)", ...	metre	1
119	4252	EPSG	4252	GEOGCS["Lome", DATUM["Lome", ELLIPSOID["Clarke 1880 (IGN)", 6378249.2, 29...	metre	1
120	4253	EPSG	4253	GEOGCS["Luzon 1911", DATUM["Luzon 1911", ELLIPSOID["Clarke 1866", 637820...	metre	1
121	4254	EPSG	4254	GEOGCS["Hito XVIII 1963", DATUM["Hito XVIII 1963", ELLIPSOID["International 19...	metre	1
122	4255	EPSG	4255	GEOGCS["Herat North", DATUM["Herat North", ELLIPSOID["International 1924", 63...	metre	1
123	4256	EPSG	4256	GEOGCS["Mahe 1971", DATUM["Mahe 1971", ELLIPSOID["Clarke 1880 (RGS)", 6...	metre	1
124	4257	EPSG	4257	GEOGCS["Makassar", DATUM["Makassar", ELLIPSOID["Bessel 1841", 6377397.15...	metre	1
125	4258	EPSG	4258	GEOGCS["ETRS89", DATUM["European Terrestrial Reference System 1989", ELLI...	metre	1
126	4259	EPSG	4259	GEOGCS["Malongo 1987", DATUM["Malongo 1987", ELLIPSOID["International 192...	metre	1
127	4261	EPSG	4261	GEOGCS["Merchich", DATUM["Merchich", ELLIPSOID["Clarke 1880 (IGN)", 63782...	metre	1
128	4262	EPSG	4262	GEOGCS["Massawa", DATUM["Massawa", ELLIPSOID["Bessel 1841", 6377397.15...	metre	1
129	4263	EPSG	4263	GEOGCS["Minna", DATUM["Minna", ELLIPSOID["Clarke 1880 (RGS)", 6378249.14...	metre	1
130	4265	EPSG	4265	GEOGCS["Monte Mario", DATUM["Monte Mario", ELLIPSOID["International 1924", ...	metre	1
131	4266	EPSG	4266	GEOGCS["M'poraloko", DATUM["M'poraloko", ELLIPSOID["Clarke 1880 (IGN)", 637...	metre	1
132	4267	EPSG	4267	GEOGCS["NAD27", DATUM["North American Datum 1927", ELLIPSOID["Clarke 18...	metre	1
133	4268	EPSG	4268	GEOGCS["NAD27 Michigan", DATUM["NAD Michigan", ELLIPSOID["Clarke 1866 ...	US survey foot	0.30480061
134	4269	EPSG	4269	GEOGCS["NAD83", DATUM["North American Datum 1983", ELLIPSOID["GRS 198...	metre	1

Figure 10-5. *Results of discovering spatial reference systems*

You will notice that the table provides various details about each SR, including its ID; the authority that develops and maintains it; the unit of measurement, along with the unit's conversion factor, against the base measure of meters; and, most interestingly, the WKT of the SR, as defined by the OGC.

Let's examine the WKT for Microsoft's implementation of SR (SRID 104001), which is detailed in Listing 10-2.

Listing 10-2. WKT for SRID 104001

```
GEOGCS["Unit Sphere",
    DATUM["Unit Sphere",
        SPHEROID["Sphere", 1.0, 0.0]
    ],
    PRIMEM["Greenwich",0.0],
    UNIT["Degree", 0.0174532925199433]
]
```

Note that the WKT uses a JSON format (see Chapters 6–9 for a detailed discussion of JSON) and specifies map projection details, such as the prime meridian and unit of measurement.

Caution   It is important to note that while a single GEOGRAPHY column can contain values based on multiple spatial reference systems, it is not possible to compare these values. Spatial functions require that all values have the same SRID, as they contain the background information required for calculations. That said, however, it is possible for a value to be converted to a different SRID before a comparison is performed.

SSMS and Spatial Data

SQL Server Management Studio (SSMS) provides graphical results, to
assist developers when working with spatial data. For example, imagine
a simple script, such as Listing 10-3, which declares a variable of type
GEOMETRY and sets it to contain a simple CurvePolygon.

Listing 10-3. Declaring a CurvePolygon with GEOMETRY

```
DECLARE @CurvePolygon GEOMETRY =
       'CURVEPOLYGON(CIRCULARSTRING(1 3, 3 5, 4 7, 7 3, 1 3))' ;

SELECT @CurvePolygon ;
```

The normal results tab will return the WKB of the surface, in
hexadecimal notation, as shown in Figure 10-6.

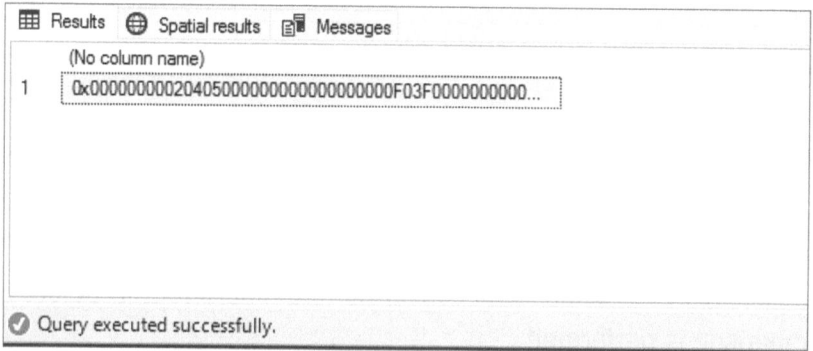

Figure 10-6. *Results in WKB*

You will notice, however, that a new tab, Spatial results, is present between the Results and Messages tabs. This pane can be seen in Figure 10-7.

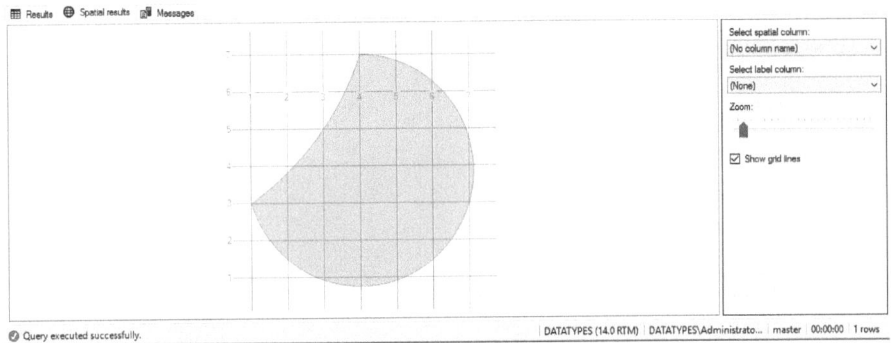

Figure 10-7. *Spatial results tab—GEOMETRY*

You will notice that we can see a graphical representation of our surface, along with some basic controls that allow us to zoom in and out and also flick between columns, if the result set contains multiple spatial columns. It is also possible to scroll around the object, by dragging the mouse.

Consider Listing 10-4. You will notice that the script is very similar to Listing 10-3, except that we are now declaring a variable of type GEOGRAPHY, instead of GEOMETRY.

Listing 10-4. Declaring a CurvePolygon with GEOGRAPHY

```
DECLARE @CurvePolygon GEOGRAPHY =
        'CURVEPOLYGON(CIRCULARSTRING(1 3, 3 5, 4 7, 7 3, 1 3))' ;

SELECT @CurvePolygon ;
```

Figure 10-8 shows the Spatial results tab for this script. You will notice that the grid has changed to degrees, as opposed to Euclidean style coordinates, to reflect that a round-earth model is now in use, and our coordinates are actually longitude and latitude.

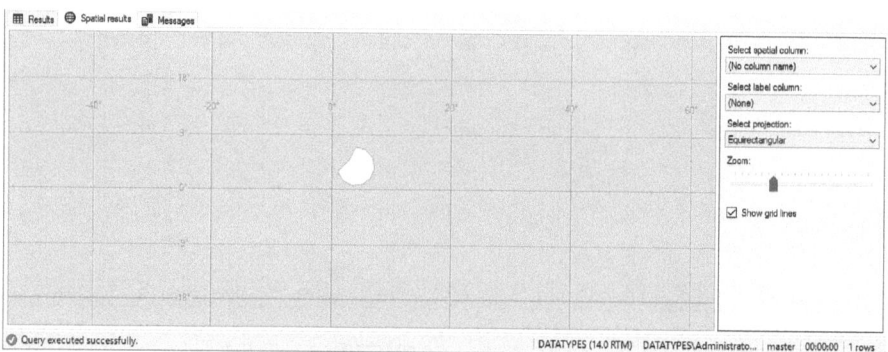

Figure 10-8. *Spatial results tab—GEOGRAPHY*

Summary

SQL Server provides two data types for working with spatial data: GEOMETRY and GEOGRAPHY. GEOMETRY allows you to work in a Euclidean (flat-earth) model, while GEOGRAPHY allows you to work in a round-earth model. SQL Server's spatial implementation is based on standards set out by the Open Geospatial Consortium (OGC).

Spatial shapes, known as surfaces, can be defined by using either well-known text (WKT) or well-known binary (WKB), which are standards set out by the OGC. When working with WKT, the surface type is defined by name, followed by its points specification. When working with WKB, you can control the order of bytes before specifying the surface type and, finally, the points specification. WKB is usually represented using hexadecimal notation.

SQL Server supports the following primitive and multipart geographies, as well as support for a FullGlobe geometry, when using GEOGRAPHY in SQL Server 2017 or later versions:

- Point

- LineString

- CircularString

- CompoundCurve

- Polygon

- CurvePolygon

- MultiPoint

- MultiLineString

- MultiPolygon

- GeometryCollection

SQL Server supports many spatial reference systems. This is important when working with GEOGRAPHY, as each SRID implements its own map projections. Surfaces with conflicting SRIDs can be stored in the same column but cannot be compared using spatial functions.

SQL Server Management Studio provides graphical results for spatial queries. The Spatial results tab allows you to move around a surface, zooming in and out. The grid will change between Euclidean coordinates and latitude/longitude, depending on the data type of the results.

CHAPTER 11

Working with Spatial Data

In Chapter 10, I discussed the concepts associated with spatial data, which SQL Server implements using the GEOMETRY and GEOGRAPHY data types. In this chapter, I will examine how to work with these data types. First, I will discuss the methods that can be used to construct surfaces, before reviewing how to query spatial data. Finally, you will see how to design and create spatial indexes.

Caution A geospatial object can be referred to as a geometry, with simple objects referred to as primitive geometries and collections of objects referred to as geometry collections. Because geometry is also the name of the data type that implements spatial data as a flat-earth model, this can cause confusion. Therefore, please note that when this chapter refers to a geospatial object, the word *geometry* will be used in lowercase. When referring to the data type, the uppercase word GEOMETRY will be used.

© Peter A. Carter 2018
P. A. Carter, *SQL Server Advanced Data Types*,
https://doi.org/10.1007/978-1-4842-3901-8_11

Constructing Spatial Data

The GEOMETRY and GEOGRAPHY data types expose a number of methods that can be used to interact with spatial data. Many of these methods form part of Open Geospatial Consortium (OGC) standards, while others are an extension of that standard. Table 11-1 details the methods that can be used for constructing geometries, all of which are from OGC specifications and are exposed through both GEOMETRY and GEOGRAPHY.

Table 11-1. *Methods for Constructing Geometries*

Spatial Type	From WKT	From WKB
Point	STPointFromText	STPointFromWKB
LineString	STLineFromText	STLineFromWKB
Polygon	STPolyFromText	STPolyFromWKB
Any Primitive Spatial Instance	STGeomFromText	STGeomFromWKB
MultiPoint	STMPointFromText	STMPointFromWKB
MultiLineString	STMLineFromText	STMLineFromWKB
MultiPolygon	STMPolyFromText	STMPolyFromWKB
Any Multi Spatial Instance	STMGeomCollFromText	STMGeomCollFromWKB

Each of these methods accepts two parameters. The first parameter is the well-known text (WKT) or well-known binary (WKB) of the spatial instance. The second parameter is the SRID (please refer to Chapter 10, for further details on SRIDs) that the spatial instance should use. When called against a column or variable of type GEOMETRY, 0 can be passed as the SRID, as map projections are not required in a Euclidean model (see Chapter 10). When called against a column or variable of type GEOGRAPHY, however, a valid SRID must be used, and passing 0 will result in an error being thrown by the .NET framework.

The script in Listing 11-1 will create a LineString in a variable of type GEOMETRY, by using well-known-text.

Listing 11-1. Creating a LineString with Well-Known Text

```
DECLARE @LineString GEOMETRY ;

SET @LineString = GEOMETRY::STLineFromText('LINESTRING(0 0, 4.5
5, 4.5 0, 0 0)', 0)

SELECT @LineString ;
```

The graphical results of this script can be found in Figure 11-1.

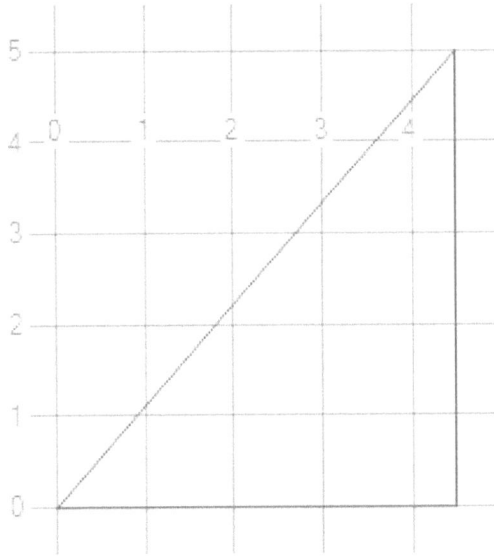

Figure 11-1. *Results of creating a LineString from WKT*

Alternatively, the same spatial instance could be created with WKB, by using the script in Listing 11-2.

Listing 11-2. Creating a LineString from a Well-Known Binary

```
DECLARE @LineString GEOMETRY ;

SET @LineString = GEOMETRY::STLineFromWKB(0x01020000000400000
000000000000000000000000000000000000000000000000012400000000000
0014400000000000000012400000000000000000000000000000000000000000
0000000, 0);

SELECT @LineString ;
```

Tip An additional extended method exists for constructing geometries. GeomFromGML allows you to instantiate an object, based on the Geography Markup Language (GML). For example, the script in Listing 11-3 will create a LineString from GML. A full discussion of GML is beyond the scope of this book, but the OGC specification can be found at www.opengeospatial.org/standards/gml.

Listing 11-3. Creating a LineString from GML

```
DECLARE @LineString GEOMETRY ;

SET @LineString =
GEOMETRY::GeomFromGml('<LineString xmlns="http://www.opengis.
net/gml">
<posList>0 0 4.5 5 4.5 0 0 0</posList> </LineString>', 0) ;

SELECT @LineString ;
```

SQL Server also provides an extended method for creating a spatial instance, by defining the x and y coordinates of a point. Listing 11-4 demonstrates the use of the Point method against a GEOMETRY variable. The method accepts three parameters. The first is the x axis coordinate, the second is the y axis coordinate, and the third is the SRID.

Listing 11-4. Using the Point Method

```
DECLARE @Point GEOMETRY ;

SET @Point = GEOMETRY::Point(10, 10, 0) ;

SELECT @Point ;
```

Spatial instances can also be instantiated by simply passing the well-known text or well-known binary as a value. For example, consider the script in Listing 11-5.

Listing 11-5. Passing Well-Known Text to a Variable

```
DECLARE @Polygon GEOMETRY ;

SET @Polygon = 'POLYGON((0 0, 10 0, 10 10, 0 10, 0 0))' ;

SELECT @Polygon ;
```

The graphical results of this script are displayed in Figure 11-2.

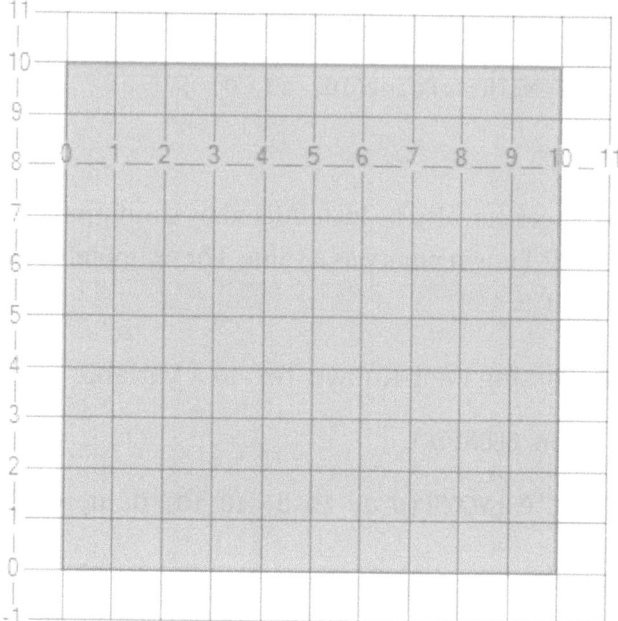

Figure 11-2. *Results of passing well-known text to a variable*

A spatial instance can be set to NULL, either by passing a NULL value directly or by using the read-only Null property of the instance. This is demonstrated in Listing 11-6.

Listing 11-6. Setting an Instance As NULL

```
--SET Variable As NULL by passing A NULL Directly

DECLARE @Polygon GEOMETRY ;

SET @Polygon = NULL ;

SELECT @Polygon ;
```

```
--Set A Variable As NULL by using the read-only Null Property
SET @Polygon = GEOMETRY::[Null] ;
SELECT @Polygon ;
```

It is possible to check the validity of your well-known text or
well-known binary by using the STIsValid method. If the instance is not
valid, it can be made valid, by using the MakeValid method. For example,
consider the script in Listing 11-7, which instantiates a Polygon that
overlaps itself.

Listing 11-7. Validating and Correcting an Instance

```
DECLARE @Polygon GEOMETRY ;
SET @Polygon = GEOMETRY::STGeomFromText('POLYGON((0 0, 10 10,
10 0, 0 10, 0 0))', 0) ;
SELECT
        @Polygon.STIsValid() AS IsValid
    , @Polygon.MakeValid().ToString() AS Fixed
    , @Polygon AS WKB ;
```

The results, shown in Figure 11-3, show that the original value has
returned 0, because it is not valid, and the fixed version has converted it to
a MultiPolygon.

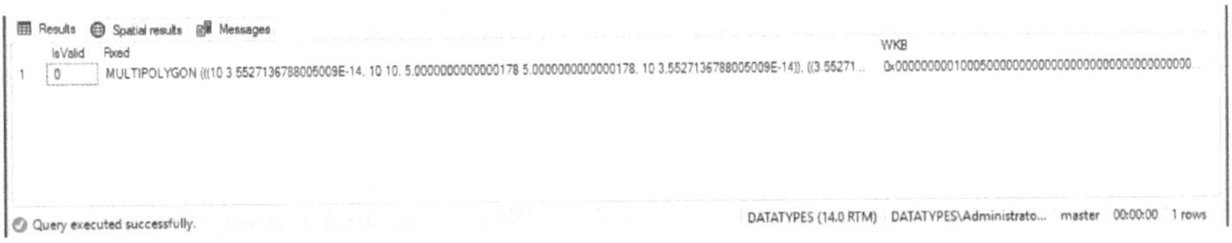

Figure 11-3. *Results of validating and correcting an instance*

The graphical results of the query are shown in Figure 11-4.

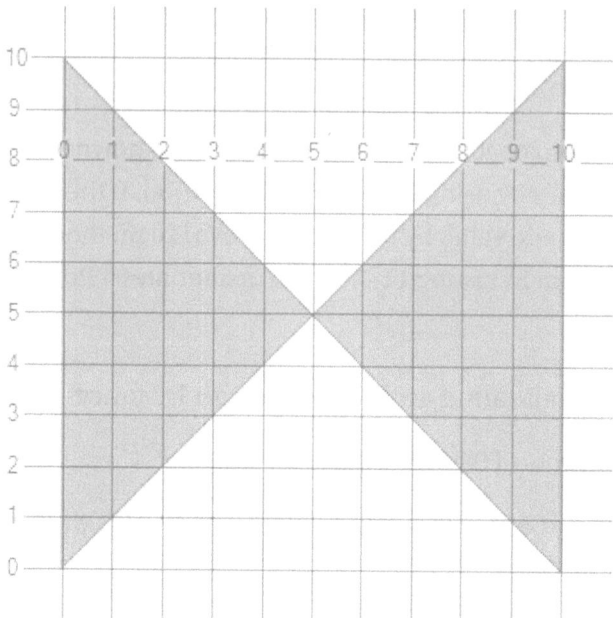

Figure 11-4. *Graphical results of validating and correcting an instance*

It is worth noting that because of the way in which spatial data is parsed, the use of STIsValid and MakeValid are somewhat limited. For example, consider the script in Listing 11-8, which attempts to instantiate a Polygon that is not enclosed.

Listing 11-8. Attempt to Instantiate a Non-enclosed Polygon

```
DECLARE @LineString GEOMETRY ;

SET @LineString = GEOMETRY::STGeomFromText('POLYGON((0 0, 10 10, 10 0, 0 10))', 0) ;
```

```
SELECT
        @LineString.STIsValid() AS IsValid
      , @LineString.MakeValid().ToString() AS Fixed
      , @LineString AS WKB ;
```

Because the Polygon is not enclosed, it fails to parse, and the error, illustrated in Figure 11-5, is thrown.

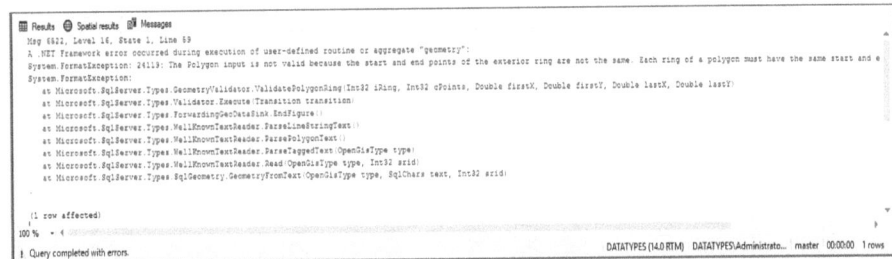

Figure 11-5. *Error thrown from instantiating a non-enclosed Polygon*

Querying Spatial Data

SQL Server provides numerous methods for interacting with spatial data. An overview of these methods can be found in Table 11-2. The table details the name of each method, whether it is an OGC standard or a Microsoft extension, and the data types the method works with. The final column provides a brief description of the method's ability.

Table 11-2. Spatial Methods

Method	OGC/Extended	Works With	Description
AsBinaryZM	Extended	GEOGRAPHY & GEOMETRY	Returns the well-known binary of a spatial instance, augmented with Z and M values, if present
AsGml	Extended	GEOGRAPHY & GEOMETRY	Returns the GML of a spatial instance
AsTextZM	Extended	GEOGRAPHY & GEOMETRY	Returns the well-known text of a spatial instance, augmented with Z and M values, if present
BufferWithCurves	Extended	GEOGRAPHY & GEOMETRY	Accepts a single parameter, which designates a distance. Returns an object representing all points, within the distance supplied, of the spatial instance against which the method was called
BufferWithTolerance	Extended	GEOGRAPHY & GEOMETRY	Accepts three parameters, denoting a distance from a spatial object, the tolerance, and a bit flag called relative that denotes if the tolerance is relative. Returns a spatial object representing the union of all points, whose distance from a geography instance is less than or equal to the distance specified, allowing for the specified tolerance

CurveToLineWithTolerance	Extended	GEOGRAPHY & GEOMETRY	Accepts two parameters, designating a tolerance, and a bit flag, indicating if the tolerance is relative. Returns a Polygon that represents an approximation of the instance against which the method was called, which contains no arc segments
EnvelopeAngle	Extended	GEOGRAPHY Only	Returns the maximum angle (in degrees) between the center point of an instance's bounding circle and a point in the geography instance
EnvelopeCenter	Extended	GEOGRAPHY Only	Returns the center of a spatial instance's bounding circle
Filter	Extended	GEOGRAPHY & GEOMETRY	Attempts to determine if a spatial object, passed as a parameter, intersects with the spatial object the method is called against. Returns 1 if the objects potentially intersect and 0 if they don't. Results may be unreliable and return false positives.
HasM	Extended	GEOGRAPHY & GEOMETRY	Validates if an M value has been specified for a spatial instance. Returns 1 if an M value exists and 0 if it does not

(continued)

Table 11-2. (continued)

Method	OGC/Extended	Works With	Description
HasZ	Extended	GEOGRAPHY & GEOMETRY	Validates if an Z value has been specified for a spatial instance. Returns 1 if a Z value exists and 0 if it does not
InstanceOf	Extended	GEOGRAPHY & GEOMETRY	Accepts a single parameter, which denotes a spatial type. Returns 1 if the spatial instance the method is called against is of the specified type or 0 if the instance is a different type
IsNull	Extended	GEOGRAPHY & GEOMETRY	Validates if a spatial instance is Null. Returns 1 if it is and 0 if it contains an object
IsValidDetailed	Extended	GEOGRAPHY & GEOMETRY	If an object is valid, the method returns 24400. If the object is not valid, it returns an error code describing why it is not valid. These error codes and their meanings can be found in Table 11-3.
Lat	Extended	GEOGRAPHY Only	Returns the latitude of a Point

Long	Extended	GEOGRAPHY Only	Returns the longitude of a Point
M	Extended	GEOGRAPHY & GEOMETRY	Returns the M value of the spatial instance
MakeValid	Extended	GEOGRAPHY & GEOMETRY	Converts a spatial instance that is not well-formed to a spatial instance that is well-formed
MinDbCompatibilityLevel	Extended	GEOGRAPHY & GEOMETRY	Returns the minimum database compatibility level, which provides support for the type of spatial object that the method is called against
NumRings	Extended	GEOGRAPHY Only	Called against a Polygon. Returns the total number of rings within the Polygon
Reduce	Extended	GEOGRAPHY & GEOMETRY	Accepts a single parameter that details a tolerance. Runs a Douglas-Peucker algorithm against a spatial instance and returns the approximate result*
ReorientObject	Extended	GEOGRAPHY Only	Changes the ring orientation of a Polygon

(continued)

311

Table 11-2. (continued)

Method	OGC/Extended	Works With	Description
RingN	Extended	GEOGRAPHY Only	Accepts a single parameter that defines a 1-based index. Returns a ring from the spatial instance the method is called against, which resides at the given index number
ShortestLineTo	Extended	GEOGRAPHY & GEOMETRY	Accepts a spatial object as a parameter. Returns a LineString that represents the shortest distance between the spatial object that the method is called against and the spatial object that is passed as a parameter
STArea	OGC	GEOGRAPHY & GEOMETRY	Returns the surface area of an instance
STAsBinary	OGC	GEOGRAPHY & GEOMETRY	Returns the WKB of an instance
STAsText	OGC	GEOGRAPHY & GEOMETRY	Returns the WKT of an instance

STBoundary	OGC	GEOMETRY Only	Returns the boundary of an instance. For example, calling the method against a Polygon will return a LineString marking the Polygon's border. Calling the method against a LineString will return a MultiPoint, with the start and end point of the LineString.
STBuffer	OGC	GEOGRAPHY & GEOMETRY	Accepts a single parameter, defining distance, and returns all points within that distance of instance. Distance can be positive or negative. When negative, the buffer will be interior to the boundary.
STCentroid	OGC	GEOMETRY Only	Returns the geometric center of an object. The instance that the method is invoked against must contain one or more Polygons; otherwise, the method returns NULL.
STContains	OGC	GEOGRAPHY & GEOMETRY	Evaluates if a spatial instance is contained by another. Should be called against the containing instance and accepts a single parameter for the contained instance. Returns 1 if the value is contained and 0 if it is not

(continued)

Table 11-2. (*continued*)

Method	OGC/Extended	Works With	Description
STConvexHull	OGC	GEOGRAPHY & GEOMETRY	Returns the smallest possible convex Polygon that contains the geometry instances that the method is called against
STCrosses	OGC	GEOMETRY Only	Validates if a given spatial instance crosses the spatial instance that the method is called against. Accepts a single parameter that describes the second spatial instance. Returns 1 if the second spatial instance crosses the first and 0 if it does not
STCurveN	OGC	GEOGRAPHY & GEOMETRY	Returns the curve of a LineString, CircularString, CompoundCurve, or MultiLineString spatial instance. Accepts a single parameter, which defines the index of the curve that should be returned, where a spatial instance has multiple curves
STCurveToLine	OGC	GEOGRAPHY & GEOMETRY	Creates an approximate polygonal spatial instance, from a curved spatial instance, such as a CircularString or CurvePolygon. Returns an instance of a LineString or Polygon, respectively.

STDifference	OGC	GEOGRAPHY & GEOMETRY	Returns the portion of a geography, which the method is called against, that does not reside within the boundaries of a second spatial instance, which is passed as a parameter to the method
STDimension	OGC	GEOGRAPHY & GEOMETRY	Returns that maximum number of dimensions of a spatial instance
STDisjoint	OGC	GEOGRAPHY & GEOMETRY	Validates if the intersection set between two geometries is empty. Returns 1 if it is empty or 0 if it is not empty. Accepts a single parameter, which is the spatial instance, to intersect with the spatial instance that the method is called against
STDistance	OGC	GEOGRAPHY & GEOMETRY	Calculates the approximate shortest distance between the spatial instance that the method is called against and a spatial instance that is passed to the method as a parameter
STEndpoint	OGC	GEOGRAPHY & GEOMETRY	Returns the final Point used to define a spatial instance

(continued)

315

Table 11-2. (*continued*)

Method	OGC/Extended	Works With	Description
STEnvelope	OGC	GEOMETRY Only	Returns a rectangular Polygon that encloses the spatial instance that the method has been called against
STEquals	OGC	GEOGRAPHY & GEOMETRY	Validates if the spatial instance that the method is called against has the same points set as a spatial instance that is passed to the method as a parameter. Returns 1 if the points sets are the same and 0 if they are not
STExteriorRing	OGC	GEOMETRY Only	When called against a Polygon, the method will return the Polygon's exterior ring.
STGeometryN	OGC	GEOGRAPHY & GEOMETRY	Returns a specific object from a geometry collection. Accepts a single parameter, which is the 1-based index of the object to return
STGeometryType	OGC	GEOGRAPHY & GEOMETRY	Returns the type of a spatial instance, as defined by the OGC

STInteriorRingN	OGC	GEOMETRY Only	When called against a Polygon, the method will return the Polygon's interior ring.
STIntersection	OGC	GEOGRAPHY & GEOMETRY	Returns a spatial instance that covers the area that is overlapped by a spatial instance that the method is called against and a spatial instance that is passed to the method as a parameter
STIntersects	OGC	GEOGRAPHY & GEOMETRY	Validates if the spatial instance, against which the method is called, overlaps with a spatial instance that is passed to the method as a parameter. Returns 1 if the instances intersect and 0 if they do not
STIsClosed	OGC	GEOGRAPHY & GEOMETRY	Checks if the start point and end point of a spatial object are the same. Returns 1 if they are the same and 0 if they are not the same
STIsEmpty	OGC	GEOGRAPHY & GEOMETRY	Validates if a spatial instance is empty or contains an object. Returns 1 if the instance is empty and 0 if it contains an object

(continued)

Table 11-2. (*continued*)

Method	OGC/Extended	Works With	Description
STIsRing	OGC	GEOMETRY Only	Validates if a spatial instance meets the following criteria: • Is a LineString • Does not intersect itself (except at end point) • Multiple objects do not intersect each other (except where the point of intersection is on both object's boundaries) • Is closed Returns 1 if the conditions are all true, or 0 if 1 or more of the conditions are false
STIsSimple	OGC	GEOMETRY Only	Validates if a spatial instance meets the following conditions: • Does not intersect itself (except at end point) • Multiple objects do not intersect each other (except where the point of intersection is on both objects' boundaries) Returns 1 if both conditions are true. Returns 0 if either condition is false

STIsValid	OGC	GEOGRAPHY & GEOMETRY	Validates that a spatial instance is well-formed. Returns 1 if the instance is well-formed and 0 if it is not well-formed
STLength	OGC	GEOGRAPHY & GEOMETRY	Returns the total length of a spatial object. For a Polygon, this is the length of the perimeter. For a Point, the length is always 0.
STNumCurves	OGC	GEOGRAPHY & GEOMETRY	Must be called against simple, primitive, one-dimensional spatial instances. Returns the number of curves in the instance
STNumGeometries	OGC	GEOGRAPHY & GEOMETRY	Returns the number of spatial objects in a multi-geometry. Returns 1 if the instance is a primitive geometry
STNumInteriorRing	OGC	GEOMETRY Only	Called against a Polygon and returns the number of interior rings that the Polygon contains
STNumPoints	OGC	GEOGRAPHY & GEOMETRY	Returns the number of Points that were used to describe a spatial instance

(continued)

319

Table 11-2. (*continued*)

Method	OGC/Extended	Works With	Description
STOverlaps	OGC	GEOGRAPHY & GEOMETRY	Validates if the spatial instance that the method was called against overlaps a spatial instance that is passed in as a parameter. Returns 1 if the objects overlap and 0 if they do not
STPointN	OGC	GEOGRAPHY & GEOMETRY	Accepts a single parameter, which describes a 1-based index location of an object within a multipart geometry. Returns the spatial object located at that index
STPointOnSurface	OGC	GEOMETRY Only	Returns an arbitrary point, within the interior of a spatial instance
STRelate	OGC	GEOMETRY Only	Validates if the spatial instance against which the method is called is related to a spatial instance that is passed as the first parameter to the method. Relationships are defined by the OGC Dimensionally Extended 9 Intersection Model (DE-9IM) pattern matrix. The pattern matrix used is the second parameter passed to the method.**

STSrid	OGC	GEOGRAPHY & GEOMETRY	Returns the SRID of the spatial instance, against which the method was called
STStartPoint	OGC	GEOGRAPHY & GEOMETRY	Returns the first Point used to define a spatial instance
STSymDifference	OGC	GEOGRAPHY & GEOMETRY	Returns a spatial instance, which includes all Point that are: • Within the spatial instance the method was called against • Within a spatial instance passed as a parameter • Not within both spatial instances
STTouches	OGC	GEOMETRY Only	Validates if the spatial instance against which the method was called spatially touches a spatial instance passed to the method as a parameter. Returns 1 if the instances touch and 0 if they do not

(continued)

321

Table 11-2. (*continued*)

Method	OGC/Extended	Works With	Description
STUnion	OGC	GEOGRAPHY & GEOMETRY	Returns a spatial instance that provides the union between the spatial instance against which the method was called and a spatial instance passed to the method as a parameter. The resultant union could be either a primitive or multipart geometry, depending on the inputs.
STWithin	OGC	GEOGRAPHY & GEOMETRY	Accepts a single parameter, which defines a spatial object. Validates if the spatial instance passed as a parameter is completely inside the spatial instance against which the method was called. Returns 1 if it is and 0 if it is not
STX	OGC	GEOMETRY Only	Called against a Point. Returns the Point's x coordinate

STY	OGC	GEOMETRY Only	Called against a Point. Returns the Point's y coordinate
ToString	Extended	GEOGRAPHY & GEOMETRY	Returns the well-known text of the spatial instance against which the method is called
Z	Extended	GEOGRAPHY & GEOMETRY	Returns the Z value of the spatial instance

*A Douglas-Peucker algorithm takes a curve composed of line segments and attempts to find a similar curve with fewer points.

**Details of the DE-9IM pattern matrices can be found at https://link.springer.com/referenceworkentry/10.1 007%2F978-3-319-17885-1_298.

Table 11-2 called out the IsValidDetailed, which has been implemented by Microsoft as an extended method. Table 11-3 details the error codes that can be thrown by the IsValidDetailed method, when a spatial instance is not valid.

Table 11-3. *IsValidDetailed Error Codes*

Error Code	Description
24400	The instance is valid.
24401	The instance is not valid, but the reason is unknown.
24402	The instance is not valid, because a point is isolated, which is not valid for the object's type.
24403	The instance is not valid, because some pair of polygon edges overlap.
24404	The instance is not valid because a polygon ring intersects itself or another ring.
24405	The instance is not valid, because a polygon ring intersects itself or another ring, and the ring number cannot be returned.
24406	The instance is not valid, because a curve degenerates to a point.
24407	The instance is not valid, because a polygon ring collapses to a line.
24408	The instance is not valid, because a polygon ring is not closed.
24409	The instance is not valid, because some portion of a polygon ring lies in the interior of a polygon.
24410	The instance is not valid, because a ring is the first ring in a polygon but is not the exterior ring.
24411	The instance is not valid, because a ring lies outside the exterior ring of its polygon.

(*continued*)

Table 11-3. (*continued*)

Error Code	Description
24412	The instance is not valid, because the interior of a polygon is not connected.
24413	The instance is not valid, because of two overlapping edges in a curve.
24414	The instance is not valid, because an edge of a curve overlaps an edge of another curve.
24415	The instance is not valid, because a polygon has an invalid ring structure.
24416	The instance is not valid, because in a curve, the edge is either a line or a degenerate arc with antipodal end points.

In addition to the methods detailed in Tables 11-1 and 11-2, there are also a number of aggregation methods available when using the GEOMETRY and GEOGRAPHY data types. These are detailed in Table 11-4.

Table 11-4. *Aggregation Methods*

Method	Description
CollectionAggregate	Creates a GeometryCollection from a set of spatial objects
ConvexHullAggregate	Returns the convex hull of a set of spatial objects
EnvelopeAggregate	Returns a bounding spatial object for a set of spatial objects
UnionAggregate	Returns a union of a set of spatial objects

Now that you are aware of the spatial methods that SQL Server exposes, you can look at how they can be employed in practice, by using the WideWorldImporters database. Imagine that we are responsible for delivery routes, and we must plan a route in Alabama.

The first thing that we want to do is validate our data. Are all our customers, with delivery locations marked as being in Alabama, actually within the Alabama state border? The Sales.Customers table contains a GEOGRAPHY column called DeliveryLocation, with each row containing a Point object that maps their delivery address. We can use the STWithin method against this column, passing in the Border column from the Application.StateProvinces table, which maps the state border. This is demonstrated in Listing 11-9.

Listing 11-9. Validating That All Addresses Are Within the Alabama State Border

```
DECLARE @StateBorder GEOGRAPHY = (
                SELECT Border
                FROM Application.StateProvinces
                WHERE StateProvinceName = 'Alabama') ;
SELECT
            Customer.CustomerName AS CustomerName
          , City.CityName AS City
          , Customer.DeliveryLocation.ToString() AS
            DeliveryLocation
FROM SALES.Customers Customer
INNER JOIN Application.Cities City
        ON City.CityID = Customer.DeliveryCityID
WHERE Customer.DeliveryLocation.STWithin(@StateBorder) = 1 ;
```

The results of this query (which are displayed in Figure 11-6) validate that all 16 customers with Alabama delivery addresses actually reside in Alabama.

	CustomerName	City	DeliveryLocation
1	Tailspin Toys (Eulaton, AL)	Eulaton	POINT (-85.9124671 33.6456587)
2	Tailspin Toys (Jemison, AL)	Jemison	POINT (-86.7466522 32.9598451)
3	Tailspin Toys (Nanafalia, AL)	Nanafalia	POINT (-87.9880691 32.1129257)
4	Tailspin Toys (Guin, AL)	Guin	POINT (-87.9147494 33.9656594)
5	Tailspin Toys (Belgreen, AL)	Belgreen	POINT (-87.8664241 34.474818)
6	Tailspin Toys (Saks, AL)	Saks	POINT (-85.8396879 33.6987135)
7	Wingtip Toys (Tuscaloosa, AL)	Tuscaloosa	POINT (-87.5691735 33.2098407)
8	Wingtip Toys (Highland Home, AL)	Highland Home	POINT (-86.3138546 31.9534835)
9	Wingtip Toys (Coker, AL)	Coker	POINT (-87.6877882 33.2459512)
10	Wingtip Toys (Robertsdale, AL)	Robertsdale	POINT (-87.7119324 30.5538048)
11	Wingtip Toys (Broomtown, AL)	Broomtown	POINT (-85.5216276 34.3606453)
12	Wingtip Toys (Marion Junction, AL)	Marion Junction	POINT (-87.2388839 32.437358)
13	Wingtip Toys (Flomaton, AL)	Flomaton	POINT (-87.2608071 31.000182)
14	Risto Valbe	Bazemore	POINT (-87.7000188 33.8945496)
15	Manca Hrastovsek	Southside	POINT (-86.0224718 33.9245425)
16	Emma Salpa	Rogersville	POINT (-87.2947417 34.8256425)

Query executed successfully.

Figure 11-6. Results of validating that all addresses are within the Alabama state border

Next, we want to check the distance of each delivery location from our depot and order the results by that distance. This will help us plan the route. This technique is known as finding nearest neighbors and is demonstrated in Listing 11-10, which calculates the distance and orders the results, by using the DeliveryLocation from the Application.SystemParameters table, which marks the location of WideWorldImporters.

Note   The WideWorldImporters depot is in California, but while the distances to the Alabama locations are vast, they still allow us to plan the driver's most sensible route.

Listing 11-10. Finding Nearest Neighbors

```
DECLARE @StateBorder GEOGRAPHY = (
                SELECT Border
                FROM Application.StateProvinces
                WHERE StateProvinceName = 'Alabama') ;

DECLARE @Office GEOGRAPHY = (
                SELECT DeliveryLocation
                FROM Application.SystemParameters) ;

DECLARE @MilesRatio INT = 0.000621371 ;

SELECT
            Customer.CustomerName AS CustomerName
          , City.CityName AS City
          , Customer.DeliveryLocation.ToString() AS
          DeliveryLocation
          , Customer.DeliveryLocation.STDistance(@Office) * @
          MilesRatio AS DeliveryDistanceMiles
FROM SALES.Customers Customer
INNER JOIN Application.Cities City
        ON City.CityID = Customer.DeliveryCityID
WHERE Customer.DeliveryLocation.STWithin(@StateBorder) = 1
ORDER BY DeliveryDistanceMiles ;
```

The results of this query can be seen in Figure 11-7.

	CustomerName	City	DeliveryLocation	DeliveryDistanceMiles
1	Tailspin Toys (Belgreen, AL)	Belgreen	POINT (-87.8664241 34.474818)	1939.75915206454
2	Tailspin Toys (Guin, AL)	Guin	POINT (-87.9147494 33.9656594)	1947.58181832539
3	Risto Valbe	Bazemore	POINT (-87.7000188 33.8945496)	1960.8273185532
4	Emma Salpa	Rogersville	POINT (-87.2947417 34.8256425)	1964.04782212196
5	Wingtip Toys (Coker, AL)	Coker	POINT (-87.6877882 33.2459512)	1975.68612346646
6	Wingtip Toys (Tuscaloosa, AL)	Tuscaloosa	POINT (-87.5691735 33.2098407)	1982.99232324433
7	Tailspin Toys (Nanafalia, AL)	Nanafalia	POINT (-87.9880691 32.1129257)	1986.00460852848
8	Wingtip Toys (Marion Junction, AL)	Marion Junction	POINT (-87.2388839 32.437358)	2019.10760853923
9	Tailspin Toys (Jemison, AL)	Jemison	POINT (-86.7466522 32.9598451)	2033.72250552745
10	Wingtip Toys (Robertsdale, AL)	Robertsdale	POINT (-87.7119324 30.5538048)	2041.87457914395
11	Manca Hrastovsek	Southside	POINT (-86.0224718 33.9245425)	2051.87676799238
12	Wingtip Toys (Flomaton, AL)	Flomaton	POINT (-87.2608071 31.000182)	2054.42859013072
13	Tailspin Toys (Eulaton, AL)	Eulaton	POINT (-85.9124671 33.6456587)	2063.91858396912
14	Tailspin Toys (Saks, AL)	Saks	POINT (-85.8396879 33.6987135)	2066.73705103033
15	Wingtip Toys (Broomtown, AL)	Broomtown	POINT (-85.5216276 34.3606453)	2070.07110349507
16	Wingtip Toys (Highland Home, AL)	Highland Home	POINT (-86.3138546 31.9534835)	2081.62431628622

Figure 11-7. *Results of finding nearest neighbors*

You will notice that in Listing 11-10, the distance is multiplied by 0.000621371. This is because the distance is natively in meters. The unit of measurement of distance is associated with the SRID, so we can double check this, by enhancing our query to expose the SRID, as shown in Listing 11-11. This query exposes the STRid property of each spatial instance and uses this value to join to the sys.spatial_reference_systems system table, to expose the unit of measure column.

Listing 11-11. Exposing the SRID

```
DECLARE @StateBorder GEOGRAPHY = (
                SELECT Border
                FROM Application.StateProvinces
                WHERE StateProvinceName = 'Alabama') ;

DECLARE @Office GEOGRAPHY = (
                SELECT DeliveryLocation
                FROM Application.SystemParameters) ;

DECLARE @MilesRatio INT = 0.000621371 ;

SELECT
            Customer.CustomerName AS CustomerName
        , City.CityName AS City
        , Customer.DeliveryLocation.ToString() AS
        DeliveryLocation
        , Customer.DeliveryLocation.STDistance(@Office) *
        @MilesRatio AS DeliveryDistanceMiles
        , Customer.DeliveryLocation.STSrid AS SRID
        , srid.unit_of_measure
FROM SALES.Customers Customer
INNER JOIN Application.Cities City
        ON City.CityID = Customer.DeliveryCityID
INNER JOIN sys.spatial_reference_systems srid
        ON srid.spatial_reference_id = Customer.
DeliveryLocation.STSrid
WHERE Customer.DeliveryLocation.STWithin(@StateBorder) = 1
ORDER BY DeliveryDistanceMiles ;
```

While we know that all deliveries are in the state of Alabama, we may wish to discover how big our actual delivery area is. We can achieve this by creating an envelope and then calculating its area. This approach uses the EnvelopeAggregate extended method and the STArea method, as demonstrated in Listing 11-12.

Listing 11-12. Calculating the Area of an Aggregate Envelope

```
DECLARE @StateBorder GEOGRAPHY = (
                SELECT Border
                FROM Application.StateProvinces
                WHERE StateProvinceName = 'Alabama') ;

SELECT
          GEOGRAPHY::EnvelopeAggregate(DeliveryLocation).
          STArea() AS AreaInSquareMetres
        , GEOGRAPHY::EnvelopeAggregate(DeliveryLocation)
          AS EnvelopeObject
FROM Sales.Customers
WHERE DeliveryLocation.STWithin(@StateBorder) = 1 ;
```

The results of this query can be seen in Figure 11-8.

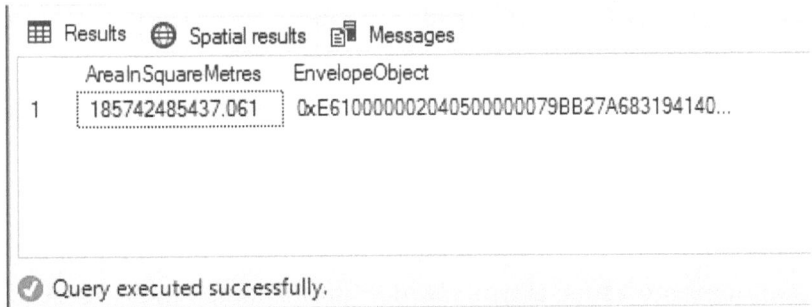

Figure 11-8. Results of calculating the area of an aggregate envelope

The graphical results of the query in Listing 11-12 are illustrated in Figure 11-9.

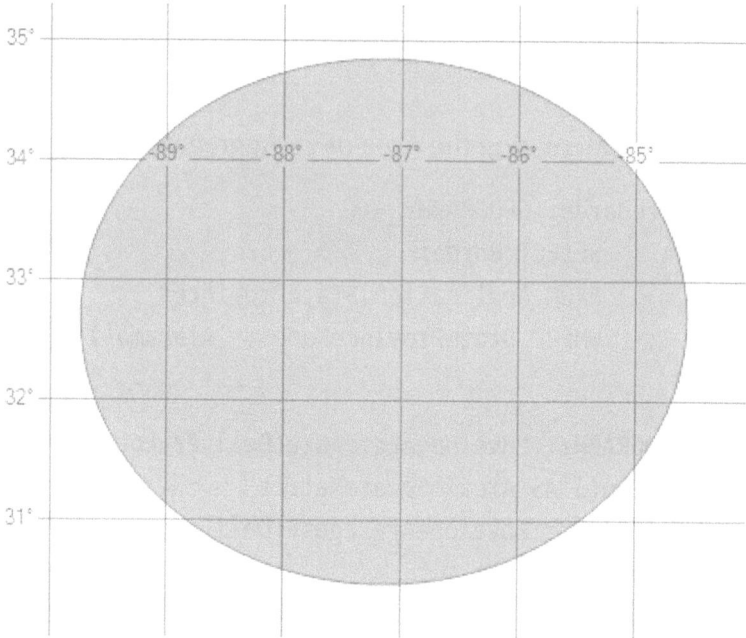

Figure 11-9. *Graphical results of calculating the area of an aggregate envelope*

Indexing Spatial Data

The following sections provide an overview of spatial indexes, before demonstrating how to create them.

Understanding Spatial Indexes

Spatial indexes are a special type of index, implemented in SQL Server, that can improve the performance of certain queries against spatial data types. Table 11-5 describes the predicate patterns that can benefit from spatial indexes, when used in a WHERE or JOIN clause.

Table 11-5. *Queries That Can Benefit from Spatial Indexes*

Data Type	Method	Operator
GEOMETRY & GEOGRAPHY	STDistance	<
		<=
GEOMETRY & GEOGRAPHY	STEquals	=
GEOMETRY & GEOGRAPHY	STIntersects	=
GEOMETRY Only	STContains	=
GEOMETRY Only	STOverlaps	=
GEOMETRY Only	STTouches	=
GEOMETRY Only	STWithin	=

Just as with traditional indexes, spatial indexes use a B-Tree structure (see Chapter 5 for further information on B-Tree indexes), meaning that the spatial data must be represented in a linear order. To achieve this, SQL Server decomposes space into a nested grid system, before building an index.

The grid will have four layers. Each cell in the first (Level 1) grid will contain another (Level 2) grid, and so on. Each of the four grid layers can be given a separate density, with low density being defined as 4 × 4 cells, medium density as 8 × 8 cells, and high density as 16 × 16 cells. Each cell within the grid is numbered using a Hilbert space-filling curve algorithm.

Tip   A full discussion of the Hilbert space-filling curve is beyond the scope of this book, but further details can be found in many locations online, including mathworld.wolfram.com/HilbertCurve.html.

Once the grid system has been created, SQL Server reads the data from the column row by row. For each row, it will associate the spatial object with each Level 1 cell that it touches. For each touched cell, it will then drop down to Level 2 and repeat the process. This then happens again for Level 3 and Level 4, as required. This process is called tessellation. The output of the process is a set of touched cells, which can be stored in the index and subsequently used to calculate their spatial position, relative to other objects.

The tessellation process requires a bounding box, and this can behave differently, depending on the tessellation system used. The tessellation systems are data-type dependent and you will have the option of using automatic coordinates for the bounding box or defining your own.

You may further configure the tessellation process, by defining how many tessellation cells should be used. What this means is that you can cap the maximum number of touched cells recorded for a single object. It is worth noting, however, that this only affects Levels 2 through 4. Level 1 will record as many cells as the object touches, regardless of your configuration.

Creating Spatial Indexes

To demonstrate the creation of a spatial index, we will create an index on the Border column of the Application.StateProvinces table in the WideWorldImporters database. We will use an auto grid system, and we will configure medium density for Levels 1 to 3, with high density for Level 4.

To create the index through SQL Server Management Studio, drill through Databases ➤ WideWorldImporters ➤ Tables ➤ Application. StateProvinces in Object Explorer. Then select New Index ➤ Spatial Index from the context menu of the Indexes folder. This will cause the General page of the New Index dialog bog to be invoked, as shown in Figure 11-10.

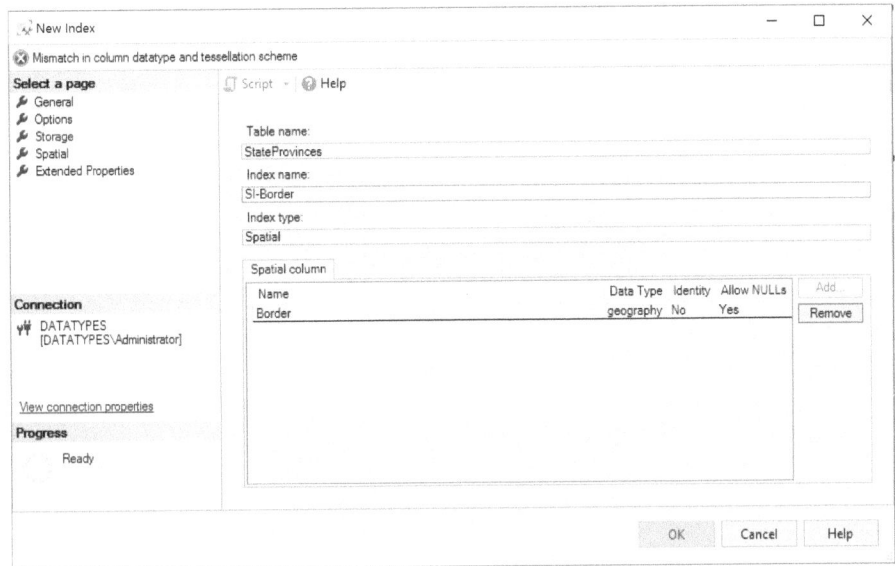

Figure 11-10. *New Index dialog box—General page*

On this page of the dialog box, we have given the index a meaningful name and used the Add button, to add the column that we wish to index. We will now progress to the Options page, which is illustrated in Figure 11-11.

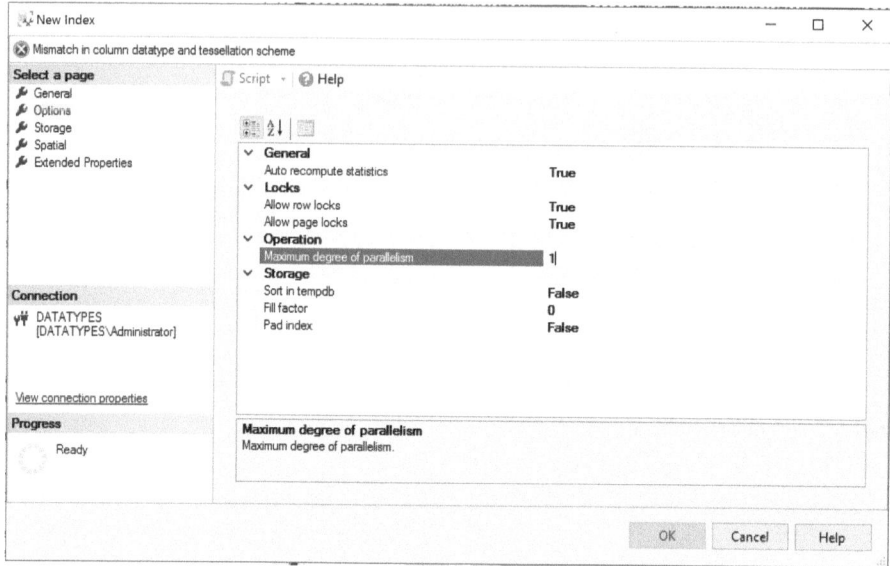

Figure 11-11. *New Index dialog box—Options page*

The Options page will look familiar to anyone who has created a traditional index. Table 11-6 details each of the options available.

Table 11-6. *Spatial Index Options*

Option	Description
Auto Recompute Statistics	Specifies if statistics should be updated automatically when they are deemed out of date
Allow Row Locks	Specifies if row locks can be acquired when accessing the index
Allow Page Locks	Specifies if page locks can be acquired when accessing the index
Maximum Degree of Parallelism	Has no effect for building primary spatial indexes, as this operation is always single-threaded

(continued)

Table 11-6. (*continued*)

Option	Description
Sort in TempDB	If specified, Sort in TempDB will cause the intermediate result set to be stored in TempDB, as opposed to the user database. This could mean that the index is built faster.
Fill Factor	Specifies a percentage of free space that will be left on each index page at the lowest level of the index. The default is 0 (100% full), meaning that only enough space for a single row will be left. Specifying a percentage lower than 100—for example, specifying 70—will leave 30% free space, which can reduce page splits, if there are likely to be frequent row inserts.
Pad Index	Applies a fill factor (see preceding) to the intermediate levels of a B-Tree

On the Storage page, illustrated in Figure 11-12, you can specify the filegroup that the index will be created on. Usually, it is best for indexes to be aligned with the same filegroup (or partition schema) as their table, for performance. From a maintenance perspective, it may be helpful to store the index on a different filegroup when the table is partitioned. If you don't, the index will have to be dropped before the table is repartitioned.

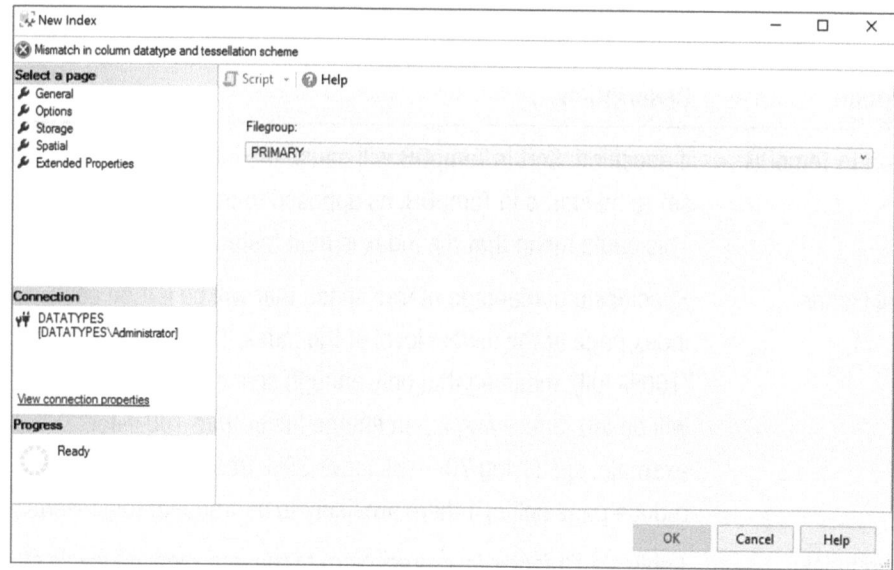

Figure 11-12. *New Index dialog box—Storage page*

The Spatial page is shown in Figure 11-13. This is where we can configure the spatial specific options of our index. In the General section of the page, we can choose our tessellation system—either automatic or manual. If we select manual, the Grids area of the page will become active, and we can select the grid densities that we would like to use. If the manual geometry system is selected, the Bounding Box area of the page will also become active, and we can specify our bounding box coordinates.

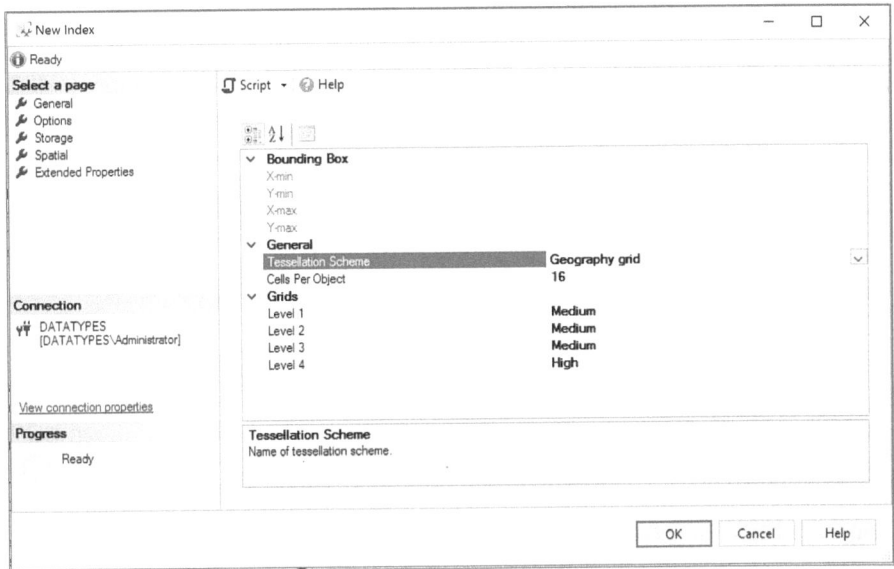

Figure 11-13. *New Index dialog box—Spatial page*

Tip   A geometry system must be used on a GEOMETRY column and a geography system must be used on a GEOGRAPHY column.

Alternatively, we could use T-SQL to create the index. The script in Listing 11-13 will create the same index as discussed previously.

Listing 11-13. Creating a Spatial Index

```
USE WideWorldImporters
GO

CREATE SPATIAL INDEX [SI-Border]
ON Application.StateProvinces (Border)
USING  GEOGRAPHY_GRID
WITH (GRIDS =(LEVEL_1 = MEDIUM,LEVEL_2 = MEDIUM,LEVEL_3 =
MEDIUM,LEVEL_4 = HIGH),
            CELLS_PER_OBJECT = 16,
```

```
        PAD_INDEX = OFF,
        STATISTICS_NORECOMPUTE = OFF,
        SORT_IN_TEMPDB = OFF,
        DROP_EXISTING = OFF,
        ONLINE = OFF,
        ALLOW_ROW_LOCKS = ON,
        ALLOW_PAGE_LOCKS = ON, MAXDOP = 1)
ON [PRIMARY] ;
```

Summary

Spatial objects can be constructed by using various means. They can be created using OGC standard methods, from either well-known text or well-known binary, or they can be constructed by using a Microsoft extended method from GML. SQL Server also supports passing well-known text directly into a variable of a table's cell.

A wealth of methods exist that allow developers to easily interact with spatial data. Commonly used methods include STDistance, which will return the distance between two geometries, and STWithin, which will check if an instance resides within the same space as another. There are also aggregate methods that allow multiple instances to have union, envelope, and convex hull applied to them as a group, as well as converting multiple instances to a single collection.

SQL Server provides spatial indexes, which can improve the performance of certain types of queries. The index support for queries depends on the data type, the method in the WHERE or JOIN clause, and the arithmetic operator used.

Spatial indexes use B-Tree structures, but before the B-Tree is created, a grid system of space is created, with four nested levels. The spatial instances from the column are then read one by one into the grid system, and their touched cells are numbered, using a Hilbert curve. This means that spatial instances can be indexes in a linear fashion, but detailing their proximity to each other.

CHAPTER 12

Working with Hierarchical Data and HierarchyID

Modeling and working with data hierarchies have long been requirements for SQL Server developers. Traditionally, hierarchical data has been modeled using a self-join on a table, between two columns. One column contains the ID of the hierarchical member, and the other, the ID of its parent hierarchical member. Newer versions of SQL Server (2008 and later versions) offer HierarchyID, however. HierarchyID is a data type written in .NET and exposed in SQL Server. Using HierarchyID can offer performance benefits and simplified code, compared to using a table with a self-join. The data type exposes many methods that can be called against the data, to allow developers to easily determine the ancestors and descendants of a hierarchical member, as well as determine other useful information, such as the level of a specific hierarchical member within the hierarchy.

In this chapter, we will examine first the use cases for hierarchical data. I will discuss how to model a traditional hierarchy, before explaining how we can remodel it using HierarchyID. Finally, we will look at the methods that are exposed against the HierarchyID data type.

© Peter A. Carter 2018
P. A. Carter, *SQL Server Advanced Data Types*,
https://doi.org/10.1007/978-1-4842-3901-8_12

Hierarchical Data Use Cases

There are many data requirements that need a hierarchy to be maintained. For example, consider an employee hierarchy, modeled from an organizational chart (see Figure 12-1). A human resources department may have reporting requirements, to determine how many staff directly or indirectly report to a manager. It may also have to report on more complex requirements, such as how much revenue has been generated by staff reporting to each group head.

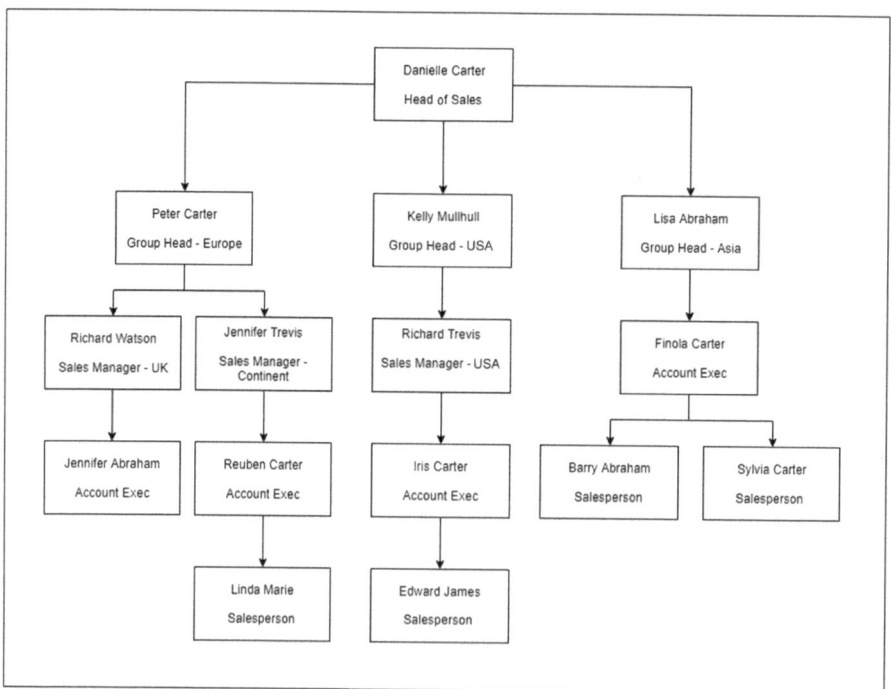

Figure 12-1. *Sales department organization chart*

Another classic use case for hierarchical data is a bill of materials (BoM). A BoM defines a hierarchy of parts that are required to produce a product. For example, Figure 12-2 illustrates a simple BoM for a home computer. A computer manufacturer would have to maintain a hierarchy of these parts for stock reporting.

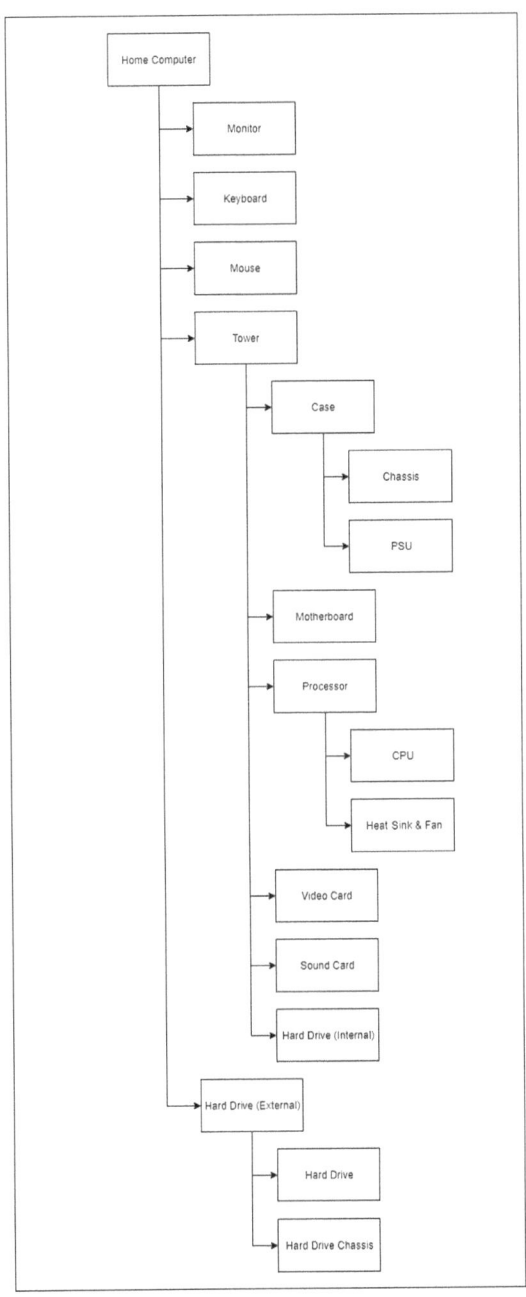

Figure 12-2. *Bill of materials*

In this chapter, we will be working with the example of a sales area hierarchy. As illustrated in Figure 12-3, we will be modeling global sales regions. The hierarchy is ragged, meaning that there can be a varying number of levels in each branch of the hierarchy.

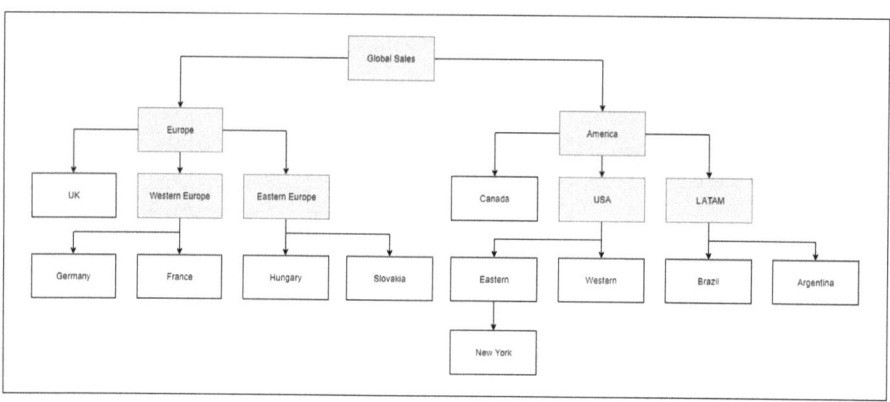

Figure 12-3. *Sales area hierarchy*

Maintaining a sales area hierarchy is important to many companies, as it allows them to report on many factors, from revenue taken in each region to the number of salespeople in each region to average revenue per salesperson and region, etc. In this example, as well as in standard sales regions, there are areas of the hierarchy that are aggregation areas. This means that no salespeople exist, and sales are not directly taken for these regions. Instead, they are reporting levels, to allow lower levels of the hierarchy to be rolled up. These aggregation areas are highlighted in blue.

Modeling Traditional Hierarchies

Let's look at how we might model a sales area hierarchy, using a traditional approach. To do this, consider the data in Table 12-1.

Table 12-1. *Sales Area Hierarchy*

SalesAreaID	ParentSalesAreaID	SalesArea Name	CountOfSalesPeople	SalesYTD
1	NULL	Global Sales	NULL	NULL
2	1	Europe	NULL	NULL
3	1	America	NULL	NULL
4	2	UK	3	300,000
5	2	Western Europe	NULL	NULL
6	2	Eastern Europe	NULL	NULL
7	3	Canada	4	350,000
8	3	USA	NULL	NULL
9	3	LATAM	NULL	NULL
10	5	Germany	3	150,000
11	5	France	2	100,000
12	6	Hungary	1	50,000
13	6	Slovakia	2	80,000
14	8	Eastern	4	140,000
15	8	Western	3	280,000
16	9	Brazil	1	100,000
17	9	Argentina	2	70,000
18	14	New York	2	120,000

In the preceding table, the SalesAreaID column would be the primary key of the table, and the ParentSalesAreaID column would be a foreign key, which references the SalesAreaID column, creating what is known as a self-join.

Note   The ParentSalesAreaID column is NULL for the GlobalSales area, because it does not have a parent. This is known as the root of the hierarchy.

The SalesAreaName column describes the sales area, while the CountOfSalesPeople and SalesYTD columns detail how each sales area is performing. We will use these columns to explore how to work with hierarchical data. You will notice that the CountOfSalesPeople and SalesYTD columns are populated with NULL values for aggregation areas. This is because they are "virtual" areas, where no salespeople are based.

This table can be created by using the script in Listing 12-1.

Listing 12-1. Creating a Traditional Hierarchical Table

```
USE WideWorldImporters
GO

CREATE TABLE Sales.SalesAreaTraditionalHierarchy
(
        SalesAreaID         INT     NOT NULL    PRIMARY KEY,
        ParentSalesAreaID   INT     NULL
                                    REFERENCES Sales.Sales
                                    AreaTraditionalHierarch
                                    y(SalesAreaID),
        SalesAreaName               NVARCHAR(20)    NOT NULL,
        CountOfSalesPeople          INT             NULL,
        SalesYTD                    MONEY           NULL
) ;

INSERT INTO Sales.SalesAreaTraditionalHierarchy (
            SalesAreaID
        , ParentSalesAreaID
        , SalesAreaName
```

```
      , CountOfSalesPeople
      , SalesYTD
)
VALUES
(1, NULL, 'GlobalSales', NULL, NULL),
(2, 1, 'Europe', NULL, NULL),
(3, 1, 'America', NULL, NULL),
(4, 2, 'UK', 3, 300000),
(5, 2, 'Western Europe', NULL, NULL),
(6, 2, 'Eastern Europe', NULL, NULL),
(7, 3, 'Canada', 4, 350000),
(8, 3, 'USA', NULL, NULL),
(9, 3, 'LATAM', NULL, NULL),
(10, 5, 'Germany', 3, 150000),
(11, 5, 'France', 2, 100000),
(12, 6, 'Hungary', 1, 50000),
(13, 6, 'Slovakia', 2, 80000),
(14, 8, 'Eastern', 4, 140000),
(15, 8, 'Western', 3, 280000),
(16, 9, 'Brazil', 1, 100000),
(17, 9, 'Agentina', 2, 70000),
(18, 14, 'New York', 2, 120000) ;
```

Let's imagine that we must answer a business question, using this traditional hierarchy. For example, we may have to answer the question, "What is the total of SalesYTD for the America region?" To determine this, we would have to write a query that joins the table to itself and rolls up the SalesYTD column for all subregions under the America region.

The best way of achieving this is to use a recursive CTE (common table expression). A CTE is a temporary result set that is defined within the context of a SELECT, UPDATE, INSERT, DELETE, or CREATE VIEW statement and can only be referenced within that query. It is similar to using a subquery as a derived table but has the benefit that it can be referenced multiple times and also reference itself. When a CTE references itself, it becomes recursive.

A CTE is declared using a WITH statement, which specifies the name of the CTE, followed by the column list that will be returned by the CTE, in parentheses. The AS keyword is then used, followed by the body of the CTE, again within parentheses. This is shown, for our example, in Listing 12-2.

Tip   The queries in Listings 12-2 to 12-14 are not meant to be run separately. Listing 12-15 brings them all together, into a useable script.

Listing 12-2. CTE Structure

```
; WITH AreaHierarchy (SalesAreaID, SalesYTD, ParentSalesAreaID)
AS
(
        [Body of CTE]
)
```

The definition of a recursive CTE has two queries, joined with a UNION ALL clause. The first query is known as the anchor query and defines the initial result set. The second query is known as the recursive query and references the CTE. The first level of recursion will join to the anchor query, and subsequent levels of recursion will join to the level of recursion immediately above them.

Therefore, in our example, the anchor query will have to return the SalesAreaID of the America sales area. Because all queries joined with UNION ALL must contain the same number of columns, our anchor query must also return the ParentSalesAreaID and SalesYTD columns, even though these values will be NULL.

The query in Listing 12-3 shows the required anchor query.

Listing 12-3. Anchor Query

```
SELECT
        SalesAreaID
      , SalesYTD
      , ParentSalesAreaID
FROM Sales.SalesAreaTraditionalHierarchy RootLevel
WHERE SalesAreaName = 'America'
```

The recursive query will return the same column list as the anchor query but will include a JOIN clause, which joins the ParentSalesAreaID column in the recursive query to the SalesAreaID column of the CTE, as demonstrated in Listing 12-4.

Listing 12-4. Recursive Query

```
SELECT
        Area.SalesAreaID
      , Area.SalesYTD
      , Area.ParentSalesAreaID
FROM Sales.SalesAreaTraditionalHierarchy Area
INNER JOIN AreaHierarchy
        ON Area.ParentSalesAreaID = AreaHierarchy.SalesAreaID
```

Following the declaration of this CTE, we will be able to run a SELECT statement, which rolls up the SalesYTD, to return the total of SalesYTD for the whole of America. The script in Listing 12-5 brings all these components together.

Listing 12-5. Bringing It All Together

```
WITH AreaHierarchy (SalesAreaID, SalesYTD, ParentSalesAreaID)
AS
(
        SELECT
                    SalesAreaID
                , SalesYTD
                , ParentSalesAreaID
        FROM Sales.SalesAreaTraditionalHierarchy RootLevel
        WHERE SalesAreaName = 'America'
        UNION ALL
        SELECT
                    Area.SalesAreaID
            , Area.SalesYTD
            , Area.ParentSalesAreaID
        FROM Sales.SalesAreaTraditionalHierarchy Area
        INNER JOIN AreaHierarchy
            ON Area.ParentSalesAreaID = AreaHierarchy.SalesAreaID
)
SELECT SUM(SalesYTD)
FROM AreaHierarchy ;
```

Modeling Hierarchies with HierarchyID

When modeling hierarchical data using HierarchyID, there is no need
to perform a self-join against a table. Therefore, instead of having a
column that references its parent area's primary key, we will instead
have a HierarchyID column, which defines each area's position within
the hierarchy. To explain this concept further, let's consider the data in
Table 12-2.

Table 12-2. *Sales Area Hierarchy with* HierarchyID

SalesAreaID	SalesAreaHierarchy	SalesAreaName	CountOfSalesPeople	SalesYTD
1	/	GlobalSales	NULL	NULL
2	/1/	Europe	NULL	NULL
3	/2/	America	NULL	NULL
4	/1/1/	UK	3	300,000
5	/1/2/	Western Europe	NULL	NULL
6	/1/3/	Eastern Europe	NULL	NULL
7	/2/1/	Canada	4	350,000
8	/2/2/	USA	NULL	NULL
9	/2/3/	LATAM	NULL	NULL
10	/1/2/1/	Germany	3	150,000
11	/1/2/2/	France	2	100,000
12	/1/3/1/	Hungary	1	50,000
13	/1/3/2/	Slovakia	2	80,000
14	/2/2/1/	Eastern	4	140,000
15	/2/2/2/	Western	3	280,000
16	/2/3/1/	Brazil	1	100,000
17	/2/3/2/	Argentina	2	70,000
18	/2/2/1/1/	New York	2	120,000

In Table 12-2, you will notice that the hierarchy is represented by the format /[Node]/[Child Node]/[GrandchildNode]/, in which a row containing just / is the root of the hierarchy. For example, we can see that the value /1/2/1/ for Germany tells us that Germany is a child of /1/2/

(Western Europe), which in turn is a child of /1/ (Europe). /1/ is the child of / (Global Sales), which is the root of the hierarchy.

We can create and populate this table by using the script in Listing 12-6.

Listing 12-6. Create Table with HierarchyID

```
USE WideWorldImporters
GO

CREATE TABLE Sales.SalesAreaHierarchyID
(
SalesAreaID                     INT                         NOT
NULL    PRIMARY KEY,
SalesAreaHierarchy   HIERARCHYID     NOT NULL,
SalesAreaName               NVARCHAR(20)    NOT NULL,
CountOfSalesPeople     INT                           NULL,
SalesYTD                         MONEY                   NULL
) ;

INSERT INTO Sales.SalesAreaHierarchyID (
            SalesAreaID
        , SalesAreaHierarchy
        , SalesAreaName
        , CountOfSalesPeople
        , SalesYTD
)
VALUES
(1, '/', 'GlobalSales', NULL, NULL),
(2, '/1/', 'Europe', NULL, NULL),
(3, '/2/', 'America', NULL, NULL),
(4, '/1/1/', 'UK', 3, 300000),
(5, '/1/2/', 'Western Europe', NULL, NULL),
(6, '/1/3/', 'Eastern Europe', NULL, NULL),
```

```
(7, '/2/1/', 'Canada', 4, 350000),
(8, '/2/2/', 'USA', NULL, NULL),
(9, '/2/3/', 'LATAM', NULL, NULL),
(10, '/1/2/1/', 'Germany', 3, 150000),
(11, '/1/2/2/', 'France', 2, 100000),
(12, '/1/3/1/', 'Hungary', 1, 50000),
(13, '/1/3/2/', 'Slovakia', 2, 80000),
(14, '/2/2/1/', 'Eastern', 4, 140000),
(15, '/2/2/2/', 'Western', 3, 280000),
(16, '/2/3/1/', 'Brazil', 1, 100000),
(17, '/2/3/2/', 'Agentina', 2, 70000),
(18, '/2/2/1/1/', 'New York', 2, 120000) ;
```

Even though we have inserted human-readable strings into the SalesAreaHierarchyID column, SQL Server converts these strings and stores them as hexadecimal values. This makes the column extremely compact and efficient. The size of the HierarchyID column and that of the INT column used for the ParentSalesAreaID column in the traditional hierarchy can be compared using the query in Listing 12-7.

Listing 12-7. Comparing the Size of a Traditional Hierarchy to HierarchyID

```
USE WideWorldImporters
GO

SELECT
        SUM(DATALENGTH(salesareahierarchy)) AS SizeOf
        HierarchyID
        , SUM(DATALENGTH(parentsalesareaid)) AS SizeOf
        Traditional
FROM Sales.SalesAreaHierarchyID SalesAreaHierarchy
```

```
INNER JOIN sales.SalesAreaTraditionalHierarchy SalesAreaTraditional
        ON SalesAreaHierarchy.SalesAreaID = SalesArea
        Traditional.SalesAreaID ;
```

The results of this query are shown in Figure 12-4. You can see that the HierarchyID column is less than half the size of the INT column used for the ParentSalesAreaID.

Figure 12-4. *Results of size comparison*

Note   In Chapter 1, you learned that it is important to use the correct data type, and if I had chosen to use a SMALLINT for the ParentSalesAreaID column, the two columns would be about the same size. This is, however, a minor example, provided for the purpose of explaining HierarchyID, but if you are implementing hierarchies on a large scale, this example is a fair representation.

If we run a normal SELECT statement against the SalesAreaHierarchyID table, we can see the hexadecimal values in their raw form. For example, consider the query in Listing 12-8.

Listing 12-8. SELECT Statement Against HierarchyID Column

```
USE WideWorldImporters
GO

SELECT
        SalesAreaName
    , SalesAreaHierarchy
FROM Sales.SalesAreaHierarchyID ;
```

The results of this query are displayed in Figure 12-5. You will notice that the contents of the SalesAreaHierarchy column are returned as hexadecimal values, instead of human-readable strings. In order to view the human-readable strings that we entered, we must use the ToString() method, which is discussed in the "Working with HierarchyID Methods" section of this chapter.

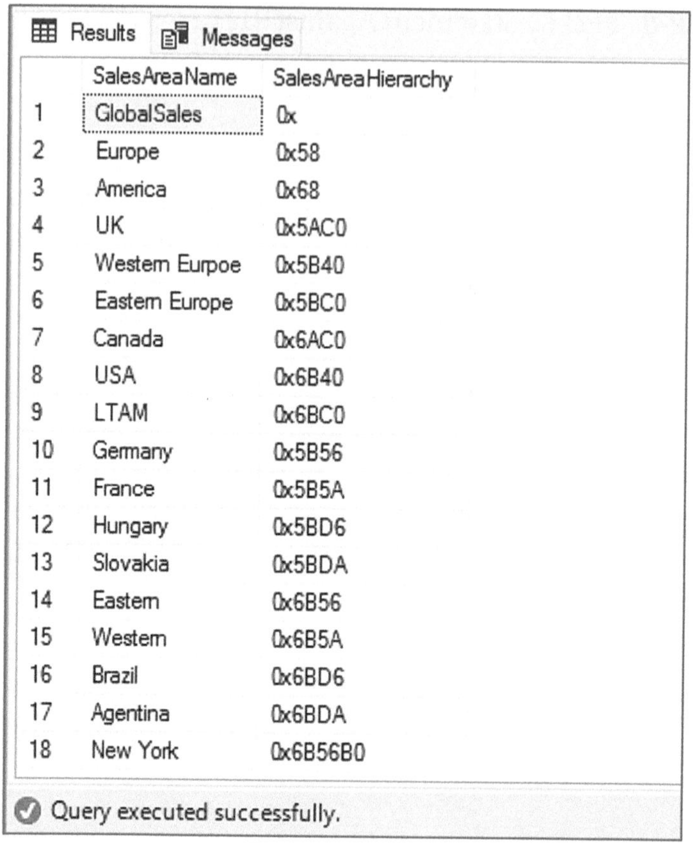

	SalesAreaName	SalesAreaHierarchy
1	GlobalSales	0x
2	Europe	0x58
3	America	0x68
4	UK	0x5AC0
5	Western Eurpoe	0x5B40
6	Eastern Europe	0x5BC0
7	Canada	0x6AC0
8	USA	0x6B40
9	LTAM	0x6BC0
10	Germany	0x5B56
11	France	0x5B5A
12	Hungary	0x5BD6
13	Slovakia	0x5BDA
14	Eastern	0x6B56
15	Western	0x6B5A
16	Brazil	0x6BD6
17	Agentina	0x6BDA
18	New York	0x6B56B0

Results ☷   Messages

✅ Query executed successfully.

Figure 12-5. *Results of SELECT statement against HierarchyID column*

HierarchyID Methods

A number of methods are exposed against the HierarchyID data type, allowing developers to quickly write efficient code when working with hierarchies. Table 12-3 details these methods.

Table 12-3. *Methods Exposed Against the* `HierarchyID` *Data Type*

Method	Description
GetAncestor	Returns the ancestor of a hierarchy node. Accepts a parameter that defines how many levels up the hierarchy the ancestor should be returned from. For example, GetAncestor(1) will return the node's parent, while GetAncestor(2) will return the node's grandparent.
GetDescendant	Returns a child node ID for a given node in the hierarchy. The GetDescendant() method is generally used in the creation of two nodes. Therefore, the method accepts two parameters, both of type HierarchyID. The generated node will sit between the two nodes specified.
GetLevel	Returns the hierarchical level of the node
GetRoot	A static method that returns the root level of a hierarchy
IsDescendantOf	The IsDescendantOf() method accepts a single parameter, of type HierarchyID, and returns 1 if a given node is a descendant of the node passed as a parameter.
Parse	Parses the string representation of a node, which is passed as a parameter, to ensure it is valid. If valid, it returns the hexadecimal representation. If invalid, it will throw an error.
Read	Reads the binary representation of SqlHierarchyId from the BinaryReader and sets the SqlHierarchyId object to that value. The Read() method can only be called from SQLCLR. It cannot be called from T-SQL. When using T-SQL, you should use CAST or CONVERT instead.

(*continued*)

Table 12-3. (*continued*)

Method	Description
GetReparentedValue	Used to move a node to a new parent. Accepts two parameters, the first being the original parent and the second being the new parent
ToString	Returns a string-formatted representation of a node within the hierarchy
Write	Writes out a binary representation of SqlHierarchyId to the BinaryWriter. For use with SQLCLR only. When using T-SQL, use CAST or CONVERT instead.

Tip   HierarchyID methods are case-sensitive. For example, calling tostring() will throw an error; calling ToString() will succeed.

Working with HierarchyID Methods

The following sections describe how to use the methods exposed against the HierarchyID data type.

Using ToString( )

If you run a SELECT statement against a column with the HierarchyID data type, the value returned will be a hexadecimal representation of the node. To see a textual representation of the node, you must use the ToString() method. For example, consider the query in Listing 12-9.

Listing 12-9. Using ToString()

```
USE WideWorldImporters
GO

SELECT
        SalesAreaName
    , SalesAreaHierarchy
    , SalesAreaHierarchy.ToString() AS SalesArea
    HierarchyString
FROM Sales.SalesAreaHierarchyID ;
```

The results of this query are displayed in Figure 12-6. You will see that the column becomes human-readable, once the ToString() method is called against it.

	SalesAreaName	SalesAreaHierarchy	SalesAreaHierarchyString
1	GlobalSales	0x	/
2	Europe	0x58	/1/
3	America	0x68	/2/
4	UK	0x5AC0	/1/1/
5	Western Eurpoe	0x5B40	/1/2/
6	Eastern Europe	0x5BC0	/1/3/
7	Canada	0x6AC0	/2/1/
8	USA	0x6B40	/2/2/
9	LATAM	0x6BC0	/2/3/
10	Germany	0x5B56	/1/2/1/
11	France	0x5B5A	/1/2/2/
12	Hungary	0x5BD6	/1/3/1/
13	Slovakia	0x5BDA	/1/3/2/
14	Eastern	0x6B56	/2/2/1/
15	Western	0x6B5A	/2/2/2/
16	Brazil	0x6BD6	/2/3/1/
17	Argentina	0x6BDA	/2/3/2/
18	New York	0x6B56B0	/2/2/1/1/

Query executed successfully.

Figure 12-6. *Results of using* ToString()

Using Parse( )

The Parse() method is called implicitly when a string representation of a node is inserted into a HierarchyID column. Essentially, the Parse() method performs the reverse function of the ToString() method. It attempts to convert a string formatted representation to the HierarchyID representation. If it fails, an error is thrown. For example, consider the script in Listing 12-10.

Listing 12-10. Using the `Parse()` Method

```
--Returns Hexidecimal Representation Of Node

SELECT HierarchyID::Parse('/1/1/2/2/') ;

--Throws An Error Because Trailing / Is Missing

SELECT HierarchyID::Parse('/1/1/2/2') ;
```

The Results tab displayed by running this script can be seen in Figure 12-7. While the first query displays the expected result, the second query returns no results.

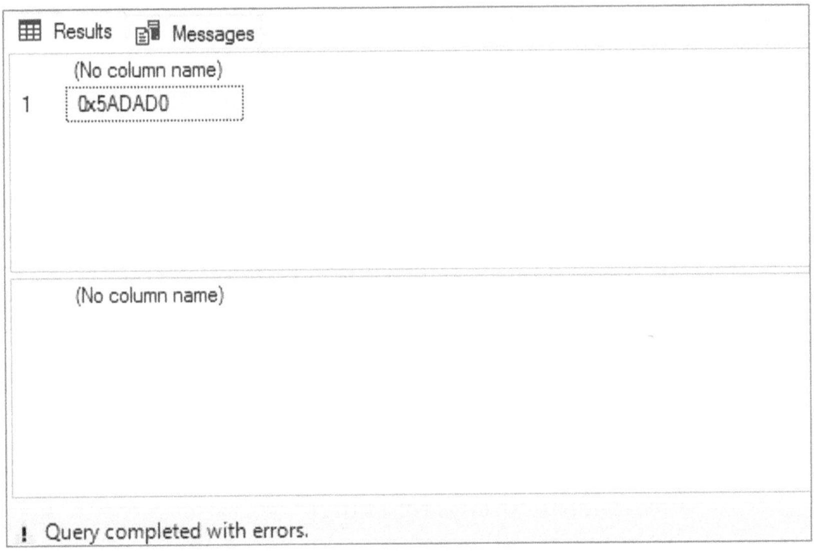

Figure 12-7. *Using `Parse()` Results tab*

Checking the Messages tab, displayed in Figure 12-8, will detail the error thrown by the .NET framework.

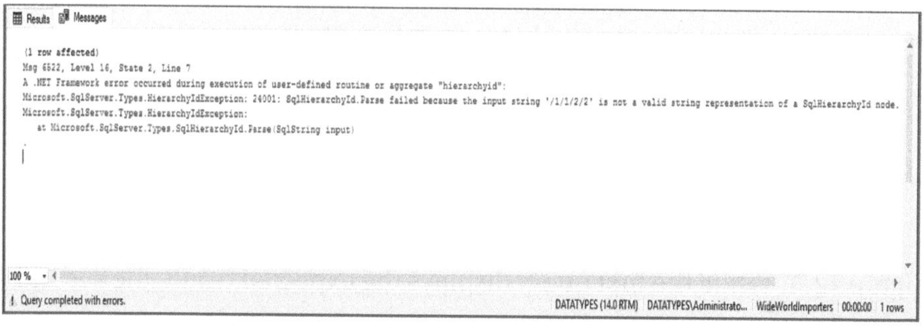

Figure 12-8. *Error thrown by .NET framework*

Using GetRoot( )

The GetRoot() method will return the root node of a hierarchy, as demonstrated in Listing 12-11.

Listing 12-11. Using GetRoot()

```
USE WideWorldImporters
GO

SELECT
        SalesAreaName
     , SalesAreaHierarchy.ToString()
FROM Sales.SalesAreaHierarchyID
WHERE SalesAreaHierarchy = HierarchyID::GetRoot() ;
```

The results of this query can be viewed in Figure 12-9.

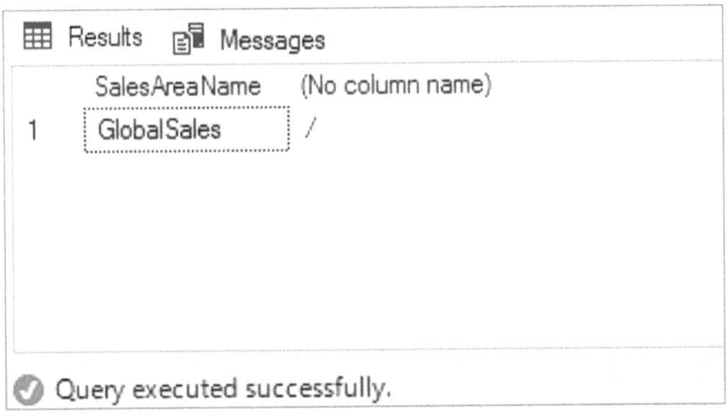

Figure 12-9. Results of using GetRoot()

Using GetLevel( )

The GetLevel() method allows you to determine at what level of the hierarchy a particular node resides. For example, the query in Listing 12-12 will return all nodes that reside on the bottom level of the hierarchy. In our case, this is just New York.

The subquery will determine the maximum level within the hierarchy, and the outer query will return all sales areas that are at that level.

Listing 12-12. Using GetLevel()

```
USE WideWorldImporters
GO

SELECT
        SalesAreaName
FROM Sales.SalesAreaHierarchyID
WHERE SalesAreaHierarchy.GetLevel() =
        (
        SELECT
                MAX(SalesAreaHierarchy.GetLevel())
        FROM Sales.SalesAreaHierarchyID
        ) ;
```

The results of this query can be found in Figure 12-10.

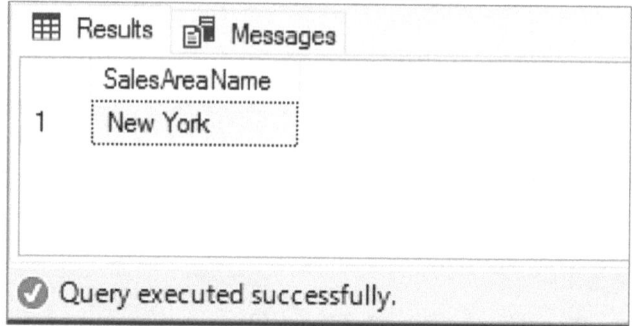

Figure 12-10. *Results of using* `GetLevel()`

Read( ) and Write( )

Because this chapter focuses on how to use `HierarchyID` within your T-SQL code and the `Read()` and `Write()` methods are only applicable to using SQLCLR (the technology that allows for managed objects to be created inside SQL Server), a full description of the `Read()` and `Write()` methods is beyond the scope of this book.

Using GetDescendant( )

Of course, a developer could insert a new node into the hierarchy, between existing nodes, but the `GetDescendant()` method helps a developer do this pragmatically. The method accepts two parameters, both of which can be `NULL` and represent existing children. The method will then generate a node value, using the following rules:

- If the parent is `NULL`, then a `NULL` value will be returned.

- If the parent is not `NULL`, and both parameters are `NULL`, the first child of the parent will be returned.

- If the parent and first parameter are not NULL, but the second parameter is NULL, a child of parent greater than the first parameter will be returned.

- If the parent and second parameter are not NULL but the first parameter is NULL, a child of parent smaller than the second parameter will be returned.

- If parent and both parameters are not NULL, a child of parent between the two parameters will be returned.

- If the first parameter is not NULL and not a child of the parent, an error is thrown.

- If the second parameter is not NULL and not a child of the parent, an error is thrown.

- If the first parameter is greater than or equal to the second parameter, an error is thrown.

For example, imagine that we want to create with the parent of America a new sales area called Spain. We want the node value to be between Canada and USA. We could achieve this with the query in Listing 12-13.

Tip   Obviously, Spain should be included under Western Europe, not under America. Don't worry, this is a deliberate error, which we will resolve in the "Using GetReparentedValue" section of this chapter.

Listing 12-13. Generating a New Hierarchy Node

```
USE WideWorldImporters
GO

SELECT NewNode.ToString()
FROM
```

```
(
SELECT
        SalesAreaHierarchy.GetDescendant(0x6AC0,0x6B40) AS
NewNode
FROM Sales.SalesAreaHierarchyID
WHERE SalesAreaName = 'America'
) NewNode ;
```

The results produced by this query are illustrated in Figure 12-11. You will see that the lowest level contains a period (1.1). This is because Canada has a value of 1 and USA has a value of 2. Therefore, to generate a node value between the two, an integer cannot be used. This guarantees that a new node can always be inserted between two existing nodes.

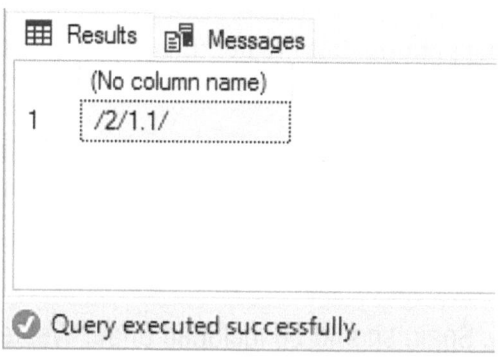

Figure 12-11. *Results of using GetDescendant()*

To programmatically add the Spain sales area to the hierarchy, we could use the query in Listing 12-14.

Listing 12-14. Insert a New Node into the Hierarchy

```
USE WideWorldImporters
GO

INSERT INTO Sales.SalesAreaHierarchyID
        (
                SalesAreaID
            , SalesAreaHierarchy
            , SalesAreaName
            , CountOfSalesPeople
            , SalesYTD
                )
SELECT
        (SELECT MAX(SalesAreaID) + 1 FROM Sales.SalesArea
        HierarchyID)
                , SalesAreaHierarchy.GetDescendant
                (0x6AC0,0x6B40)
            , 'Spain'
            , 2
            , 200000
FROM Sales.SalesAreaHierarchyID
WHERE SalesAreaName = 'America' ;
```

Using GetReparentedValue( )

As you probably noticed in the "Using GetDescendant()" section, the
Spain sales area was incorrectly created under the America aggregation
area, as opposed to the Western Europe aggregation area. We can resolve
this issue by using the GetReparentedValue() method.

Consider the script in Listing 12-15. First, we declare two variables,
with the type HierarchyID. These will be passed as parameters into the
GetReparentedValue() method. The @America variable is populated

with the sales area hierarchy node pertaining to the original parent sales area, and the @WesternEurope variable is populated with the sales area hierarchy node pertaining to the target parent sales area.

Listing 12-15. Use GetReparentedValue()

```
USE WideWorldImporters
GO

DECLARE @America HIERARCHYID =
(
    SELECT SalesAreaHierarchy
    FROM Sales.SalesAreaHierarchyID
    WHERE SalesAreaName = 'America'
) ;

DECLARE @WesternEurope HIERARCHYID =
(
    SELECT SalesAreaHierarchy
    FROM Sales.SalesAreaHierarchyID
    WHERE SalesAreaName = 'Western Europe'
) ;

SELECT Area.ToString()
FROM
(
SELECT SalesAreaHierarchy.GetReparentedValue(@America,
@WesternEurope) AS Area
FROM Sales.SalesAreaHierarchyID
WHERE SalesAreaHierarchy = 0x6B16
) NewNodePath ;
```

The results of this script can be seen in Figure 12-12. You will notice that the leaf node value has remained the same, while the path (parent nodes) have been changed, so that the node sits under the Western Europe aggregation area.

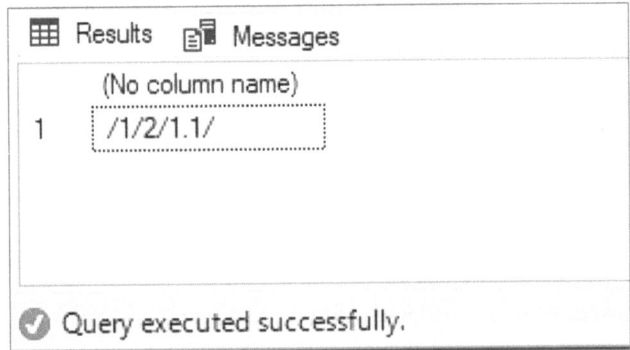

Figure 12-12. *Results of using* `GetReparentedValue()`

We could update the ancestry of the Spain sales area, in the Sales. SalesAreaHierarchyID table, by using the script in Listing 12-16.

Listing 12-16. Updating the Ancestry of the Spain Sales Area

```
USE WideWorldImporters
GO

DECLARE @America HIERARCHYID =
(
    SELECT SalesAreaHierarchy
    FROM Sales.SalesAreaHierarchyID
    WHERE SalesAreaName = 'America'
) ;

DECLARE @WesternEurope HIERARCHYID =
(
    SELECT SalesAreaHierarchy
```

```
        FROM Sales.SalesAreaHierarchyID
        WHERE SalesAreaName = 'Western Europe'
) ;

UPDATE Sales.SalesAreaHierarchyID
SET SalesAreaHierarchy =
(
SELECT SalesAreaHierarchy.GetReparentedValue(@America,
@WesternEurope)
FROM Sales.SalesAreaHierarchyID
WHERE SalesAreaHierarchy = 0x6B16
)
WHERE SalesAreaHierarchy = 0x6B16 ;
```

Using GetAncestor( )

The GetAncestor() method can be used to return the ancestor node
of a given hierarchical node at the number of levels based on an input
parameter to the method. For example, consider the query in
Listing 12-17. This query will return the grandparent of Spain, the parent
of Spain, and Spain itself, by passing different parameters into the
GetAncestor() method.

Caution   For this query to work as expected, you first must have
run the previous examples in the chapter. Specifically, the insert
and update queries in the "Using GetDescendant()" and "Using
GetReparentedValue()" sections, as well as Listing 12-2, which
creates and populates the table.

Listing 12-17. Using GetAncestor()

```
USE WideWorldImporters
GO

SELECT
                CurrentNode.SalesAreaName AS SalesArea
        , ParentNode.SalesAreaName AS ParentSalesArea
        , GrandParentNode.SalesAreaName AS GrandParentSalesArea
FROM Sales.SalesAreaHierarchyID Base
INNER JOIN Sales.SalesAreaHierarchyID CurrentNode
        ON CurrentNode.SalesAreaHierarchy = Base.
        SalesAreaHierarchy.GetAncestor(0)
INNER JOIN Sales.SalesAreaHierarchyID ParentNode
        ON ParentNode.SalesAreaHierarchy = Base.
        SalesAreaHierarchy.GetAncestor(1)
INNER JOIN Sales.SalesAreaHierarchyID GrandParentNode
        ON GrandParentNode.SalesAreaHierarchy = Base.
        SalesAreaHierarchy.GetAncestor(2)
WHERE Base.SalesAreaName = 'Spain' ;
```

Using IsDescendantOf( )

The IsDescendantOf() method evaluates if a node within the hierarchy
is a descendant (at any level) of a node that is passed to it as a parameter.
It is this method that we can use to rewrite the query in Listing 12-5, which
rolled up the SalesYTD for all sales areas under the America aggregation
area, using a traditional hierarchy.

You will remember, that when using a traditional hierarchy, we had
to implement a recursive CTE, which rolled up the SalesYTD column, for
all hierarchical levels, which are descendants of America. When using
a HierarchyID column to maintain the hierarchy, however, our code is
greatly simplified, as demonstrated in Listing 12-18.

Listing 12-18. Using IsDescendantOf()

```
USE WideWorldImporters
GO

SELECT
    SUM(SalesYTD) AS TotalSalesYTD
FROM Sales.SalesAreaHierarchyID
WHERE SalesAreaHierarchy.IsDescendantOf(0x68) = 1 ;
```

Instead of a recursive CTE, the functionally equivalent code is a simple query with a WHERE clause that filters hierarchical nodes, based on whether they are descendants of the America aggregation area. Listing 12-19 shows a more complex example. Here, we are parameterizing the sales area and calculating not only the total SalesYTD but also the TotalSalesPeople and the regions AverageSalesPerSalesPerson.

Listing 12-19. Parameterizing IsDescendantOf() Queries

```
USE WideWorldImporters
GO

DECLARE @Region NVARCHAR(20) = 'America' ;

DECLARE @RegionHierarchy HIERARCHYID =
    (
        SELECT SalesAreaHierarchy
        FROM Sales.SalesAreaHierarchyID
        WHERE SalesAreaName = @Region
    ) ;
SELECT
      SUM(SalesYTD) AS TotalSalesYTD
    , SUM(CountOfSalesPeople) AS TotalSalesPeople
```

```
, SUM(SalesYTD) / SUM(CountOfSalesPeople) AS
 AverageSalesPerSalesPerson
FROM Sales.SalesAreaHierarchyID
WHERE SalesAreaHierarchy.IsDescendantOf(@RegionHierarchy) = 1 ;
```

You can clearly see how the Region parameter could be passed into a stored procedure, so that this code could be accessed by an application.

Let us now add a SalesAreaName to the SELECT list, and group by this column, as demonstrated in Listing 12-20.

Listing 12-20. Adding a GROUP BY

```
USE WideWorldImporters
GO

DECLARE @Region NVARCHAR(20) = 'America' ;

DECLARE @RegionHierarchy HIERARCHYID =
    (
        SELECT SalesAreaHierarchy
        FROM Sales.SalesAreaHierarchyID
        WHERE SalesAreaName = @Region
    ) ;

SELECT
    SUM(SalesYTD) AS TotalSalesYTD
  , SUM(CountOfSalesPeople) AS TotalSalesPeople
  , SUM(SalesYTD) / SUM(CountOfSalesPeople) AS
    AverageSalesPerSalesPerson
  , SalesAreaName
FROM Sales.SalesAreaHierarchyID
WHERE SalesAreaHierarchy.IsDescendantOf(@RegionHierarchy) = 1
GROUP BY SalesAreaName ;
```

The results of this query are illustrated in Figure 12-13.

	TotalSalesYTD	TotalSalesPeople	AverageSalesPerSalesPerson	SalesAreaName
1	70000.00	2	35000.00	Argentina
2	NULL	NULL	NULL	America
3	100000.00	1	100000.00	Brazil
4	350000.00	4	87500.00	Canada
5	140000.00	4	35000.00	Eastern
6	NULL	NULL	NULL	LATAM
7	120000.00	2	60000.00	New York
8	NULL	NULL	NULL	USA
9	280000.00	3	93333.3333	Western

Query executed successfully.   DATATYPES

Figure 12-13. Results of using `IsDescendantOf()` *with* `GROUP BY`

The interesting behavior exposed by the results of this query is that America is included. This is because `HierarchyID` regards America as a descendant of itself. This does not create an issue for us, because the aggregations are not pre-calculated. However, in some instances, you may have to exclude America from the result set. This can easily be achieved by adding an additional filter to the `WHERE` clause, as demonstrated in Listing 12-21.

Listing 12-21. Filtering the Current Node from Descendants

```
USE WideWorldImporters
GO

DECLARE @Region NVARCHAR(20) = 'America' ;

DECLARE @RegionHierarchy HIERARCHYID =
    (
```

```
    SELECT SalesAreaHierarchy
    FROM Sales.SalesAreaHierarchyID
    WHERE SalesAreaName = @Region
    ) ;

SELECT
    SUM(SalesYTD) AS TotalSalesYTD
    , SUM(CountOfSalesPeople) AS TotalSalesPeople
    , SUM(SalesYTD) / SUM(CountOfSalesPeople) AS
    AverageSalesPerSalesPerson
    , SalesAreaName
FROM Sales.SalesAreaHierarchyID
WHERE SalesAreaHierarchy.IsDescendantOf(@RegionHierarchy) = 1
        AND SalesAreaHierarchy <> @RegionHierarchy
GROUP BY SalesAreaName ;
```

This query filters the result set to exclude the sales area, the hierarchical node of which is equal to the hierarchical node that is being passed to the IsDescendantOf() method. This technique allows us to use the WITH ROLLUP clause on the GROUP BY, in conjunction with wrapping SalesAreaName in an ISNULL() function, to produce a subtotal row for the whole of America. This is demonstrated in Listing 12-22.

Listing 12-22. Producing a Total Row for America

```
USE WideWorldImporters
GO

DECLARE @Region NVARCHAR(20) = 'America' ;

DECLARE @RegionHierarchy HIERARCHYID =
    (
        SELECT SalesAreaHierarchy
        FROM Sales.SalesAreaHicrarchyID
```

```
                WHERE SalesAreaName = @Region
            ) ;

SELECT
        SUM(SalesYTD) AS TotalSalesYTD
      , SUM(CountOfSalesPeople) AS TotalSalesPeople
      , SUM(SalesYTD) / SUM(CountOfSalesPeople) AS
      AverageSalesPerSalesPerson
      , ISNULL(SalesAreaName, @Region)
FROM Sales.SalesAreaHierarchyID
WHERE SalesAreaHierarchy.IsDescendantOf(@RegionHierarchy) = 1
        AND SalesAreaHierarchy <> @RegionHierarchy
GROUP BY SalesAreaName  WITH ROLLUP ;
```

The results of this query can be seen in Figure 12-14.

	TotalSalesYTD	TotalSalesPeople	AverageSalesPerSalesPerson	(No column name)
1	70000.00	2	35000.00	Argentina
2	100000.00	1	100000.00	Brazil
3	350000.00	4	87500.00	Canada
4	140000.00	4	35000.00	Eastern
5	NULL	NULL	NULL	LATAM
6	120000.00	2	60000.00	New York
7	NULL	NULL	NULL	USA
8	280000.00	3	93333.3333	Western
9	1060000.00	16	66250.00	America

Query executed successfully.   DATATYPES

Figure 12-14. *Results of adding a total row*

Indexing HierarchyID Columns

There are no "special" index types that support HierarchyID, as there are for XML or geospatial data types. Instead, the performance of HierarchyID columns can be improved by using traditional clustered and nonclustered indexes. When creating indexes to support HierarchyID, there are two strategies that can be employed, depending on the nature of the queries that will use the indexes.

By default, creating an index on a HierarchyID column will create a depth-first index. This means that descendants will be stored close to their parents. In our example, New York would be stored close to Eastern, which in turn would be stored close to USA, and so on. The script in Listing 12-23 demonstrates how to create a clustered index on the SalesAreaHierarchy column, which uses a depth-first approach.

Caution   The script first drops the primary key on the SalesAreaID column, which implicitly drops the clustered index on this column. The primary key name, in this case, is system-generated, however. Therefore, to run this script, you must change the name of the constraint, to reflect your own system.

Listing 12-23. Creating a Depth-First Clustered Index

```
USE WideWorldImporters
GO

ALTER TABLE Sales.SalesAreaHierarchyID
        DROP CONSTRAINT PK__SalesAre__DB0A1ED5D7B258FB ;
GO

CREATE CLUSTERED INDEX SalesAreaHierarchyDepthFirst
        ON Sales.SalesAreaHierarchyID(SalesAreaHierarchy) ;
GO
```

We can see how SQL Server has organized this data,
by running the query in Listing 12-24. This query uses the undocumented
sys.physlocformatter() function to return the exact location of each
record, in the format FileID:PageID:SlotID.

Listing 12-24. View Location of Rows

```
USE WideWorldImporters
GO

SELECT
      SalesAreaName
    , sys.fn_PhysLocFormatter(%%physloc%%) AS PhysicalLocation
FROM Sales.SalesAreaHierarchyID ;
```

This query returns the results shown in Figure 12-15. You can see that
each node is stored under its parent. This is even true for Spain, despite us
adding it after the other regions, which means its original location would
have been the final used slot in the page.

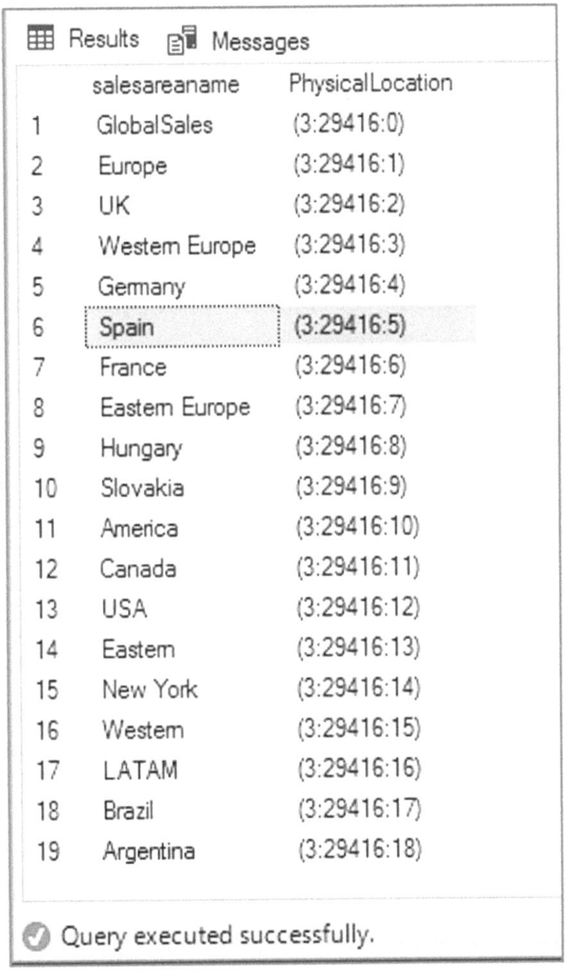
Results
Messages
salesareaname PhysicalLocation
1 GlobalSales (3:29416:0)
2 Europe (3:29416:1)
3 UK (3:29416:2)
4 Western Europe (3:29416:3)
5 Germany (3:29416:4)
6 Spain (3:29416:5)
7 France (3:29416:6)
8 Eastern Europe (3:29416:7)
9 Hungary (3:29416:8)
10 Slovakia (3:29416:9)
11 America (3:29416:10)
12 Canada (3:29416:11)
13 USA (3:29416:12)
14 Eastern (3:29416:13)
15 New York (3:29416:14)
16 Western (3:29416:15)
17 LATAM (3:29416:16)
18 Brazil (3:29416:17)
19 Argentina (3:29416:18)
Query executed successfully.

***Figure 12-15.** Results of viewing row locations*

Tip The row's physical location is likely to be different when you run the query yourself.

The other possible indexing strategy is a breadth-first technique. Here, sibling nodes will be stored close to each other, instead of storing descendants close to each other. To implement a breadth-first indexing strategy, we must add to our table an additional column that stores the hierarchical level of each node. This column can be created and populated by using the script in Listing 12-25.

Listing 12-25. Adding a Level Column to Support Breadth-First Indexing

```
USE WideWorldImporters
GO

ALTER TABLE Sales.SalesAreaHierarchyID ADD
        SalesAreaLevel INT NULL ;
GO

UPDATE Sales.SalesAreaHierarchyID
SET SalesAreaLevel = SalesAreaHierarchy.GetLevel() ;
```

Using the script in Listing 12-26, we can now create a clustered index, which is first order by the hierarchical level of the node and then by the HierarchyID column. This will cause siblings to be stored close to one another.

Note   The script first drops the existing clustered index, because a table can only support a single clustered index.

Listing 12-26. Creating a Breadth-First Index

```
USE WideWorldImporters
GO

DROP INDEX SalesAreaHierarchyDepthFirst ON Sales.
SalesAreaHierarchyID ;
GO

CREATE CLUSTERED INDEX SalesAreaHierarchyBredthFirst
       ON Sales.SalesAreaHierarchyID(SalesAreaLevel,
       SalesAreaHierarchy) ;
```

Listing 12-27 demonstrates how we can use the same technique as in Listing 12-24, to view the actual location of each node within the hierarchy. This time, as well as returning the sales area name, we will also return the SalesAreaLevel for easy analysis.

Listing 12-27. View Rows Location with a Breadth-First Strategy

```
USE WideWorldImporters
GO

SELECT
      SalesAreaName
    , SalesAreaLevel
    , sys.fn_PhysLocFormatter(%%physloc%%) AS PhysicalLocation
FROM Sales.SalesAreaHierarchyID ;
```

The results of this query can be found in Figure 12-16. You will notice that the order of rows has changed and that UK, Western Europe, Eastern Europe, Canada, USA, and LATAM are now next to one another, as they are all at Level 2 of the hierarchy.

	salesareaname	salesarealevel	PhysicalLocation
1	GlobalSales	0	(3:37688:0)
2	Europe	1	(3:37688:1)
3	America	1	(3:37688:2)
4	UK	2	(3:37688:3)
5	Western Europe	2	(3:37688:4)
6	Eastern Europe	2	(3:37688:5)
7	Canada	2	(3:37688:6)
8	USA	2	(3:37688:7)
9	LATAM	2	(3:37688:8)
10	Germany	3	(3:37688:9)
11	Spain	3	(3:37688:10)
12	France	3	(3:37688:11)
13	Hungary	3	(3:37688:12)
14	Slovakia	3	(3:37688:13)
15	Eastern	3	(3:37688:14)
16	Western	3	(3:37688:15)
17	Brazil	3	(3:37688:16)
18	Argentina	3	(3:37688:17)
19	New York	4	(3:37688:18)

Query executed successfully.

Figure 12-16. *Results of viewing row locations in a breadth-first hierarchy*

Summary

HierarchyID is created as a .NET class and implemented as a data type in SQL Server. Using HierarchyID over a traditional approach to modeling hierarchies in SQL Server has the benefits both of reducing code complexity and improving performance. The HierarchyID data type exposes several methods that can be used by developers to easily navigate a hierarchy, insert new hierarchical nodes, or update existing nodes so that they sit under a new parent.

The two most commonly used methods, in my experience, are the ToString() method, which allows a developer to format a hierarchical node as a human-readable string representation, and IsDescendantOf(), which performs an evaluation of hierarchical node lineage and returns 1 when a node is a descendant of an input parameter and 0 if it is not.

The Read() and Write() methods offer data type conversion functionality to SQLCLR, but these are not implemented in T-SQL, as the CAST and CONVERT functions can easily be used instead.

When indexing HierarchyID columns, either a depth-first strategy or a breadth-first strategy can be applied. Depth-first is the default option and stores child nodes close to their parents. A breadth-first strategy requires an additional column in the table, which stores the node's level with the hierarchy. This allows a multicolumn index to store sibling nodes close to one another. The indexing option that you choose should reflect the nature of the queries run against the HierarchyID column.

Index

A

Advanced data types
    GEOGRAPHY, 25
    GEOMETRY, 25
    HIERARCHYID, 25
    JSON, 25
    XML, 25
Aggregation methods, 325

B

Bill of materials (BoM), 342–343
Binary data types
    BINARY, 14
    CONVERT function, 15
    converting to character
        string, 17
    encrypted password, 15–16
    IMAGE, 14
    style options, 15
    VARBINARY, 14

C

CAST function, 7, 9–10
Character data types
    CHAR, 11
    NCHAR, 11
    NTEXT, 12
    NVARCHAR, 12
    string storage
        sizes, 13
    TEXT, 12
    VARCHAR, 11
Clustered indexes
    creating, 165–167
    description, 159
    inserts, 164
    primary key, 162–163
    tables
        B-Tree structure, 161–162
        heap structure, 160–161
    updates, 164
Common table expression (CTE),
    347–348
Configuration management
    database (CMDB), 197–198
CONVERT function, 7

D

Date and time data types
    casting, 22
    DATE, 18
    DATETIME, 18
    DATETIME2, 19

© Peter A. Carter 2018
P. A. Carter, *SQL Server Advanced Data Types*,
https://doi.org/10.1007/978-1-4842-3901-8

S